FLAG
AND
NATION

AUSTRALIANS AND THEIR NATIONAL FLAGS SINCE 1901

UNSW
PRESS

In memory of my parents:
grandchildren of immigrants from Devon and Cornwall

A UNSW Press book

Published by
University of New South Wales Press Ltd
University of New South Wales
Sydney NSW 2052
AUSTRALIA
www.unswpress.com.au

© Elizabeth Kwan 2006
First published 2006

Aboriginal and Torres Strait Islander readers are
advised that this book contains images and details
of deceased persons.

National Library of Australia
Cataloguing-in-Publication entry
  Kwan, Elizabeth, 1945– .
  Flag and nation: Australians and their national
    flags since 1901.
  Bibliography.
  Includes index.
  ISBN 0 86840 567 1.
  1. Flags - Australia. 2. Australia - History -
  20th century. I. Title.
  929.920994

Design Di Quick
Print Everbest, China

Contents

Introduction   4

Chapter 1 | Australian federation, British flag   13

Chapter 2 | Empire Day and Australia Day   34

Chapter 3 | War and the question of loyalty   55

Chapter 4 | The red and the blue   78

Chapter 5 | Choosing between ensigns   93

Chapter 6 | Searching for Australian symbols   108

Chapter 7 | British or Australian?   123

Conclusion   149

Appendices   159

Notes   160

Sources and select bibliography   168

Illustration credits   170

Acknowledgments   172

Index   173

Introduction

AUSTRALIANS
and their
NATIONAL FLAG

Most Australians know their national flag: the blue flag with the Union Jack, the Commonwealth Star and the Southern Cross constellation. Some know that the red flag with the same design, the Australian red ensign, is the flag Australian merchant ships fly.

When the Australian colonies federated in 1901 to create the Commonwealth of Australia, the national flag was Britain's Union Jack. Australia (like Canada and New Zealand) acquired two flags to fly at the stern of ships: blue for official and naval ships; red for merchant ships. They were ensigns of the national flag, the Union Jack, which had the place of honour, while the Commonwealth Star and Southern Cross constellation were Australian symbols (see Chapter 1: Flag, ensign and jack).

When and why one of these ensigns, the blue ensign, replaced the Union Jack as the national flag is a story not many Australians know. Yet they need to know that story to understand why they are divided over their national flag (see: The 1901 flag competition).

How could, how would Australians replace the Union Jack as the national flag with one of these two ensigns? Most Australians, as British people, were attached to the Union Jack. Besides, the two ensigns were essentially shipping flags, not intended to be used on shore. The transition from British to Australian national flag would be demanding, whether Australians flew an ensign with the Union Jack or an ensign on its own. Which ensign should they choose, the blue or the red? Should they give the Union Jack precedence (see: National flags)?

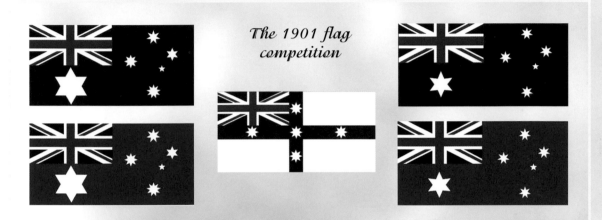

The 1901 flag competition

Australians were more concerned than their government that their new Commonwealth should have a flag. Ministers thought there were more important issues to resolve until Britain's secretary of state wrote asking the Commonwealth government to submit a design. Unable to agree on one, ministers decided to hold a competition since the public had been so interested in the issue. Already two competitions had been launched in Melbourne, where the parliament was to meet until a federal capital was built.

The debate about changing the Australian national flag since 1983 has caused a closer examination of the competition of 1901. The debate about the flag has become just as much a debate about the significance of the competition.

Those who oppose change to the flag emphasise the importance of the competition: the lack of requirements restricting the design; the more than 30 000 entrants, some from overseas; the judges' selection of a design submitted by five different entrants; the display of the design as a blue, not red ensign in announcing the winners; and the king's approval of the design.

Those who favour changing the flag question the significance of the competition: the British government required a design for two ensigns in the British tradition, not one flag; and the marine and naval judges conformed to that tradition (figure 1.12). The Admiralty confirmed their choice, rather than the design of a flag favoured by the Australian government – Australia's federation flag (figures 1.16, 1.3). After the selected design was formally gazetted in 1903 as two ensigns, the national flag remained the Union Jack.

By the 1980s most Australians accepted their blue ensign, rather than the Union Jack, as their national flag. But an increasing percentage of them felt that as long as the Union Jack – the flag of Britain – remained a part of it, their flag could not be truly Australian. Others disagreed. The division between the two groups had widened by 1992, in the process prompting this book. My hope is that exploring the history of this divide will help Australians to cross it.

A DISPUTE

There was uproar over Australia's flag in the House of Representatives in April 1992. 'In 1953, the *Flags Act* for the first time formally established it [the Australian blue ensign] as the national flag', insisted Paul Keating, Labor prime minister. 'It was gazetted before World War I, you mug', John

National flags

The national flag in Australia before federation was the Union Jack, flown on special days, such as the Queen's birthday. The six Australian colonies each had their own British blue ensign with a colonial badge in the fly for government ships. All but Victoria, which had its own red ensign, used the British red ensign for merchant ships.

After federation and the selection of a design for two ensigns, the national flag in Australia remained the Union Jack. The two ensigns in the British tradition were gazetted in 1903 as the Australian Commonwealth Ensign – a blue ensign for the Commonwealth government to use on official and naval ships; and the Australian Commonwealth Merchant Flag – a red ensign for merchant ships.

About this time people in Australia as in other parts of the British Empire began to see shipping ensigns as flags to use on land. But the tradition of seeing the blue ensign as the Commonwealth government's flag continued. State and local governments, individuals and organisations

wishing to use an Australian flag had to use the red ensign. From 1924 this tradition began to change, especially after 1938 in Victoria and then from 1941 federally.

From 1903 to 1953 people used a variety of terms for the two ensigns: the Australian/Commonwealth ensign, flag or blue ensign, or just blue ensign; and the Australian/ Commonwealth merchant flag, flag or red ensign, or just red ensign.

The Union Jack remained the national flag in Australia with precedence over the Australian blue and red ensigns until the Queen assented early in 1954 to the *Flags Act 1953*, which designated the Ensign as the 'Australian National Flag' and the Merchant Flag as the 'Australian Red Ensign'.

In 1980 the Commonwealth government tried to make the Australian national flag the flag for merchant ships but failed. Australia has two national flags, or more precisely two ensigns, since the Union Jack has been retained in the place of honour on both flags.

Howard, the Liberal industrial relations shadow minister, responded impatiently. Tourists drawn to the theatrics of question time watched with fascination the emotions being played out below, as cries of 'traitor' by National Party MP Michael Cobb punctuated the proceedings.[1]

Almost two years later a similar dispute about the flag's history erupted in Old Parliament House between Harold Scruby, executive director of Ausflag, and John Vaughan, spokesman of the Australian National Flag Association (ANFA). Their debate about the national flag coincided with an exhibition on its history and use. Again emotions ran high, stirred by the presence of flag-waving association supporters.[2]

Both incidents were as much about the present as the past. Keating and Ausflag wanted to change the national flag, believing that the Union Jack – the emblem of British nationality – in the place of honour made it an ambiguous symbol. Howard and the flag association opposed change, arguing that the Union Jack symbolised Australia's political and legal system.

When the blue ensign became the national flag of Australia was important to both sides: after the *Flags Act 1953* favoured the argument for changing the flag; before World War I, the argument for keeping it. Also important, especially to protagonists for change, was which flag preceded the blue ensign as the national flag. Keating mentioned two: the Union Jack and the Australian red ensign.

MISSING HISTORY

Surely, observers of these incidents might have thought, such a dispute about the history of the blue ensign could be easily settled. But contemporary sources raised more questions than they answered. Angus and Robertson's *Illustrated Australian Encyclopaedia* contained no entry on flags in its first edition (1925). The same publisher supplied only an ambiguous one in its *Australian Encyclopaedia* in 1958. The status of the Australian blue ensign as the national flag was not 'finally established' until 1953, the compiler, Frederick Phillips, explained. Even then, for 'official occasions both the national flag and the Union Flag are generally flown', he continued.

This practice raised doubts about the status of the blue ensign as the national flag. If, as Phillips implied, the Union Jack was the national flag before 1953, when did the blue ensign supplant it? The Commonwealth government's first edition of its booklet, *The Australian National Flag* (1956), was similarly unhelpful, being concerned more with the detail of the 1901 competition (to choose a design for two ensigns) and its winners than the status and use of those ensigns. 'For over fifty years … the flag has been the symbol of a united Australian people' was its superficial summary.

Checking the *Flags Act 1953* and the parliamentary debate surrounding it provides some clues. The Act designated for the first time the two Australian ensigns as the 'Australian National Flag' and the 'Australian Red Ensign'. But in introducing the bill then prime minister Robert Menzies assured Australians that 'on notable public occasions' the Union Jack and the Australian national flag would continue to be flown together. Which of these two flags would take precedence as the national flag?

The questions seem endless in the search for the Australian national flag's history. Some think that the *Commonwealth of Australia Gazette* notice of 1903 established the blue ensign as the national flag. It proclaimed two ensigns: the blue 'Ensign' for official and naval ships; and the red 'Merchant Flag' for merchant ships.[3] But which flag could the people use? Which flag did they use?

FLAG CEREMONIES

The flag I saluted every week when I started school in Kadina on South Australia's Yorke Peninsula in 1951 was not an Australian flag but the Union Jack. When we moved to Adelaide, then Jamestown in the state's mid-north during the 1950s, the school flag was still the Union Jack. Years later, while researching South Australia's public school system from the 1870s to the 1950s, I read in the *Education Gazette* the continuing requirement of ministers of education from 1911 until 1956 that schools fly the Union Jack for 'the national salute'. After that time principals were allowed to choose between the Union Jack and the Australian national flag.[4]

A comparison of flag ceremonies in public schools across the Australian states revealed differences in the words spoken and flags flown during the first 50 years of federation.[5] South Australians were not the only ones using the Union Jack. However, flags were becoming useful markers of a changing sense of nationhood – from British to Australian – during the 20th century. Schools were one obvious place to look for this change. State and military funerals were another: in 1931 the pall for the coffin of Sir John Monash, Australia's most famous general, was the Union Jack – as it was the next year for Albert Jacka, Australia's first World War I recipient of a Victoria Cross. Citizenship ceremonies also revealed differing allegiances: when it came to power in 1949 the Menzies Government required the Union Jack to be used on such occasions, as well as the Australian flag Labor had stipulated.

But the most significant place for observing the use of flags was Parliament House. How was the seat of government dressed for special occasions, such as its opening in 1927 and Queen Elizabeth II's coronation tour in 1954? Which flag took precedence – the Union Jack or an Australian flag? To establish the role of the blue ensign in Australia after federation requires looking beyond the *Gazette* notice of 1903 and the *Flags Act 1953* to see how governments and people used it, especially in relation to the red ensign and the Union Jack.

Finding the FLAG'S HISTORY

GAPS AND CLUES

Historians with an interest in flags have not explored in depth the roles of the three flags in the 20th century. In his book *Flag of Stars* (1966), revised as *Beneath the Southern Cross: The Story of Australia through Flags* (1980), Frank Cayley went beyond the details of the 1901 competition to mention criticism of the winning design by people and governments. But after observing that the chosen design was not seen much until World War I, he jumped to the 1940s to mention Labor minister Arthur Calwell's use of the blue ensign on cinema screens and at citizenship ceremonies. Only his comment in the undocumented history that 'public confusion continued' hinted at a more complex story. Cayley's entries under 'flags' in editions of the *Australian Encyclopaedia* from 1977 were equally restrained. As the son of an Australian naval officer his particular interest was in Australia's early flags, which were popularised in a 1984 poster for schools by John Vaughan, vexillographer and flag association spokesman.

Arthur Smout was a strong campaigner for the Australian national flag after 1953. In the three editions of his *Flag Book: Australia* published between 1968 and 1982, Smout urged Australians to fly the Australian national flag instead of the Union Jack, and to give the former precedence when the two flags were flown together.[6] His crusade confirmed that even in the 1970s and early 80s many Australians persisted in regarding the Union Jack as the national flag.

AN ANSWER AND A QUESTION

The Commonwealth government's booklet *The Australian National Flag*, published in several editions from 1956, said that the Australian flag should not be 'displayed in a position inferior to any other flag'. But not until 1977 did an edition include a 'Brief history of the flag', indicating that 'for many years' the blue ensign was seen as the official or government flag, while private individuals and organisations were advised to use the red ensign. Although that distinction began to change during the 1940s, the booklet said – with governments permitting, even encouraging Australians to use the blue ensign – 'it had not been clearly established that any particular flag was the "National Flag"'. There was 'confusion'.

Here at last was some explanation for the 1903–53 omission under 'flag' in the encyclopaedia and previous government booklets. But there was no acknowledgement of the role of the Union Jack after federation in 1901, let alone after the *Flags Act 1953*. Why had I been saluting the Union Jack at school in the 1950s?

OTHER NATIONAL FLAGS

The 1979 booklet and subsequent editions to 1985 dropped references to the red ensign being used by private individuals and organisations. The red ensign was written out of history as the people's flag until the complete revision of the booklet in 1995. *Australian Flags*, in its 'Evolution of a national flag' section, acknowledged that there had been 'several decades' of 'confusion' about the use of the two ensigns. More significant was its recognition that the Union Jack 'also continued to be used widely in the community'. Previous booklets since the first in 1956 had led the reader to think that after federation Australia no longer used the Union Jack or its British ensigns. These particular revisions were recommended as part of a comprehensive submission by Flag Society of Australia members Ralph Kelly and Tony Burton.[7]

The booklet's acknowledgement of the national flag's more complex history was refreshing, as was its mention of the debate about it. In launching it at Homebush West Public School, then minister for administrative services Frank Walker QC hoped the booklet would 'help contribute to sensible debate about our flag and its future'.[8] Such a contribution was badly needed. The more powerful the antagonists in the flag debate became during the 1990s, the more fiercely they promoted their rival versions of the flag's history in campaigns to preserve or change the current flag (see: Flag organisations in Australia).

CONTESTING THE FLAG'S HISTORY

Both sides of the debate complained about each other's misinformation. The Australian National Flag Association, drawing on the *Gazette* of 1903, insisted that the blue ensign had been Australia's national flag since 1901, when the flag competition judges selected a design for the two ensigns. Ausflag, querying the appropriateness of the design, argued that the rules

Flag organisations in Australia

Three flag organisations, emerging early in the 1980s, became active in the debate about the Australian national flag as Australians looked towards the bicentenary of 1988. Ausflag promoted flag change; the Australian National Flag Association opposed flag change. The Flag Society of Australia, a neutral body in the flag debate, encouraged interest in the history and design of flags through vexillology, the study of flags.

Incorporated in January 1983, Ausflag campaigned for a distinctively Australian national anthem, flag and colours. One of its founders, Harold Scruby, a Sydney consultant in management and marketing, remains Ausflag's executive director. On its board are prominent Australians from business, the media, politics and sport.

The RSL, concerned about Ausflag's campaign and Labor's win in March 1983, sponsored Australian National Flag Association (ANFA) branches later that year. John Vaughan, one of the NSW branch founders and its president from 1991, became the association's national spokesman in June 2000. Long interested in flags, especially early Australian flags, he had gradually developed that interest into a business. His experience marketing for a bank in schools and administering the Royal Australian Historical Society facilitated the association's work in promoting the flag. Ausflag looked to a series of flag design competitions between 1985 and 2000 to raise interest in and enthusiasm for designing a distinctively Australian flag. The groups' competition for Australian hearts and minds entered a new stage with Ausflag's move to the internet in 1995.

The Flag Society of Australia played an important role: correcting misinformation, providing advice, and publishing research in its journal *Crux Australis*. Not to be confused with this society is the Australian Flag Society of 2003 (once the Australian National Flag Association (ACT) branch), headed by Nigel Morris, with broader aims than opposing flag change.

of the competition required it to be based on British ensigns. Sydney vexillologist Ralph Kelly corrected both organisations in revealing the facts behind the myths about the competition and its aftermath.[9] His views represented the neutral expertise of the Flag Society of Australia, established in August 1983 to encourage interest in flag design and history.

Others were also concerned to verify the historical basis of the debate. This author's work in 1994 on flags in the early 1920s showed the continuing importance of the Union Jack in validating the use of Australian ensigns. Further work by the author in 1995 explained the Commonwealth government's selection in 1950 of the blue ensign as the national flag.[10] Carol Foley, a member of the law faculty at Monash University, analysed in 1996 the opposing versions of the blue ensign's history.[11] But her particular interest was to assess the Commonwealth government's executive power over the selection of the Australian national flag.

One flag association supporter who did not accept the results of this research sought unsuccessfully to 'correct' this author's entry on flags in *The Oxford Companion to Australian History*.[12]

QUESTIONS

Questions about the flag's history inevitably prompt questions about the groups taking an interest in it. Clearly they were locked in a battle for the hearts and minds of Australians who were so closely divided on change to the flag. By early 1998 for the first time a poll found that a small majority favoured change. The National Council for the Centenary of Federation considered the issue 'too controversial' to be the subject of its cheeky 1999 advertisements aimed at making Australians curious about their nation's history (see: What kind of country ...).[13]

Such questions touched too closely on the Australian flag's most important element – and the main cause of Australians' division over their flag – Britain's Union Jack.[14]

The debate about the Australian flag is as much about the place of the Union Jack on it as about a new design. But further, it is a debate about whether being British is the determining factor in being Australian. A nation's flag is its chief symbol, typifying or representing both people and country. Australia's national flag not only includes the flag of another country, but gives it the place of honour.

This book explains Australians' changing relationship to their national flags: the Union Jack since 1901; and the Australian national flag since 1954.

What kind of country ...

The $2.5 million official centenary of federation advertising campaign in 1999 posed questions on cinema screens, on posters in buses and trams, and in magazines. For example:

> What kind of country would have a national cricket team before it had a national parliament?
> What kind of country would forget the name of its first prime minister?

However, the campaign was as notable for the questions it did not ask, such as: What kind of country would celebrate federation in 1901 by introducing the British flag, the Union Jack, into its public schools? What kind of country would be unsure about which ensign – the blue or the red – to present to its schools in 1951 to celebrate 50 years of federation?

What kind of country would be so divided over its national symbol as it approached the centenary of federation?

Chapter one
Australian federation, British flag

figure 1.1
The Union flag of 1801, known as the Union Jack, symbolised the union of the English, Scots and Irish by incorporating the crosses of their patron saints in its design. It became the national flag of Britain and the British Empire.

A new flag for their new nation was on the minds of many Australians as they prepared for the inauguration of the Commonwealth. How would its design reflect their flag traditions?

Flag
TRADITIONS

BRITISH FLAG TRADITION

Britain's Union flag was likely to be an important part of any design. Commonly known as the Union Jack (figure 1.1) because it was originally flown from the jackstaff at the bow of ships, it symbolised the 1801 union of England and Scotland with Ireland by incorporating the crosses of the patron saints of the three countries: St George for England (the dominant cross in red), St Andrew for Scotland (white diagonal cross) and Ireland's St Patrick (red diagonal cross). The chief purpose of flags from early times was to indicate the nationality of ships. By 1864 three British ensigns – ships' flags with the Union Jack as the national flag in the upper hoist – had evolved to identify different kinds of vessels (see: Flag, ensign and jack).

EARLY UNOFFICIAL AUSTRALIAN FLAGS

Most of Australia's early flags were in the style of the British white ensign, featuring the St George cross with the stars of the Southern Cross, a distinctive constellation in southern hemisphere skies (figure 1.3). But there were two other quite different flags. One represented groups opposed to the transportation of British convicts to Australia and New Zealand; these united in 1851 under the flag of the Australasian League, from Launceston, Tasmania (figure 1.4). The other was the Eureka flag, the symbol under which the miners of Victoria rallied in 1854 to protest against arbitrary government (figure 1.4). Also known as the Southern Cross, it did not feature the Union Jack and was the flag by which the more radical miners swore to fight together in defending their rights and liberties.[1]

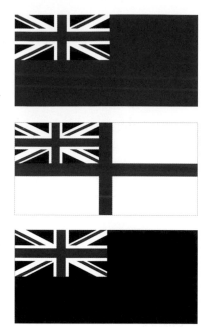

figure 1.2
The three British ensigns were shipping flags. Flown from the stern of vessels from 1864, they identified British government ships (blue ensign) from merchantmen (red) and naval ships (white).

Flag, ensign and jack

The flag evolved from prehistoric times. Its prototype, a vexilloid, was a staff with an emblem made from bones, feathers, wood or metal. The word 'vexilloid' is associated with the term for the study of flags: vexillology. The fabric flag, developed in China as a silk banner, later appeared in countries to the west.

At first used as military and ceremonial symbols, flags came to identify the rulers of countries and the nationality of their ships at sea. Their most important role was as shipping flags. One of the earliest, in the 13th century, was the English flag, white with the red cross of St George. This flag formed one element of Britain's Union flag, which evolved after Scotland's union with England in 1606 and Ireland's in 1801 (figure 1.1). British ensigns – flags with the national flag in the place of honour – evolved to identify

from 1864 three different kinds of ships which wore them at the stern: blue for government ships, red for merchant ships, and white for warships (figure 1.2).

The place of honour on a flag is the upper hoist, the first quarter (or 'canton') of the flag next to the flagpole. While flag is a general term, ensign describes a more specific kind of flag. Jack is another type of ship's flag: the small flag flown on the jackstaff at the bow of a warship. For British warships, the jack was a small Union flag – hence the term Union Jack, which became the common name for the British national flag.

From 1865 the Admiralty required every British colony to use a British blue (government) ensign with its colonial badge in the fly (the second or outer half of the flag). Most British colonies also used the British red (merchant) ensign, without a badge.

COLONIAL ENSIGNS

From 1865 Britain required its colonies to use a British blue ensign with the badge of the colony in the fly.

By 1901 the NSW and Victorian blue ensigns (figure 1.5) revealed the different choices of symbols those colonies had made in the 1870s. Merchant ships in most British colonies flew the British red ensign, but Victoria had its own red ensign with the Southern Cross, which had been approved by Britain's Board of Trade in 1870.[2]

Flag COMPETITIONS

Many Australians assumed that the Commonwealth would follow the British pattern of ensigns for ships. The only issue to settle seemed to be the choice of Australian and/or federal symbols.

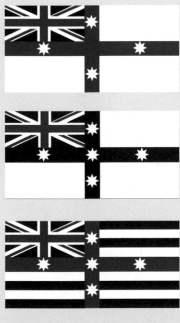

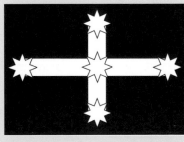

figure 1.3
These unofficial Australian flags are styled on the British white ensign with stars from the Southern Cross added: the 1823–24 national colonial flag; the 1832 NSW ensign – the 1890s federation flag; the 1850s Murray River flag.

figure 1.4
The 1851 Australasian League flag represented colonial groups opposing the transportation of British convicts to Australia and New Zealand. Protesting Victorian miners rallied under the Eureka or Southern Cross flag of 1854, a symbol of protest against arbitrary government.

figure 1.5
By 1901 the ensigns of Australia's two largest colonies had quite different symbols: NSW's St George cross with stars from early Australian flags; and Victoria's representations of the Southern Cross based on the Australasian League's flag.

DIFFERENT COMPETITIONS, DIFFERENT RULES

A newspaper competition

In June 1900 Melbourne's *Herald Standard* newspaper launched a design competition for two Australian ensigns. Rules stipulated that entries had to include the Union Jack and, as constellation or symbol, the Southern Cross. In September 1900 the judges, a soldier, a mariner and four laymen, chose a design based on the British red ensign, with the Southern Cross in the fly and six red bands to represent the states (figure 1.6) (see: Canada sets an example).

Canada sets an example

The judge's choice of winner in *The Herald Standard* competition suggested they were looking for a flag that Australians could fly on land and sea. In this, they were following the example of Canadians, who had made their red ensign a popular flag. 'The blood-red fighting flag of Britain, with a Commonwealth emblem in the fly, would tell us that you are of us and with us', one prominent Canadian urged. Even so, the British Admiralty would also require a blue ensign (figure 1.6).[3]

A second competition

The Melbourne journal *The Review of Reviews for Australasia* featured both *Herald Standard* ensigns on the covers of its October and November 1900 issues, and immediately launched a second competition for red and blue ensigns – this time without the requirement that British or Australian symbols be incorporated. However, the editor, William Fitchett, admitted that designs without these elements would probably not be successful.[4]

Two very different representations of the Southern Cross had emerged by the end of the 19th century. One was NSW's version of the St George cross with stars; the other Victoria's representation of the constellation (figures 1.7–1.11). Would either of these be chosen as Commonwealth ensigns? How would federation be represented?

The Commonwealth government competition

Edmund Barton, the prime minister, was reluctant at the beginning of 1901 to respond to the British government's request for a flag design for the new Commonwealth. It was all very well for one Australian to complain to him that 'every city, village, house, school and steamer is anxious to proclaim the Union of Australia, but not one can do so through the non-existence of our Flag'.[5] There were federal elections and the opening of the new parliament by royalty to organise, as well as legislation to prepare.

figure 1.6
Frederick Thompson, of Melbourne, won **The Herald Standard** *competition with this design for blue and red ensigns. To the specified Union Jack and Southern Cross, he added six red bands for the states*

It was also clear that choosing a flag design for the Commonwealth would be difficult, given the rivalry between Victoria and New South Wales over their symbols. Commonwealth ministers could not agree on a design. Since the public seemed to be so interested in the issue, the government launched in April 1901 a competition for two ensigns – one for naval and official use, the other for merchant ships – without specifying symbols.[6]

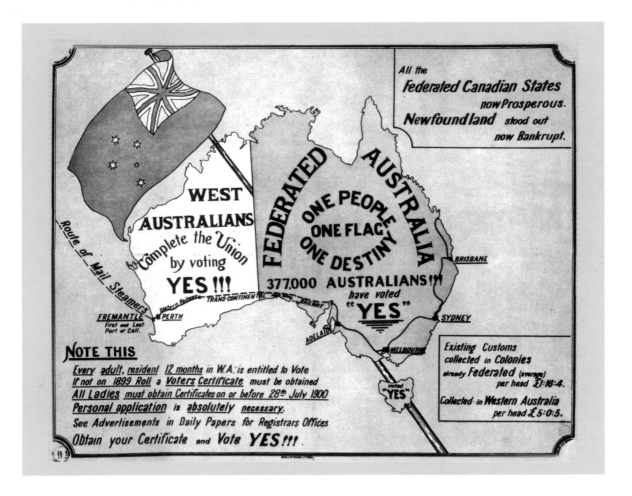

figure 1.7
Victoria's red ensign with the Southern Cross constellation featured in this illustration encouraging West Australians to choose federation when voting on the proposed constitution in July 1900, as other Australians had done the year before.

WINNERS AND DISSENTING VOICES

There were more than 30 000 entries in the government competition, many forwarded from the one begun by *The Review of Reviews*. But the judges took less than a week at the end of August 1901 to choose a similar design submitted separately by five entrants: Annie Dorrington of Perth, Ivor Evans and Egbert Nuttall, both of Melbourne, Leslie Hawkins of Sydney, and William Stevens of Auckland (figure 1.12).

The choice reflected the judges' seafaring backgrounds: a design for two British ensigns with the Southern Cross constellation in the fly for Australian sentiment, and a large six-pointed star (the Commonwealth Star) pointing to the St George cross in the Union Jack above, to represent the six federating states. Aware of the need to satisfy 'the Home Authorities', they thought the Admiralty could not object to the Southern Cross – already approved in the Victorian and NZ ensigns, or to the 'star under the "Jack"', though it was unusual to have two separate symbols on colonial ensigns.[7]

figure 1.8
The NSW government's invitation to the inaugural celebrations for the Commonwealth of Australia in Sydney in January 1901 featured a boat to represent the Commonwealth. On board were the states with their symbols, but it was the NSW-style federation flag that featured most prominently.

Barton announced the winners at a ceremony in the Royal Exhibition Building on 3 September 1901, at which the blue ensign was flown above the dome for the first time. But criticism of the design began at once, especially in New South Wales: it was too Victorian (compare figures 1.12 and 1.5). Critics, including the pro-federation Australian Natives Association (for Australian-born European men) wanted the St George cross with stars – 'the principal feature of the old Australian flag' (figures 1.3, 1.13). Dissension in Cabinet showed the extent of agreement with this point of view. After all, the

St George cross with stars had been the symbol of the campaign for federation. Barton himself had persuaded the Australasian Federation League of New South Wales to adopt and promote it as the federal flag.[8]

When queried about that flag, the competition judges said they believed that it would be difficult, and therefore costly, to make.[9] They were faced with the problem of how to make the old Australian flag fit the British pattern of red and blue ensigns. There was also criticism of the Commonwealth Star, seen by some as too large. William Lumley of Melbourne had submitted a design that foreshadowed the Royal Australian Navy's choice of an Australian white ensign more than 60 years later. Afterwards he modified the large star (figure 1.15).

figure 1.9
'One flag', proclaimed the government of Victoria's invitation to celebrate federation in May 1901. What would the symbols for that flag be: the St George cross with stars or the Southern Cross constellation?

For some months Barton delayed sending the competition-winning design to London for approval. When he did, in February 1902, he also sent the NSW-style alternative design, explaining

AUSTRALIAN COMMONWEALTH CELEBRATIONS.

THE GOVERNMENT OF VICTORIA requests the honor of the presence of Mr and Mrs J. G. Watson at a Conversazione in the Exhibition Building on the Evening of Tuesday 7th May 1901, at 8 p.m.

The Young Queen.

Her hand was still on her sword hilt—the spur was still on her heel—
She had not cast her harness of grey war=dinted steel;
High on her red=splashed charger, beautiful, bold, and browned,
Bright=eyed out of the battle, the young Queen rode to be crowned
Loyal she gave the greeting, royal she bowed her head,
Crying "Crown me, my mother," and the old Queen stood and said
—Kipling's Commonwealth Ode.

figure 1.10
The most important of the Commonwealth government's invitations – for the opening of the first Commonwealth parliament in Melbourne in May 1901 – declared Britain's recognition of Australia's maturity by featuring Victoria's Southern Cross.

figure 1.11
The Commonwealth government's invitation to meet the Duke and Duchess of Cornwall and York in Melbourne in May 1901 represented Australia as a young woman with a shield bearing the NSW-style federation flag – without the Union Jack.

The Young Queen.

Her hand was still on her sword hilt—the spur was still on her heel—
She had not cast her harness of grey war=dinted steel ;
High on her red=splashed charger, beautiful, bold, and browned,
Bright=eyed out of the battle, the young Queen rode to be crowned
Loyal she gave the greeting, royal she bowed her head,
Crying "Crown me, my mother," and the old Queen stood and said
—Kipling's Commonwealth Ode.

figure 1.12
The similar winning designs for the two Commonwealth ensigns in the Victorian style included the Commonwealth Star. The winners announced on 3 September 1901 were Annie Dorrington (Perth), Ivor Evans and Egbert Nuttall (Melbourne), Leslie Hawkins (Sydney), and William Stevens (Auckland).

figure 1.13
The 1898 referendum badge of the Australasian Federation League of New South Wales had the words 'One Flag' added to Henry Parkes' slogan of 'One People, One Destiny'. The league promoted the federation flag as the flag for the new Commonwealth.

that it was 'originally known as the Australian flag' (figure 1.3).[10] How would the Admiralty rule? New Zealand had legislated in September 1900 for its blue ensign to serve as its national flag for all purposes, official and general, on land and water. But the Admiralty had refused to approve this change to British tradition, forcing amendment in November 1901. Even so, while accepting a red ensign for merchant ships, New Zealand retained its chosen flag for all purposes ashore, where the Admiralty had no control.[11]

CONFUSION REIGNS

The desire for a national flag that could be used by people and government was evident in Britain as well as Canada, New Zealand and Australia. The celebrations for Edward VII's coronation in Britain in June 1902 revealed confusion among officials and citizens as to what was the national flag – the Union Jack or the British red ensign – and whether the Union Jack could be used by people as well as government. Clearly, a change was occurring in the use of flags.

Having begun as emblems to identify and protect subjects at sea, flags now also served as symbols of national sentiment at home. The British government and monarchy encouraged such displays as a way of developing social cohesion at a time when

figure 1.14
Union Jacks and federation flags decorating Swanston Street, Melbourne, for celebrations marking the opening of the first Commonwealth parliament by the Duke of Cornwall and York on 9 May 1901.

figure 1.15
William Lumley's design for the 1901 flag competition foreshadowed the Australian white ensign of 1967. His modified design, filling the large 'empty' Commonwealth Star, flew at the Melbourne Cricket Ground on 2 January 1902 for the England–Australia Test.

it was being challenged politically by class interests: better a British flag than the red flag of socialism. But which British flag could they use? *The Times* rejected the assumption that the Union Jack was only for government, but looked to schools to teach people how to fly it properly: many had flown it upside down at the time of the coronation.[12]

figure 1.16
The Admiralty approved (but modified) the competition-winning design for two ensigns, rather than the federation flag. The Commonwealth ensign for official and naval use and the Commonwealth merchant flag for merchant ships were formally gazetted in February 1903.

The Admiralty decides

The Admiralty's preference for the competition-winning design for two ensigns (with modified stars) was predictable (figure 1.16). Consistent with its decision on the NZ ensigns, the choice emphasised Australia's colonial status. The Union Jack, honoured in the ensigns, was the symbol of British sovereignty. As an Australian official remarked two generations later when trying to explain Australians' continuing confusion about their blue ensign:

> It would in all the circumstances appear that the grant to the Commonwealth of a flag had no greater significance than had that to say Tasmania in pre-federation days … The Commonwealth was merely another Colonial unit and the flag was merely a Colonial Ensign.[13]

The new (blue) Commonwealth ensign wasn't and could not be the national flag. That remained the Union Jack – the flag sent to schools to celebrate Australian nationhood.

Flying the flag in
THE SCHOOL YARD

SEIZING THE MOMENT

Sir Frederick Sargood was a highly respected Melbourne merchant and unofficial leader of Victoria's Legislative Council (figure 1.17). Sargood, who was an English immigrant, had become involved in the Victorian Volunteer Artillery and founded the St Kilda Rifle Corps. In 1884, as Victoria's first defence minister, he created the school cadet corps. Since 1898 Sargood had been pushing for provision of the Union Jack to public schools in Victoria, as a reminder to children of their British heritage, but governments baulked at the cost. Now, with the approach of celebrations for the opening of the Commonwealth parliament at the Royal Exhibition Building on 9 May 1901, he seized his opportunity.

figure 1.17
English immigrant, Melbourne merchant and politician, and a judge of The Herald Standard *flag competition, Sir Frederick Sargood (1834–1903) introduced Union Jacks into public schools at the time of federation to remind future generations of Australians that they were British.*

Sargood knew of moves to find a design for Australian flags and public interest in the issue – he was chairman of the panel of judges for *The Herald Standard* competition. The panel's choice and the exhibition of some 8000 entries attracted such crowds that the opening hours were extended. Important people had begun talking about an Australian flag in schools, and Sargood expected that sooner or later a design would gain official approval.[14] Australians' enthusiasm for federation foreshadowed the role their flag could have in developing Australian patriotism in schools. Imperial sentiment was likely to wane (see: Symbol under siege).

For Sargood it was time to renew his campaign to make the British symbol a permanent reminder to future generations of Australians of their rights and responsibilities as citizens of the empire. School boards would want their schools to participate in federation celebrations: they would help with the cost of flags and poles.

Sargood wrote to Melbourne's *Argus* and *Age* newspapers and to country papers on 2 October 1900, offering 200 Union Jacks to launch his proposal: a flag ceremony 'would be a very suitable means of enabling our State school children to take part in the general rejoicings'. But the detail of the letter revealed his true purpose: to make children 'realise the fact of our being part of the greatest empire in the world'; and to promote 'a love of the old mother country and a pride in the "old flag"'.[15] His generous offer of flags might also be seen as an astute marketing exercise for his successful wholesale softgoods business.

PLAYING POLITICS

The mixture of Australian and British sentiment in Sargood's proposal attracted public support, with both the conservative *Argus* and the liberal *Age* listing donors – among them James Moore, a timber merchant, who matched Sargood's 200 flags with poles.

Relieved of the cost, the government approved the scheme, which was to lend itself to political manipulation over the following months. In March 1901, HB Higgins, a liberal radical candidate for the working-class seat of North Melbourne in the new parliament, refused to prove his loyalty by donating a Union Jack to the public school at Fitzroy. Opposed to Australia's involvement in the war in South Africa, Higgins thought those backing the conflict were exploiting Victorians' imperial sentiment. In the colony's election a few months before, Geelong electors had successfully broken up a political meeting he was addressing, waving Union Jacks against him.[16]

Enough donors came forward for one perceptive Melbourne observer to estimate that 'the national flag seems likely to fill a very large space in the

Symbol under siege

The Union Jack had been the focus of much anxiety as it symbolised the fate of British troops in South Africa. 'Thank God, we kept the flag flying', the British commander at Ladysmith had said in February 1900 at the lifting of its siege. There were further instances of British endurance: Mafeking in May, after a seven months' siege; in China, too, in August, with the Boxer rebels.

These, the Victorian chief justice and lieutenant-governor declared at the opening of the flag competition exhibition, were 'magnificent lessons of the value of the national flag', the rallying point for Britons under threat. The fate of the Union Jack had drawn Australians together. The flag symbolised their common British origins, history and destiny, their ethnicity, or as one editor later put it, their 'British stick-together-ism'.[17] Yet, while Australians were serving with British forces in South Africa, some at home opposed the war.

Australian landscape'. Dr Fitchett, *The Review of Reviews* editor, had a particular interest in the Union Jack. The English-born Wesleyan clergyman was author of the extraordinarily popular *Deeds that Won the Empire* (1897), and *Fights for the Flag* (1898), issued in a new edition in 1900. Fitchett was happy to promote in his journal the efforts of Sargood's State School Flag Committee, whose members included Victoria's military commandant and the president of the Marine Board – both of whom had been members of *The Herald Standard's* panel of judges – the secretary of the education department, the deputy postmaster-general and the chairman of the Council of Boards of Advice for schools. With the committee made up in this way, the scheme's success seemed assured.

Bunting and empire

'Though the National Flag is primarily just so much silk or bunting, its design and colouring are full of meaning; and, though its prime cost may be but a few shillings, its value is priceless, for the national honour is enwrapped in its folds, and the history of centuries is figured in the symbolism of its devices. It represents to us all that patriotism means. It is the flag of freedom, and of the greatest empire that the world has ever known.'[18]

Extract from F Edward Hulme, *The Flags of the World: their History, Blazonry, and Associations from the Banner of the Crusades to the Burgee of the Yachtsman*, Warne, London, 1897.

While school boards placed orders for flags and poles, the railway commissioner and postmaster-general agreed to transport them free. Sargood's immediate concern was to supply all public schools in Victoria, but he hoped to involve schools beyond the colony's borders and wrote to premiers and newspapers in other colonies. He even invited schools in New Zealand, where he had business interests, and Fiji to participate.[19]

TELEGRAPHIC TIMING

To raise Union Jacks simultaneously across Australia on 14 May 1901, Sargood refined a strategy used by the labour movements in the United States and Europe for May Day, 1890. Australian children, coordinated by telegraph across three time zones, would raise their Union Jacks together. In preparation, teachers and children followed departmental directions.[20] The description of the Union Jack (figure 1.18) for older children to memorise suited Sargood's purpose perfectly (see: Bunting and empire).

FLAG RHETORIC

Sargood believed that teaching children to love the Union Jack and the empire it represented was necessary in public schools but not in private ones, where it was only displayed on special occasions, and then with the restraint of the tradition they had inherited from England. Rudyard Kipling's

Stalky & Co, a story of life in an English school for the sons of men in the armed forces, gives a glimpse of that tradition with the boys' disparagement of anything resembling 'flag-flapping'. The patriotism of such pupils was assumed, their schools regarded as 'nurseries of unselfish citizenship'.

These were the schools of the middle class, which saw itself as 'the backbone of the nation'.[21] For that reason Sargood placed its representatives at the very centre of the ceremony he orchestrated on 14 May in the Royal Exhibition Building, where the Commonwealth parliament had met five days before. There, boys from Victoria's elite private schools – Scotch College, St Patrick's College, Melbourne Grammar School, Geelong Grammar School, Wesley College and Xavier College – gathered for a prize-giving ceremony attended by the Duke and Duchess of Cornwall and York.

THE MESSAGE GOES OUT

*figure 1.18
While the Education Gazette and Teachers' Aid's diagram of the 'National Flag for Schools' of 1900 revealed the dominance of the St George cross, The School Paper explained to pupils that red stood for 'ardent love', blue for 'truth' and white for 'purity'.*

Meanwhile, public school children waited far off for the duchess's telegraphic signal at the end of the Melbourne ceremony to raise the flags bought or donated in the preceding months. In Newcastle, boys with flags were stationed between the telegraph office and local schools, ready to relay its arrival. At precisely 12.50 pm Eastern Standard Time, as the Union Jack rose up a gilded flagpole within the exhibition building, thousands of public school children around Australia watched the raising of their Union Jacks to the sound of gunfire (figures 1.19, 1.20).

The response was widespread, particularly in Victoria, New South Wales and Tasmania, but also in South Australia. Newspapers reported the

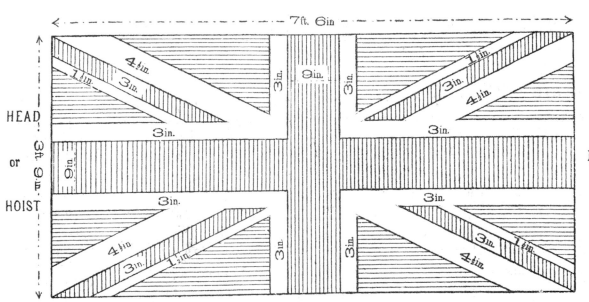

The Union Flag, commonly called the "Union Jack."

Red—Vertical Lines ; White—Plain Spaces ; Blue—Horizontal Lines.

hoisting and saluting of the flag, cheers for king, duke and duchess, and the new nation, school cadets firing three volleys – Sargood had been sure that they would oblige – the singing of patriotic songs, giving of speeches, presenting of commemorative medals, and handing out bags of lollies, the children's long-awaited reward.[22]

figure 1.19
Pupils saluting the
Union Jack at King-street
State School, West
Melbourne, on
14 May 1901 to
mark the opening
of the first Common-
wealth parliament
in Melbourne.

MISSION ACCOMPLISHED

The ceremonies emphasised the British Empire rather than the Commonwealth of Australia. A speaker at Sutherland, near Sydney, might tell his young listeners that the 'British flag' was 'a symbol of Australian unity', but Melbourne's conservative *Argus* recognised the importance of the other message: 'In the mind of every schoolboy and schoolgirl … the accomplishment of federation will ever be associated with an unprecedented and universal expression of loyalty to the British Throne and Empire'. *The Sydney Morning Herald* agreed: the ceremony was 'an object lesson in loyalty', it reported.

But as Sargood indicated, most important would be 'the lasting impression' left on children as, week by week, they saw the Union Jack, 'the symbol of unity, strength and protection', flying over their schools. Others developed the same theme. In working-class Collingwood, the mayor, a London-born Labor MLA, believed that the flag would be a

figure 1.20
Coordinated by a tele-
graph message from
Melbourne's Royal
Exhibition Building,
many schools across
Australia, including
Fort-street Public
School in Sydney,
raised the Union Jack
at 12.50 pm Eastern
Standard Time on
14 May 1901.

constant reminder of 'the greatest freedom and liberty for the people' and a guarantee of the empire's support. Freedom and strength: these were the qualities presented to children through the symbol of the Union Jack. Sargood, now a senator in the new parliament, could be well satisfied. The Victorian government hoped every public school would buy the picture, 'The Opening of the First Federal Parliament', but the flag was a much more potent symbol.[23]

DISSENTING VOICES

The Union Jack, however, did not fly unchallenged. At least three NSW schools also flew the flag of the campaign for federation, variously referred to as the Australian, Commonwealth or Federal flag (figure 1.3). Phillip Nelligan, the headmaster of Smith-street Superior Public School in working-class Balmain, Sydney, made a point of using both flags, and having the children sing *Advance Australia Fair* as well as *God Save the King*.

Nelligan's even-handed approach to country and empire was unusual. Perhaps his education, outside the imperial mould at the Catholic St Stanislaus' College in Bathurst, had something to do with it.[24] He realised the importance of developing in children a love for the Australian nation within the wider loyalty they gave to their British nation.

The cheerful salute

The idea of pledging allegiance to the flag came from the Canadians, who in turn had copied the Americans. Flying the flag over US schools had become common from the time of the civil war and was promoted from the late 1880s by the powerful veterans' pressure group, the Grand Army of the Republic, which presented flags to schools and encouraged them to adopt the American patriotic salute: 'We give our Heads! – and our Hearts! – to God! and our Country! One Country! One Language! One Flag!'

The Grand Army's campaign had become part of a wider movement to Americanise the children of immigrants pouring into cities from central, eastern and southern Europe. It was a time of rapid industrialisation, marked by fierce clashes between capital and labour. The ritual evolved, with the words of the salute changing to: 'I pledge allegiance to my Flag and the Republic for which it stands: one Nation indivisible, with Liberty and Justice for All'.

Assimilating large numbers of non-English-speaking immigrants posed even more of a challenge for Canada, where the majority saw themselves as both Canadian and British. The Canadians adapted both forms: 'We give our heads and our hearts to God and our Country – One Flag, One Fleet, One Throne'; and 'I pledge allegiance to my Flag and to the Empire for which it stands – one Empire, indivisible, with Liberty and Justice for All'.[25]

By contrast, the Victorian pledge was firmly grounded in the practicalities of the child's world – parents, teachers and the laws: 'I love God and my country; I honour the flag; I will serve the King, and cheerfully obey my parents, teachers and the laws', pupils recited (figure 1.21).[26]

Country rather than the British Empire was the focus of the Victorian school salute, though reinforced by service to the sovereign and honour to the Union Jack. But then 'country' could be ambiguous. It was the word 'cheerfully' in the salute that was to linger in many minds down the years. Perhaps William Gillies, the Australian-born teacher and writer of Victorian textbooks, had put it in. He argued that Australians had better reason than most peoples of the world to obey their laws cheerfully since they had a more widespread right to elect their lawmakers.[27] At least most of them had that right after 1902, which was when women were given the franchise for federal (but not all state) elections. Indigenous voters were largely denied it until 1962.

FROM SPECIAL CEREMONY TO WEEKLY TIMETABLE

While federal ministers argued about the design the competition judges had chosen for the Australian ensigns, Victoria's minister for public instruction consolidated the role of the Union Jack as the national flag in the state's public schools. Sargood's ceremony of saluting the Union Jack would continue beyond the celebrations of May 1901. Together with patriotic songs and poems, a salute of the flag would mark the new king's birthday, the return of Australians from the Boer War, and other 'national occasions'.

More significantly, the minister required a simplified version of the ceremony every Monday morning – the hoisting of the flag and the children's declaration of loyalty – an idea that had come from the USA via Canada (see: The cheerful salute). Many schools already had their national flag. Others would now have to get one. Fitchett had been right about the Union Jack. Replacing it with an Australian flag would be difficult.

A lukewarm reception for AUSTRALIAN ENSIGNS

Barton's government was unsure what to do with the blue ensign when authorisation for its use finally came from Britain in 1903. Questions from the naval commandant in Brisbane were bounced from the defence minister to the external affairs department without receiving a definitive answer.[28] There was one MP, the youngest in the House of Representatives, who did

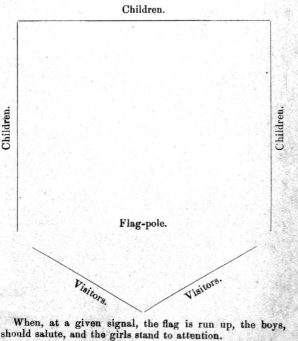

SALUTING THE FLAG.

The children should be drawn up in the form of a hollow square facing the flag-pole. If the school has a cadet corps, its place will be in the hollow square. Visitors should face the children, standing, if possible, behind the flag-pole.

Children.

Children.

Children.

Flag-pole.

Visitors.

Visitors.

When, at a given signal, the flag is run up, the boys, should salute, and the girls stand to attention.

figure 1.21
The Union Jack was the focus of new instructions issued by the Victorian government in October 1901 to public schools. An extract explained how to organise the compulsory flag ceremony to be held each week and on national occasions.

figure 1.22
In June 1904, Richard Armstrong Crouch (1868–1949), a Melbourne barrister, persuaded the House of Representatives to pass a motion urging the Commonwealth government to use the Commonwealth ensign. The government was reluctant.

have an answer. Richard Crouch, a Melbourne barrister and member of the Australian Natives Association, wanted the blue ensign to be used by the militia, in which he was involved, and on forts and naval ships (figure 1.22). Defence authorities, he argued, were treating it as an 'inferior ensign'. The defence minister insisted on the Union Jack for Australian forts, but allowed the blue ensign to be flown by Commonwealth Naval Forces – though not ships Australia subsidised in the Royal Navy's Australian squadron.[29]

Replacing the Union Jack on Australian forts was to take much longer. The defence department head was adamant that on forts, according to *King's Regulations*, 'The Union Jack is not in any way superseded by the Commonwealth ensign'.[30] Richard Crouch was not one to give up easily. Impatient with the Commonwealth government, he persuaded the House of Representatives in June 1904 to pass his motion 'that … the Australian flag, as officially selected, should be flown upon all forts, vessels, saluting places, and public buildings of the Commonwealth upon all occasions when flags are used'. The first Labor Commonwealth government, which took office briefly that year, agreed to fly the blue ensign on special days on Commonwealth buildings in Sydney and Melbourne; also on post offices as long there was no additional expense – a qualification which undermined the decision.[31]

Expense was one problem. Design was another. The new Labor prime minister, Chris Watson, did not like the design of the ensign: 'Though it includes the Southern Cross … it is not sufficiently indicative of Australian unity', he said. Watson wanted 'a more distinctive design for a national flag', which his government would seek. His words echoed the earlier complaint about the design being too Victorian. As to flags on forts, Watson followed defence department advice. It was 'custom to display the Union Jack', not an ensign, on forts: 'The Commonwealth flag is regarded as an ensign to be used in the same way as the British ensign. The British ensign is not displayed from forts.'[32]

COMPETING LOYALTIES, AND A CHALLENGE

Australian sentiment had been critical in bringing about federation, yet at the core of this sentiment there remained a strong sense of being British: father of federation, Henry Parkes' 'crimson thread of kinship' drew the Australian colonists together.[33] British legislation established their Commonwealth. British royalty opened Australia's first parliament. Melbourne's *Table Talk*, an investigative journal of politics and finance, showed the king conferring nationhood on a federated Australia (figure 1.23). The fact that federation had been achieved in the midst of an imperial war strengthened the British core of Australian nationhood. The challenge for Australians was to develop an identity distinct from that strong British, even English, core.

figure 1.23
To Melbourne's
Table Talk of
9 May 1901, King
Edward VII had
bestowed nation-
hood on the
Commonwealth,
not the Australian
people who
approved its
constitution.

CROWNING THE YOUNG QUEEN!

It was the message of British poet Rudyard Kipling in the last line of his poem 'The Young Queen', honouring the new Commonwealth (figure 1.10): 'And make thy people to love thee, as thou has loved me', the old queen (Britain) advised the young queen (Australia).[34]

The search for an Australian flag design showed how difficult that challenge would be. Both the competition-winning design favoured by Britain and the federation flag Barton and others preferred were British ensigns, honouring the Union Jack and emphasising Australia's colonial status. Officialdom's dislike of the chosen design and caution as to protocol made it reluctant to use the blue ensign, the flag of the Commonwealth government, not the Australian people. As to the red ensign, legislation would not require merchant ships registered in Australia to use it until section 406 of the *Navigation Act 1920* took effect in February 1922.[35] In the meantime, with Sir Frederick Sargood's help, the Union Jack rather than an Australian flag became established in public schools, reinforcing children's sense of being British.

Chapter two
Empire Day and Australia Day

The Labor government's 1904 decision to use the Commonwealth ensign, however reluctantly taken, gave heart to Richard Crouch of the Australian Natives Association and others who saw it as the symbol of an emerging Australian nationality (see chapter 1: A lukewarm reception for Australian ensigns). But clearly government regarded the Union Jack as the national flag and the Australian flag an ensign primarily reserved for ships. In this situation the use of an Australian flag was going to be difficult. Just how difficult became apparent, first with the introduction of Empire Day on 24 May 1905, and then the Irish-Catholic-inspired move to replace it with Australia Day.

PARTY POLITICS –
the introduction of
EMPIRE DAY, 1905

BRITISH EMPIRE LEAGUE

Most British colonies had agreed by early 1903 to celebrate 24 May, the birthday of the late Queen Victoria, as Empire Day, marking it by a public holiday or a special day in schools. Australia, however, was an exception, and in 1905 was one of the few places in the empire where the day was not officially celebrated. Three years earlier, the British Empire League (BEL) had been established in Sydney to counter the influence of the Australian Anti-War League. Giving a British emphasis to the motto it borrowed from Parkes, 'One People,

One Destiny', the BEL had enthusiastically endorsed the idea of Empire Day, proposed by its advocate, Lord Meath, to delegates at the Colonial Conference in London in 1902. It would be a 'Britons' day', reminding Australians of their British nationality under the Union Jack, the league said.[1]

Neither the prime minister, Sir Edmund Barton, nor the state premiers supported the BEL's 1903 proposal to establish Empire Day in Australia. Barton thought it would be divisive – likely to provoke those who had opposed the war in South Africa and his government's decision to increase its subsidy to Britain for a naval squadron, rather than develop an Australian navy. Australians, Barton said, would do better to celebrate their new federation. But the league looked to Empire Day to counter the 'dangerous tendency' towards Australian independence stimulated by federation. It wanted to give Australians who valued the British connection 'the chance to demonstrate openly and enthusiastically their loyalty to King and Empire'.[2]

GEORGE REID'S ANTI-LABOR CAMPAIGN

When the BEL tried again in February 1905 to get Empire Day officially recognised, a different prime minister, Scottish-born George Reid, who was also a vice-president of the league, was in power, and most of the state premiers did not belong to Labor. The introduction of Empire Day was approved. However, the decision appeared to be a minimal response to badgering by the league: instead of the public holiday it wanted, it was to be a day for public schools to learn about and celebrate the empire. But political circumstances, especially in New South Wales, pointed to party political motives at work in the decision. Joseph Carruthers, the NSW premier who had put the item on the premiers' conference agenda, knew how useful Empire Day could be in consolidating his new Liberal Party as a broad anti-Labor grouping.

Cultivating a support base
Carruthers, an Australian-born Sydney solicitor, had defeated the Labor Party the previous year by carefully drawing together a range of political groups with similar interests: the Liberal and Reform Association, the Women's Liberal League, the temperance movement and the Australian Protestant Defence Association. Critical to his electoral success had been the support of recently enfranchised women voters. He knew how important the formation of a women's branch had been to the revival of the BEL in 1903 and how determined the women were to promote loyalty to the empire in public schools as a means of countering socialist influence.[3]

Events within the NSW Labor Party just a few days before the premiers' conference increased the consolidation of Carruthers' support base when a conference of Labor leagues and trade unions in Sydney approved as a party objective the development of Australia as a self-reliant socialist community. This made Labor even more of a target for the BEL and the Liberal Party. Well might one Labor delegate fear that those voting for a motion put to the conference by the federal party leader, Chris Watson for 'the cultivation of an Australian national sentiment' could be giving 'the enemy a rod with which to beat the Labor movement'. There were already accusations that Labor wanted to 'cut the painter' (ties with Britain). Watson acknowledged that 'national' was too radical a word and withdrew it.[4]

For Carruthers, special Empire Day lessons in public schools would undermine Labor and bolster its opponents. The other premiers, most generally opposed to Labor, agreed with the NSW premier.

For Reid, the prime minister, the implications were clear. Aware of the growing electoral success of the highly organised and disciplined NSW and federal Labor parties, he was seeking ways of binding conservative free trade supporters and Liberal protectionists together against Labor. The day after the decision to introduce Empire Day, Reid launched his nationwide campaign against socialism.

Exploiting the sectarian divide
Now developments in Sydney suggested further possibilities. Cardinal Patrick Moran, Archbishop of Sydney, defended the words and spirit of Labor's new objective by encouraging Irish-Australian Catholics to go on supporting the Labor Party. In the context of attracting the Protestant middle class and working class vote, Reid had much to gain from emphasising the Catholic–Labor link – especially if he could present Labor's Australian sentiment as anti-British and disloyal.[5] Schools, by encouraging widespread public involvement in celebrating Empire Day, could serve political as well as imperial ends.

Uncertain PREPARATIONS

Ministers and directors of education were unprepared for Australia's first Empire Day. In South Australia, where some 20 schools affiliated with the League of Empire (as the BEL became known there and in Victoria) had celebrated the day in 1904, the education minister hastened to direct all 700 public schools to participate in special activities. In Victoria, where the league was not yet established, Melbourne's lord mayor urged local councils to organise a celebration with the help of 'national societies', such as the

Australian Natives Association, St George's Society, and the Caledonian Society. How to involve schools became a central issue. Geelong's Empire Day Celebration Committee found teachers reluctant to organise large numbers of children to salute the Union Jack in Market Square. It had to make do with school cadets, bands and a choir.[6]

Elsewhere in NSW public discussion about Empire Day revealed a tangle of political, ethnic and religious tensions around the issues of country and empire, of being Australian and British. Preparations for the event in the town of Bathurst revealed these tensions in microcosm (see: Cultural baggage).

Cultural baggage

Bathurst's experience showed that organising Empire Day celebrations would not be easy. Most people stayed away from the mayor's first public meeting, suspicious that the president of the BEL, English-born Bruce Smith, a Member of the House of Representatives and free trade supporter, was promoting Empire Day for political purposes. Bathurst's rival newspapers, the protectionist *National Advocate*, with strong links to Labor, and the free trade *Bathurst Daily Argus* mirrored the conflicting views of the day.

Some feared that if enough people stayed away from the mayor's second meeting, Empire Day would have to be abandoned. Elizabeth Edgeley, wife of Bathurst general merchant Louis Edgeley, of Imperial Warehouse, had much at stake. As a BEL representative, she had attended the first meeting. As president of the Bathurst branch of the Women's Liberal League, she was also about to welcome state delegates to its third biennial conference – the first to be held outside Sydney. Delegates were to discuss the dangers of socialism for Australia: an appropriate topic, the *Argus* thought; anti-Labor propaganda, according to the *Advocate*.

The second meeting went ahead, but so few attended that supporters of Empire Day decided to abandon the celebrations rather than give their opponents the satisfaction of seeing them fail. But Louis Edgeley revived the idea and further meetings followed to organise a bonfire for the evening of 24 May. Organisers struggled to understand the divisions Empire Day was revealing in their community – divisions discussed at length in the press. To the *Argus*, those born in Australia were British; to the *Advocate*, they were Australian.[7]

Even the proposed bonfire revealed deeper concerns, religious as well as ethnic. Bonfires and fireworks had strong English Protestant associations, linked through memory and custom to England's defeat of Catholic Spain's invading Armada and of Catholic Guy Fawkes' gunpowder plot to blow up the Houses of Parliament. These were English events, and bonfires in the English calendar defined a national culture which was distinctly Protestant and anti-Catholic. Transferred to Australia, bonfires also became anti-Irish. Using bonfires to mark Empire Day reinforced these associations.

'AN INTELLIGENT PATRIOTISM'

Carruthers, the Liberal premier who had proposed Empire Day, showed awareness of the sensitivities surrounding the event when he urged schools to use British and Australian flags – a striking contrast to instructions issued in South Australia and Victoria, which specified only the Union Jack.[8]

Directions about the nature of the patriotism to be taught on Empire Day were as important as the flags to be used. Government ministers and departments spoke of the need to teach 'an intelligent patriotism', to teach children to see themselves as 'citizens, not merely of Australia, but also of a great empire'. They cautioned teachers against placing Australia at the centre of the curriculum, as had been happening under the reformist ideas of the New Education. There was a fine line between developing children's Australian sentiment and maintaining their Britishness. The simplest of poems conveyed that tension:

> Let England boast her Rose so red,
> Scotland her Thistle blue,
> Ireland its Shamrock leaf so green
> The Wattle blooms for you.

Victorian regulations introducing Empire Day assured teachers that while it was 'extremely desirable that a national Australian sentiment should be engendered', they should also 'give the children clear ideas of the relation of Australia to the Empire as a whole'.[9] In other words, imperial sentiment should not be neglected. The celebration of Empire Day in schools would embody that view (see: Buns and bonfires).

Self-reliance,
NOT INDEPENDENCE

The phrase, 'good Australians', aimed at school children and used to describe Australians who acknowledged their British nationality first, was to persist. The fear was that in developing allegiance to their new Commonwealth, Australians would neglect imperial loyalty. Certainly the NSW Labor Party wanted Australians to take pride in their country, but talked of self-reliance rather than independence.

The radical journal *The Bulletin* went further, insisting that patriotism in Australia meant love of Australia, not empire (figure 2.1). Believing that Empire Day had 'an evil subtlety … in corrupting the young', the journal pleaded with 'those Australian parents who are Australians first' to teach

For children, the best part of Empire Day came after the special lessons and speeches. There were games and picnics, buns, lollies and fruit. Fitzroy cricket ground in Melbourne offered donkey rides, Punch and Judy shows, merry-go-rounds and sideshows, as well as sports. In Ballarat the mayor and officials gave between four and five thousand children 'a real good time' with moving picture shows.

It was unusual for mayors and councils not to cooperate – although that happened in Oakleigh, Melbourne, where there were complaints, and Broken Hill. In New South Wales celebrations featured parades, bonfires and fireworks. At the centre of the day's proceedings was the Union Jack, hoisted and saluted by children or cadets, and the subject of many speeches. Australian flags were conspicuous by their absence – even in New South Wales, where the press reported only seven. In Sydney's Rozelle, Phillip Nelligan, the former headmaster of Balmain's Smith-street Superior Public School and then head of Darling-street Superior Public School, continued the even-handed approach to flags and anthems he had adopted in 1901 (see chapter 1: Dissenting voices).[10]

The message of Empire Day almost always declared the supremacy of imperial sentiment. Public figures, especially in New South Wales, acknowledged Australian senti-ment but insisted that it take second place. The governor told the children of Fort-street School that although 'they had a … country they had a right to be proud of … [and] also an Australian flag, they should remember that the chief part of that flag was the little Union Jack'. State premier Carruthers, an old Fort-street boy, agreed, later telling children at Kogarah, south of Sydney, that their love of Australia must take second place to their love of the empire. Victoria's minister for public instruction went further at a children's demonstration in Melbourne Town Hall, warning Australians not to forget that they were British, that 'to be good Australians they must of necessity be good Britishers'.[11]

Bathurst continued to be a microcosm of the conflicting attitudes to Empire Day being played out in Sydney. Children from public schools gathered around the Union Jack at the Bathurst Superior Public School, where all speakers referred to the disagreement in the community about the day's significance. The climax was the bonfire and fireworks. A procession of bands, citizen soldiers, fire brigade and voluntary societies, including the Protestant Alliance, led a crowd of some 10 000 to the ordnance ground to hear the gun salute and sing *God Save the King*, before cheering King, Empire, and mayor. Local papers reflected on the result, hoping the troublemakers – local disloyalists according to the *Argus*, Liberal Party leaders in Sydney according to the *Advocate* – had learned a lesson.[12]

The women's committee of the BEL had ensured the success of the first Empire Day by presenting Union Jacks to schools. As John Dacey, a Labor MLA, observed, 'No one comes forward to present a flag of Australia to this or that school. But there is something to be got by presenting the flag of the Empire'.[13]

While public schools were the prime target of the celebrations, private schools were encouraged to participate. Responses varied: at Kew and Hawthorn, the heart of Melbourne's private-school domain, boys from several schools gathered at the post office and town hall, including the pupils of the Jesuits' Xavier College. But their rector and prefect of studies, Irish-born Father Patrick Keating, complained in his journal about the invention of '[a]nother of those great days of the Great British Empire … the cause of no end of trouble', and of the boys' participation in 'unfurling some flag or other'.

Charles O'Driscoll, headmaster of the Catholic St Ambrose's Boys School, Brunswick, in Melbourne, was less accommo-dating. He refused to accept tickets for the mayor's magic lantern show on the develop-ment of the Empire. O'Driscoll trained as a Christian Brother and was Australian-born of Irish parents.[14]

their children to love their own land. This drew a response: 'No more
vicious teaching could be published', said an outraged Joseph Cook to a
meeting at the Parramatta Town Hall. The former Labor, now conservative,
MHR had migrated from England at 25 and was Reid's deputy in the Free
Trade Party.[15]

The former prime minister
Edmund Barton, a hesitant supporter of Empire Day in 1903 and
now a High Court judge, agreed. On
the same platform in comfortable
Woollahra as Bruce Smith, BEL president and Free Trade MHR, he urged
his audience not to listen to those
who talked of separation from the
British Empire, warning that its
break-up would jeopardise the new
Commonwealth of Australia. He
had in mind the need to protect
the egalitarian society this small
European outpost on the edge of Asia
was trying to develop by excluding
non-European immigrants. The
same point was on the governor's
mind when he told the lord mayor's
gathering that until Australians could
defend themselves, they should
double their subsidy to Britain to
cover the cost of stationing a
squadron in their waters.[16]

SOWING THE SEEDS OF DUAL PATRIOTISM

The introduction of Empire Day in Australia in 1905 reveals a society struggling with contending visions of national identity. The achievement of
federation had encouraged Australians to imagine themselves as a distinct
nation emerging from, and contrasting with, the wider British nation. The
NSW Labor Party's decision in February to promote the development of
Australian sentiment and self-reliance reflected that new confidence. In
July, the Australian Labor Party unanimously adopted the same objective.[17]

Conservative politicians, seeking an issue to unite non-Labor
forces against the growing power of Labor, seized on the party's vision of a

self-reliant socialist Australia. Their promotion of Empire Day and imperial sentiment became part of that campaign, reinforcing the role of the Union Jack as the national flag.

In schools, Empire Day rapidly became the main celebration of the academic year. The British Empire League had been disappointed by the politicians' refusal of a public holiday but the alternative gave it unusual power: a captive audience in public schools, as Victoria's director of education, Frank Tate recognised. At a meeting in August 1905 called to establish the League of Empire in Victoria, Tate complimented the league on adopting 'the wise method of beginning with the children, who were more impressionable … than the adults'. Children knew that 24 May was a special day. *The Sydney Morning Herald* doubted that they could grasp its 'full significance', but it was satisfied that 'the chief object was realised, for seeds were planted that will grow' – which was just what *The Bulletin* feared.

Those seeds of a dual patriotism had germinated. But how would the rose and wattle grow? And what of the shamrock?[18]

Realigning LOYALTIES

AUSTRALIAN FLAG FOR FORTS

figure 2.1 Illustrator on The Bulletin, *Livingston Hopkins, was critical of the newly introduced Empire Day. 'Australian father of family: "An Empire Day, by all means, but let this be your empire!"' ran the caption under this illustration in the 18 May 1905 edition.*

The Australian blue ensign was about to gain a champion in Alfred Deakin, the Liberal protectionist who followed the divisive Reid as prime minister in July 1905. In March 1908 his government decided to replace the Union Jack with the blue ensign on forts and barracks around the country. An unobtrusive notice in the *Commonwealth of Australia Gazette* simply advised amendment to *Commonwealth Military Regulation 35*, with details available at the Government Printing Office, and invited comment 'before finally settling the proposed Regulation'.[19]

In parliament, anti-socialists, encouraged by *The Sydney Morning Herald's* bold headline 'Exit – Union Jack', saw the move as anti-British. But the government insisted that it was simply following a unanimous resolution of the House of Representatives. Richard Crouch, still a member, had the satisfaction of seeing his motion of 1904 finally being implemented – at least on forts (see chapter 1: A lukewarm reception for Australian ensigns). The government made much of the fact that the Union Jack was part of the Australian blue ensign, but when pressed by Bruce Smith, agreed to also fly the Union Jack on Empire Day. The transition to the blue ensign on forts took effect from 1 June 1908.[20]

figure 2.2
Indentured Japanese crews and
divers, brought to northern Australia
to work in the pearling industry,
flew several flags at the Japanese
Club in Broome, c. 1911.

figure 2.3
George Rose's photograph of
the public schools' flag drill
demonstration of Australian
and American flags indicates
Australia's warm welcome to

the American fleet in Sydney
on 12 September 1908. Britain's
Union Jack was conspicuous by
its absence. Australia feared
Japan's growing power.

This change signalled Deakin's determination to use Australian patriotism to persuade Australians to look to their own defence. Uneasy about Australia's dependence on the Royal Navy, Deakin believed that the Japanese naval defeat of the Russians in May 1905 and the renewal of the Anglo-Japanese alliance in August revealed Australia's vulnerability to the new power in the Pacific (figure 2.2). He had never been happy with the 1902 naval agreement's annual payment of a subsidy for ships in the Royal Navy's Australian squadron, over which Australia had no control.

Dissatisfied with Britain's response to his 1907 proposals for more Australian control, Deakin presented to Australians in December his vision of a navy flying 'the White Ensign with the Southern Cross ... altogether Australian in cost and control', and a citizen army. At the same time he encouraged an American presence in the Pacific by inviting the US fleet to visit Australian ports during its proposed world cruise – an unconventional initiative for a colony, which upset the British Foreign Office.[21]

The Australian Natives Association (ANA) in Victoria, of which Deakin was a member, had been paying more attention to an Australian flag. Previously wary of promoting Australian sentiment too directly, the ANA now saw it as essential. In its March 1908 annual conference the association insisted that it was not enough to ask branches, as it had in 1907, to celebrate Australian unity annually: they should use an Australian flag at all public events.

A member from Hawthorn had raised the issue, annoyed that his branch had been accused of disloyalty to the Union Jack when it displayed an Australian flag. The defence of an Australian flag at the conference was the same as in parliament: an Australian flag, with the Union Jack in the place of honour clearly identifying Australia as part of the empire, was a symbol of loyalty not disloyalty.[22] By the time the American fleet arrived in Sydney late in August 1908, the Australian blue ensign on forts was well established (figure 2.3).

ONE STAR OR MANY: THE COAT OF ARMS

The federal symbol of the Australian flags – the Commonwealth Star – had been gazetted in August 1908 as the crest of the Commonwealth Coat of Arms. The search for an appropriate coat of arms began in 1906. The initial design suggested by Deakin and approved by his ministers used the symbols of the old unofficial Australian coat of arms and flags (figures 1.9, 1.3) so clearly associated with New South Wales: the St George cross bearing the stars of the Southern Cross, with the rising sun as crest.

Popular in Australia from early 1850, the old coat of arms served a variety of purposes (figures 2.4–2.6). Deakin's design surrounded the central shield of red cross and stars (the Commonwealth) with six small shields (the states). The crest, against a rising sun, was six stars (the states), surmounted by a citizen's or mural crown (a crown or garland given to the soldier who was first to scale the wall of a besieged town).[23] In suggesting the symbol of the old coat of arms Deakin was perhaps seeking to please Australia's oldest and largest state after the NSW outcry against the 'Victorian' design of the Australian ensigns just six years before.

There was much discussion in Australia and Britain about the coat of arms, especially the inclusion of the St George cross, seen as too English by the Victorian Scottish Union and Scottish societies in Britain. The Garter King at Arms had intended to use the Southern Cross constellation. The ANA suggested a Union Jack

figure 2.4
The Australian cricket team used from 1899 the old Australian arms, as seen here on Bill Woodfull's faded baggy green cap of 1929–30. The old motto, 'Advance Australia', became simply 'Australia' for the cricketers in 1934.

figure 2.5
The old Australian arms (with St George cross and stars), flag (federation flag) and British arms and flags (Union Jack and royal standard) featured on a NSW government invitation for inaugural Commonwealth celebrations, January 1901.

COMMONWEALTH OF AUSTRALIA.

INAUGURAL CELEBRATIONS AT SYDNEY. JANUARY. 1901.

VICTORIA R.I.

N.S. WALES VICTORIA QUEENSLAND SOUTH AUSTRALIA WEST AUSTRALIA TASMANIA

EARL OF HOPETOUN
First Governor General.

The Government of New South Wales requests the honor of

presence at a Municipal & Civil Luncheon in the Town Hall, Sydney on the 7th January, 1901 at 1 P.M. in commemoration of the Ceremonial of Swearing in of The Earl of Hopetoun as first Governor General of The Commonwealth of Australia.

Opening of the Parliament of the Commonwealth
By his Royal Highness
The Duke of Cornwall and York.

The Government of Victoria requests the honour of the presence of

Lieutenant Cyril B. Hampshire R.N. "H.M.S." June

At the Celebrations in Melbourne in connection with the Opening of the Parliament of the Commonwealth of Australia.

figure 2.6
The Australian Natives Association, a keen supporter of federation, experimented with more than one version of Australian arms in the masthead of its Victorian journal, The Advance Australia, *as in this issue of 15 July 1902.*

figure 2.7
Only one of the official invitations for Commonwealth celebrations (issued by the Victorian government) imagined an Australian coat of arms with the badges of all the states, foreshadowing the second Commonwealth Coat of Arms of 1912.

design for the central shield. Deakin decided to retain the red St George cross, but agreed to add the other Union colours to acknowledge the Scots. Also discussed, but rejected as too detailed, were the state badges (from their flags and seals) for the small shields (compare the arms in figures 2.8 and 2.7). The crest became much simpler: a single six- then seven-pointed star replacing the six stars; no rising sun (already used as the NSW crest); and no citizen's crown (figure 2.8).[24] This was the design approved and

gazetted in August 1908. (Later that year the Commonwealth Star on the ensigns gained a seventh point to represent Australian territories.)

However, Labor's Andrew Fisher, who succeeded Deakin in April 1910, was quick to replace the English symbol. A Scottish immigrant who had come to Queensland at the age of 22 in 1885, he had a strong interest in Scottish history and literature. The badges of the states on a central shield, he thought, were more appropriate for a federal Australia. His Cabinet agreed. Combining the states' symbols in this way was a pragmatic solution to the search for an Australian symbol not already identified with any single one of them or one of the nations of Britain. Approved by the king in 1912, the design was gazetted in January 1913 (figure 2.9).

Fisher, like Barton and Watson before him, was also dissatisfied with the design of the Australian flag. But his response, when questioned about altering it, was 'One thing at a time'.[25] An Australian flag to represent the country overseas had appeared for the first time at the Olympics in 1908, heading an Australasian team; the New Zealanders did not compete separately until 1920 (figure 2.10).

figure 2.8
The Commonwealth Coat of Arms of 1908, using the NSW symbol of the old arms, added six small shields to represent the states, with the Commonwealth Star from the Australian ensigns as crest, but with seven points.

Making
'GOOD AUSTRALIANS'

Education circulars after the first Empire Day of 1905 showed a subtle re-alignment of loyalties. Within five years of the first message – that by being 'good Britishers' they would become 'good Australians' – children were hearing its reverse, that by being 'good Australians' they would become 'good Britishers'. In 1908 the NSW director of education wanted teachers to use Empire Day lessons to strengthen children's ties to Australia so that 'allegiance to their own country' became the basis of their service to the empire. His South Australian counterpart put it more simply in 1910: 'What we must strive to do first is to make good Australians of our children … in this matter of patriotism, as in all else in teaching, we must begin at home'. Unless teachers could 'arouse in the hearts of the children a love for their native land', he warned, 'it [was] hopeless to expect any true "Empire" feeling'.[26]

figure 2.9
The second and current Common-wealth Coat of Arms of 1912 replaced the St George cross with stars with the symbols of the six states, but retained the Commonwealth Star, emphasising more strongly the federal nature of the Commonwealth.

AUSTRALIA

Although instructions for Empire Day began to emphasise Australia, the Union Jack remained at the centre of the celebrations. In New South Wales this happened despite instruction that the Union and Australian flags should be displayed. Schools did not see the need or did not have the money to buy an Australian flag. Donors were not interested. Perhaps the Labor MLA John Dacey was right: there seemed no honour in presenting Australian flags to schools. In Western Australia the ANA began to address the problem, suggesting that the state government provide schools with Australian flags (figure 2.11). The association found, when seeking cooperation on the issue from branches in the eastern states, that there would not be widespread and immediate change: provision of flags was a matter for local communities.[27]

Some members of the ANA were not satisfied with merely making Empire Day more Australian. The WA branch wanted an Australia Day to teach children in public schools about Australian history and to salute the Australian flag. In the eastern states there was much discussion about an Australian national day. The NSW branch of the association suggested replacing Anniversary Day on 26 January, a NSW 19th century creation, with Foundation Day on 28 April to mark Captain Cook's landing in Australia. For many in that state 26 January was the 'day which gave us a bad start' (the day Captain Arthur Phillip of the First Fleet took possession of New South Wales at Sydney Cove). But the association's interstate conference in 1910 outvoted the branch on the issue. Nevertheless, the discussions suggested a shift was occurring in the balance of Australians' allegiances.[28]

figure 2.10
For the second time an Australian flag headed the Australasian team of Australians and New Zealanders at the Olympics in Stockholm in 1912. The team's women competed for the first time.

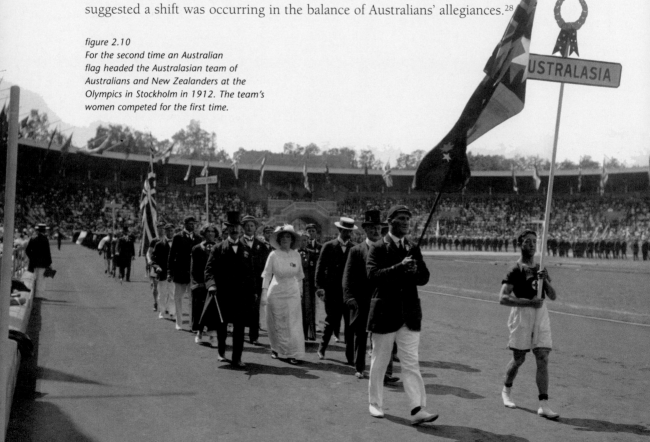

figure 2.11
Australian flags began to appear more often at Empire Day celebrations after 1908. In Perth a small boy carried one past the governor of Western Australia taking the salute beneath the Union Jack on the Esplanade in 1909.

WHICH FLAG TO SALUTE?

Flying the Australian blue ensign on forts was a significant step in that shift of allegiances. Another was making it the saluting flag at all reviews and parades. At the request of the WA branch of the ANA, Labor's defence minister, George Pearce, issued a military order in April 1911 directing that 'in future the Australian Flag is to be used as the saluting flag at all reviews and ceremonial parades'. When Pearce left for England for talks with the Admiralty and to attend the coronation of George V, his department laboured over the repercussions of his order. Faced with a governor-general who refused to take the salute on coronation day without the Union Jack, defence officials compromised: the Union Jack would be flown when vice-regal representatives were present; and the Australian flag on all other occasions.[29]

A similar problem was evident in negotiations between Australia and Britain over which flag was to fly at the stern of ships of the Australian navy. At the Imperial Defence Conference of 1909 Australian and Canadian representatives had raised the issue of using the white ensign with a dominion emblem in the fly, but the Admiralty seemed unable or unwilling to appreciate their desire to use their own flags. Negotiations continued, with Pearce insisting on the white ensign 'with a seven-pointed star in blue'. Would he be able to withstand the Admiralty at meetings in June 1911?[30]

CHALLENGE *from the* CATHOLIC HIERARCHY

'THE FLAGSHIP OF AUSTRALIAN PATRIOTISM'

Sydney's Cardinal Moran took heart from the increasing Australian emphasis in Empire Day celebrations and on the growing acceptance of an Australian flag. Since arriving in Australia in 1884, the Irish-born Moran had rapidly become known as a public figure who identified with Australian concerns. To his supporters, including Richard O'Connor, justice of the High Court and a former Commonwealth minister, he was 'the Flagship of Australian Patriotism', who had done more than anyone to encourage Australian sentiment.[31]

Moran's interest in encouraging Australian patriotism in the new Commonwealth had as much to do with his hopes for Ireland as Australia. He thought the two countries had much to offer each other. Australia's self-governing status within the empire provided an example for Ireland to follow in its campaign for Home Rule, which Moran supported financially. But the Irish could give Australians a lesson in patriotism.[32] The introduction of Empire Day in Australia made that lesson seem even more pressing to Moran, long used to the charge that Irish Catholics were disloyal. For many of his background, to celebrate imperialism was to celebrate English Protestant oppression of Irish Catholics.

A TIME FOR ACTION

With Labor in power both federally and in New South Wales, Moran decided to challenge Empire Day in 1911. He was to be assisted by Father Maurice O'Reilly, a Vincentian priest and principal of St Stanislaus' College in Bathurst, Australia's oldest Catholic boarding school. The Irish-born O'Reilly had been in Australia since 1892 and principal of 'Stannies' since 1903. He was a tall, well-built articulate man who, like Moran, followed every twist and turn in the fortunes of the Home Rule movement. The college had never participated in Empire Day celebrations in Bathurst, and O'Reilly was now determined to replace Empire Day with Australia Day, at least in Catholic schools.

Persuaded by Moran and O'Reilly, the first Catholic Education Conference in Sydney in January 1911 agreed that schools should celebrate two days: St Patrick's Day; and 24 May – the feast day of Our Lady, Help of Christians, Chief Patroness of Australia – as Australia Day. While admitting that his college's pupils were Australian not Irish, O'Reilly argued that since Australia lacked traditions of its own, its people had to draw on older ones. For Catholics that meant the traditions of Ireland. After all, he said, 'everything that was best and noblest in Australia was Irish'.[33]

By emphasising an Australian-based patriotism at a time when there was growing support for it, Moran and O'Reilly were attempting to deflect criticism of Catholics as disloyal and anti-British. But given the bitter division between Catholics and Protestants, and between those of English and Irish descent, they were naïve to think that replacing Empire Day with Australia Day under the guise of a Catholic feast day would gain the support of the Australian community. Those divisions were about to be sharpened as Moran pressed the new NSW Labor government for aid to Catholic schools, the reward expected by Irish Catholics for helping to put Labor into government.[34]

CHARGE AND COUNTERCHARGE

The press doubted that Australians would tolerate Moran's 'rival demonstration', which it saw as a 'lure' to involve them in 'sectarian squabbles', and questioned why there should be Australian and Irish days but not a British day. O'Reilly responded by criticising those builders of empire who had 'cruelly oppressed' the Irish; they were 'land sharks of the world, who … sweep nations … into the maw of capitalism', he said. The Catholic *Freeman's Journal* thought it was inevitable that Moran's critics would misunderstand his motives for the Australia Day movement, and blamed 'the maffickers of St Jingo' (that is, blustering patriots – in a play on the name of the town, Mafeking, under siege in the Boer War). Moran persisted, directing that Catholic schools in his archdiocese should celebrate the day by singing an Australian national hymn, O'Reilly's *God Bless Our Lovely Morning-land*, and flying an Australian flag.[35]

The stage was set for conflict as schools prepared for 24 May. The date had become something of a sectarian battle zone, with the Catholic leadership and an Australian flag ranged on one side and the rest of the community (with few exceptions) and the Union Jack on the other. Sydney's press urged people to answer Moran and O'Reilly with a renewed show of enthusiasm for the empire. John Perry, a member of the NSW Loyal Orange Institution (a Protestant secret society originating in Ireland) and a former minister of public instruction, declared in parliament that he hoped the Union Jack would fly the next day from all public schools and

A hymn and a salute

On 24 May 1911, Cardinal Moran greeted some 400 children at St Mary's Cathedral in Sydney to celebrate Australia Day. Aged 80, the cardinal was enjoying what was to be his last stand in Australian politics. Above the cathedral flew two flags: an Australian flag; and the much larger Irish flag of Home Rule (figure 2.12).

At Bathurst, St Stanislaus' boys gave the military salute to an Australian flag as they marched past the main door. Later they heard O'Reilly speak of their duty to the flag – to love it, to fight for it, to die for it. When he had first come to the college, boys had nicknamed him John Bull, supposedly for his huge size and aloof manner. But perhaps giving the name of the English icon to an Irishman with no love for the English was simply schoolboy humour. However, on the occasion of their first Australia Day, O'Reilly's words moved the boys to tears. The ceremony ended with a further salute and the Australian national hymn.[36]

ON EMPIRE DAY.

HIS EMINENCE: "Come with me, and you may wave this flag."
YOUNG AUSTRALIA: "Why don't you come with me? You must be lonely. You've got a good flag, but this is my flag's day."

figure 2.12
Hal Eyre on Empire Day,
The Daily Telegraph,
25 May 1911: 'His Eminence [Moran]: "Come with me, and you may wave this flag." Young Australia: "Why don't you come with me? ... You've got a good flag, but this is my flag's day."'

buildings 'and that no section of the community will hoist the Australian flag in its place'[37] (see: A hymn and a salute).

SUCCESS AND FAILURE

In New South Wales generally, there was a noticeable withdrawal of Catholic children from the celebrations of Empire Day. In Bathurst, only Protestant children gathered under the Union Jack. There were reports of separate celebrations for Catholics in other country centres: at Katoomba they met at the Falls Reserve while others congregated in Katoomba Park; at Murwillumbah they went to the coast, not the showground; and at Yass the local convent simply gave children a day's holiday. But, despite Moran's hope, Catholics in other states did not celebrate Australia Day. Not until 1922 did the Catholic archbishops and bishops of Australasia agree to observe 24 May as Australia Day.[38]

In NSW public schools there were fewer reports of Australian flags being flown on Empire Day in 1911 than in 1905. Only at schools in Rozelle (where Nelligan still worked) and Hurstville in Sydney, and in Tamworth in the north did they fly – accompanied by the Union Jack. The reluctance of schools on Empire Day to fly an Australian flag – even with the Union Jack – reflected the ethnic and sectarian animosity of 1911. The wrapping of Irish causes in its folds was a disincentive to others to display it.

Moran and O'Reilly's attempt to turn Empire Day into Australia Day backfired. It reinforced the view that the NSW Catholic hierarchy was divisive as well as disloyal. By associating Australian patriotism with Irish patriotism against British imperialism, they alienated wider Australian society as well as some Catholics. Patriotism for most Australians meant love of Australia and the British Empire. A 'good Australian' was Australian and British, not Australian and Irish. As the congregational minister warned public school children at Katoomba's Empire Day celebrations, 'Australians who forgot the Motherland certainly could not be called good Australians'.[39]

In this context an Australian flag, so closely associated with Irish Catholic purposes by Moran and O'Reilly, became a symbol of suspicion for the wider community. One of Moran's correspondents at the Irish College in Rome recognised his Australia Day strategy for what it was: 'a party pill wrapped up in sugar', and urged Moran 'to speak regularly & openly of the *Australian nation*'.[40] Moran never read his letter; he died before it could be delivered. Moran's Australia Day, celebrating Australian rather than British nationality, had touched a sensitive nerve in the Australian community.

A place at the jackstaff
BUT NOT AT THE STERN

George Pearce, the defence minister, returned to Australia from England, via Russia and Japan, having had to accept that the white ensign, 'as the symbol of authority of the Crown', without Australia's Commonwealth Star, would fly at the stern of ships of the Commonwealth Naval Forces – known from July 1911 as the Royal Australian Navy. Pearce had been persuaded that 'foreign powers would recognise only one flag and that was the flag of the British Empire'. However, the Australian blue ensign would be flown from the jackstaff.[41]

One matter held over for Pearce's return was the saluting flag. The defence department had provided the Union Jack for the governor-general to take the salute on coronation day in June (figure 2.13). The naval agreement made in London at the end of that month emphasised, in effect, that Pearce could not ignore the Union Jack as a saluting flag: it was the national flag. But the subsequent navy order indicated that the Union Jack would be in addition to not instead of an Australian flag when vice-regal representatives reviewed Commonwealth forces. A similar military order was issued in September.[42] The Commonwealth government could go only so far in asserting its blue ensign: both the Admiralty and governor-general made clear that Australia's national flag was still the Union Jack.

figure 2.13
Robert Ward and William Farran's photograph records the Governor-General Lord Dudley taking the salute with the national flag, the Union Jack not the Commonwealth Ensign, on Coronation Day 1911 at the Royal Agricultural Ground, Moore Park, Sydney.

Chapter three
War and the question of loyalty

The Union Jack represented Australians' determination to support Britain in war in 1914. The Australian government placed its navy under the command of the Royal Navy and began enlisting men for an Australian Imperial Force (AIF). British flags marked recruiting depots and ports of embarkation. But there were also Australian flags, blue and red ensigns, especially after pride in AIF achievements at Gallipoli gave them a new potency as national symbols. But did the campaign and the growing sense of nationhood it engendered lessen Australians' sense of being British? Could loyalty to Australia mean disloyalty to Britain? These questions unsettled Australians struggling with the volatile politics of the war and its aftermath, causing many to wonder whether an Australian flag could serve as the national flag without being a disloyal symbol.

Flags on the
WAR FRONT

Australian forces entered the war with two flags to represent their dual nationality – the Union Jack and the Australian blue ensign – but as military and navy orders in 1911 had shown, the two did not have equal status. Establishing a role for the blue ensign took some time. Australian Natives Association (ANA) members in Perth were shocked to note its absence at the lieutenant-governor's March 1913 review in Fremantle of the men of the *Melbourne*, the first Australian cruiser for the RAN to arrive from Britain. Naval officers had to be reminded that the Australian flag must always be used.[1]

Australian flags would play a secondary role in an imperial war, however important victory was to Australia. The surge in imperial fervour when Britain declared war led people waiting at the Melbourne office of *The Age* for overseas cables to lift high onto shoulders those with Union Jacks and sing *Rule Britannia*, *Songs of the Sea* and *Soldiers of the King*. However, the Australian blue ensign was not completely forgotten; at a parade of the 1st Victorian Regiment in Melbourne in late September 1914, it flew beside the Union Jack at the saluting point on the steps of Parliament House. But the hands of the thousands lining Spring Street held small Union Jacks[2] (see: Recruitment symbols).

figure 3.1
World War I recruiting posters in Australia often portrayed the Union Jack as the national flag. James Northfield featured it in this poster used by the Victorian State Recruiting Committee.

figure 3.2
Australian red ensigns were used as often if not more frequently than Australian blue ensigns on World War I posters. The South Australian State Recruiting Committee liked the appearance of the red ensign against the German flag.

figure 3.3
Harry J. Weston's poster, a plea for help in 1916, when Australian losses were so heavy and the year of the first conscription referendum, used the Australian blue ensign.

"Were **YOU** there then?"

Recruitment symbols

As the simplest and most eye-catching of national symbols, flags – Union Jacks, and blue and red Australian ensigns – appeared on posters in towns and suburbs after recruiting drives began early in 1915 (figures 3.1–3.3). Posters advertising war bonds also featured flags, as did fundraising badges sold by organisations such as South Australia's Cheer-Up Society, which provided free meals and entertainment for men going to or returning from the war; the Australian Comforts Fund, which sent food parcels and socks to men at the front; and the Red Cross (figures 3.4, 3.10).

Recruiting marches in New South Wales between November 1915 and February 1916 used flags to draw men into the AIF. The 'Cooees', a group of recruits in Gilgandra calling others to join them as they marched to Sydney in late 1915, carried the Australian red ensign and Union Jack. Women in the small border town of Delegate made a banner of British and Australian red ensigns for their men marching to Goulburn's recruiting depot in January 1916 (figures 3.5–3.6).[3]

figure 3.4
This poster on the Royal Bank of Australasia in Melbourne seeking men and money appeared towards the end of the war in September–October 1918 and featured an Australian flag.

figure 3.5
Men carrying this banner, made from British and Australian red ensigns, gathered 142 recruits during their march from Delegate to Goulburn, New South Wales, in January 1916. The banner made a similar journey by vehicle during World War II.

THE MEN FROM SNOWY RIVER

IN THE MIDST OF ACTION

For some soldiers leaving for war, an Australian flag became a treasured possession. Corporal George Watson, aged 20, of the 3rd Field Company Engineers, received a red ensign from the Labor attorney-general, WM (Billy) Hughes, in Melbourne in September 1914. The fitter from Ipswich, who was born near Belfast in Ireland, kept the flag through the battlefields of France, and still had it when he returned to Australia in 1919.

Eighteen-year-old John McKay, a salesman from Northcote in Melbourne, embarked in November 1915 with a red ensign that was handed to him by a woman in the crowd. McKay kept the flag as a symbol of home, covering it with an indelible pencil record of his service with the 59th Battalion, and had it in his kitbag when he returned in 1919.

By contrast, English-born company sergeant major, David Bacon, aged 25, of North Sydney, took a Union Jack with him when he left for Europe in June 1917 – and the same flag went with him when he departed for service in World War II. Some chaplains used Australian flags: a padre in the 9th Battalion draped one over his Gallipoli dugout. Another used one donated by the Women's Chaplaincy Association for burial services in the Middle East and France.[4]

figure 3.6
The Men from Snowy River marched from Delegate through Bombala, Nimmitabel, Cooma, Michelago, Queanbeyan (shown here on Queen's Bridge), Bungendore and Tarago to Goulburn in January 1916.

Personal preference rather than official policy seemed to determine AIF headquarters' use of an Australian flag. General Sir William Birdwood, British commander of the AIF, and of the Australian Corps until May 1918, flew the Australian blue ensign over his headquarters in France and on his Rolls-Royce, as did his Australian successor in the corps, Lieutenant-General Sir John Monash. But not every sectional headquarters had an Australian flag.

While 6th Brigade in France flew the red ensign from 1916 to 1918, staff of 7th Infantry Brigade had to improvise one with cardboard when Billy Hughes, now prime minister, visited them in 1916. Australian flags also identified Australian casualty clearing stations and Australian general hospitals: the one at Abbeville in France had been presented by a committee of Sydney ladies organised by the wife of the chief justice.[5]

On the battlefield, Australian flags sometimes marked objectives reached. During the battle of Polygon Wood in Belgium early on 20 September 1917, Lieutenant Arthur Hull, a signalling officer with the 18th Battalion, placed one on Anzac Redoubt, a German pillbox the Australians had named as their objective. The flag lasted a day before heavy shelling destroyed it. Hull, a farmer from Lockhart, southwest of Wagga Wagga, was killed in action three weeks later. The sale of postcards (figure 3.8) with a picture of the incident – somewhat different from what happened – raised money for the Australian Comforts Fund[6] (see: 'Australian flag flying').

figure 3.7 This postcard, dated 9 June 1915, portrayed the Union Jack as the symbol of freedom in the design of Britain's colonial ensigns.

'Australian flag flying'

'I went back to Anzac House [Redoubt] and saw the captain write a message to battalion headquarters. It read: "Consolidating objective. Australian flag flying on Anzac House."

'Such heroics I suppose were pardonable in the circumstances. Lord knows what the message read after it had been flashed through corps headquarters and reached England. Some days later the incident was featured in illustrated papers in colour and long after I returned to Australia I saw postcards that depicted a lone Digger holding aloft an outsize in Australian flags and gallantly charging a formidable pillbox. The fact was that Lieutenant Hull, who was killed a few days later, had just before the attack received a parcel from home. In it was a small Australian flag of paper about three inches by four inches. He stuck this in a tin of bully-beef and placed it on the corner of Anzac House where it was blown to pieces by a shell later in the day.'

From the book *Hell's Bells and Mademoiselles* by J Maxwell VC, MC, DSO. Published by Angus & Robertson, Sydney, 1932.

figure 3.8
Arthur Hull's Australian flag on a German pillbox in the Battle of Polygon Wood, as painted by Alfred Pearse, differed from the miniature paper flag (7.5cm by 10cm) that he stuck in a tin of bully-beef in 1917.

An Australian blue ensign, sent by General Birdwood to the 15th Infantry Brigade to fly above the church spire in Harbonnières, was hoisted there on 8 August 1918 to signal the taking of the French town. The commander of the 59th Battalion had promised the honour of raising the flag to the first man to reach the town. He was Private Ernest Forty, a 22-year-old coachbuilder from Fairfield Park, Melbourne, who had served since Gallipoli. Forty had been wounded twice in action and was to be wounded a third time before he returned to Australia in 1919 with the Harbonnières flag. Monash cabled news of the Australian troops' astonishing success in

THE
ANZAC

BOOK

Written and Illustrated in Gallipoli by the Men of Anzac

taking the town to the Fourth Army Headquarters, asking its commander to relay the news to Australia's governor-general.[7]

But despite the increasingly familiar sight of Australian flags at the front, they did not replace the Union Jack. That flag alone had pride of place on the cover of *The Anzac Book*, written and illustrated by the men of the Australian and New Zealand Army Corps at Gallipoli (figure 3.9). Its editor was Charles Bean, the Australian-born, British-educated war correspondent and later official historian. The vision expressed in the book helped shape perceptions of Anzac in the minds of the thousands of soldiers and citizens who bought copies. In Australia, British and Australian flags veiled the memorials to those who had volunteered to go to war, with the Union Jack taking precedence as the national flag. And, for all their readiness to unfurl an Australian ensign, most returned soldiers would only do so if there was a Union Jack fluttering beside it (figure 3.10).[8]

FLAGS ON THE HOME FRONT

Back in Australia, schools, especially public ones, began to take flag ritual more seriously. The Union Jack continued to dominate classrooms and school grounds, but there was greater interest in the Australian nation and its flags after Gallipoli. In June 1915 Victoria's education department circulated instructions to teachers on how to draw an Australian flag accurately. The next year, celebration of Foundation Day (26 January) included 'a lesson on the Australian Flag'. For Anzac Day (25 April), which now replaced Discovery Day (20 April), schools welcomed returned Anzacs and added the second stanza to the national anthem: 'God bless our splendid men/ Send them safe home again…'[9]

But the major occasion involving flags in public schools remained the flag ceremony, in which governments showed renewed interest after the outbreak of war. Victoria's education department reminded teachers in October 1914 to observe the Monday morning ritual, although the choice and provision of a flag was still left to individual school boards. In New South Wales, public schools had been encouraged to fly both flags, but that changed in 1917, when they were allowed to fly whichever was available.[10] The South Australian government, however, insisted on the Union Jack.

Pride in Australia and its soldiers was a powerful force in promoting a national identity and the use of Australian symbols both overseas and at home. But why did neither generals nor prime ministers promote an Australian flag as the national flag, able to fly on its own without being validated by the Union Jack? Why could the government of South Australia not tolerate an Australian flag, even when the Union Jack flew beside it?

Country
AND EMPIRE

TESTING LOYALTIES IN BATTLE

Pressures of war at the front and at home forced Australians to define more clearly their loyalties to Australia and Britain. Monash, at first a brigadier general of the 4th Infantry Brigade at Gallipoli, then a major general of the 3rd Division and finally commander of the Australian Corps in France, deplored the waste of Australian lives by some British commanders. He urged the Australianisation of the senior commands of the AIF and the merging of the five Australian divisions into one force as a means of gaining greater Australian control over the use of their troops. In this he had the support in 1917 of the Melbourne *Herald* journalist Keith Murdoch, who knew both the Australian and British prime ministers, and the editor of *The Anzac Book*, Charles Bean. In the view these two put to Lloyd George, the British leader, Australian nationalism was, as quoted by Geoffrey Serle, Monash's biographer, 'the one great motive working in our people', a view British military leaders rejected 'as a sort of treachery to the Empire'. The Australian prime minister, Billy Hughes, strengthened their cause with his own cable to the British government.[11]

Although sympathy for the British cause had led Monash to enlist in 1914, he inspired his men with an appeal to Australian as well as imperial patriotism. He delighted in being known as an Australian commander and in the victories Australians won in battle. Monash liked the stories critical of the British Army that circulated among his troops (although he advised his commanders to discourage them). In letters home he wrote about the 'bad troops, bad staffs and bad commanders' of the 'Tommy Divisions'. After the spectacular Australian achievements of August 1918 were largely ignored in reports of 'British' successes, Monash complained to his British superiors that his men 'would refuse to go on playing any game in which their scores were not put up on the scoring board'. His protest had the desired effect.[12]

Australian achievements at war, Bean told children at home, 'made our people a famous people … so famous that every Australian is proud for the world to know that he is Australian'. But some members of British associations in Australia were uneasy with that view. They complained that children noticed only the achievements of Australian soldiers and that the press ignored 'the backbone of the army … the English Tommy'. Far from seeing Australian as a term of praise, one association member said that it 'shelters anything from a Hun to a Greek dago'. For the editor of *The British Sentinel*, journal of the All British League, the British Women's Alliance and the British Empire Union, the men of the AIF were the only Australians 'in the real sense of the word' because they had proved their Britishness by going to war.[13]

CONSCRIPTION: CRISIS IN LOYALTY

Proving loyalty to Britain was at the centre of the conscription crisis in Australia in 1916–17. At the beginning of the war Australians had volunteered enthusiastically. Then pride in Anzac achievements at Gallipoli boosted enlistments for a time in 1915. But severe AIF losses on the Somme in mid-1916 led Britain's Army Council to call for large reinforcements to maintain the five Australian divisions. Britain had introduced conscription in January 1916. New Zealand followed in August. Hughes felt he had no alternative but to do the same.[14] Divided on the issue, his government called a referendum for October 1916.

Hughes presented the referendum as a test of whether Australians were for or against Britain: whether they were loyal. Describing the anti-conscriptionists as 'every enemy of Britain open and secret in our midst', he appealed to voters not to 'dishonour' Australia by voting no. The prime minister believed Australia's fate, tied to Britain's, was being determined on the battlefields of France. Only by ensuring an allied victory could Australians hope to benefit from a peace settlement. Defeated in war, Australia would be at the mercy of Germany and her allies. His campaign provoked a deeply divisive debate. Supporters tended to be mostly middle-class and Protestant. Opponents – whether on moral, economic or ethnic grounds, or because they distrusted the government's reinforcement figures and heavy-handed approach – were more likely to be working-class, trade-unionist and have an Irish Catholic background.[15]

Although a majority of voters supported Australian involvement in the war, they opposed conscription and Hughes narrowly lost the referendum, despite the support of most major newspapers, nearly all state govern-ments, the federal Liberal opposition, and the professions. When the Labor Party split over conscription, Hughes and his mostly Protestant followers joined former Liberals to form a Nationalist government, with Hughes still in control. With even greater losses on the Western Front in 1917 than the previous year, the prime minister called a second referendum on conscrip-tion for December. The campaign was more extreme than the first as supporters of conscription, alarmed by their first defeat, tried to dissuade voters from following 'the evil and mischievous' advice of putting Australia first and the Empire second.[16]

PUTTING AUSTRALIA FIRST: MANNIX AND THE IRISH CONNECTION

Dr Daniel Mannix was the most outspoken advocate of the slogan 'Australia first and the Empire second' during the second conscription campaign. He had supported the war at its outbreak but was the only member of the Catholic hierarchy to speak publicly against conscription in 1916. As the Catholic archbishop of Melbourne from May 1917, his rhetoric on the war marked Australia's most bitter period of sectarianism. Mannix pitched his appeal to working-class Irish-Australian Catholics, drawing on a renewed Catholic militancy led by the Catholic Federation – which had been formed in Victoria in 1911 to fight for educational, social and economic equality for Catholics. By December 1917 Mannix had become the main target for Hughes, the press and others supporting conscription.[17]

The issue had as much to do with Irish as Australian politics. Mannix, like most of the Catholic clergy in Australia, had come from Ireland and identified closely with the Irish struggle for Home Rule.[18] While only 3 per cent of Australians had been born in Ireland, some 20 per cent were of Irish Catholic background. Home Rule seemed assured by British legislation of September 1914, but awaited the end of the war to be implemented. Meanwhile, thousands of Irishmen had volunteered to fight for the empire in Europe. However, the brutal suppression by Britain of the Easter Uprising of 1916 turned Irish opinion away from the goal of self-government promised by the moderate Irish Party and towards the more radical independence policy of Sinn Fein (Ourselves Alone) (see: Words like firecrackers).

> ### *Words like firecrackers*
>
> When Mannix addressed a crowd estimated at possibly 100 000 people at Richmond racecourse on Guy Fawkes night in 1917 his words exploded like firecrackers. Next day *The Argus* reported the archbishop's words 'You are Sinn Feiners', spoken to the assembled throng. Mannix was drawing a direct parallel between the Australian and Irish people: '... Australia was first and the Empire second', the newspaper commented.

LOYALIST REACTION

The Victorian Protestant Federation, established in July 1917 'To maintain loyalty to the Throne, the unity of the Empire and to promote the national development of Australia', was quick to counter the archbishop's views. Leagues of Loyalty sprang up in other states, epitomising the Protestant response to the war. The style and substance of Mannix's rhetoric also alarmed some Catholics. Sydney solicitor and politician Sir Thomas Hughes, an Australian-born Irish Catholic who supported conscription, declared in November 1917 that 'Loyalty to the Empire is loyalty to Australia, and anything else is hateful to every true Australian'. Some Catholics paid a price for Mannix's words by being refused jobs or lodgings, or being ostracised as a despised minority. Yet Catholics had been just as willing as Protestants to enlist during the war.[19]

The second conscription referendum delivered a larger 'no' vote than the first one, reinforcing the Protestant view that Australian Catholics were disloyal, that their ties to the Irish cause made them anti-British. The renewed sectarianism hardened the political and religious divide: after it split in 1916, the Labor Party became more Catholic and the Nationalists more militantly Protestant. By opposing conscription, Labor appeared to be putting Australia first – a view the Nationalists strongly condemned in rhetoric that centred on the Union Jack.[20]

figure 3.11
Labor's Adelaide Daily
Herald *of 27 May*
1911 showed over
500 children at
suburban Norwood
Infants School salut-
ing the Union Jack.

'MY COUNTRY (THE BRITISH EMPIRE)'

The war was both sharpening and blurring the distinction between 'country' and 'empire'. 'For King and Country' and 'For King and Empire' were used interchangeably as inscriptions on Australian war memorials. Charles Long, the Victorian writer of school textbooks, had found 'country' an ambiguous word when explaining citizenship to Australian children. The British Empire, he said, was 'our Country', but Australia was 'more particularly *our* Country'. Yet only South Australia had thought it necessary in October 1916 to end that ambiguity for its public schools by insisting that 'I love my country' in the national salute become 'I love my country (the British Empire)'.[21]

South Australia's salute had differed from Victoria's of 1901 – there was no mention of God (reflecting Protestant dissenters' belief in the separation of church and state), teachers or parents, nor was a flag mentioned, though South Australia had always insisted on the Union Jack (figure 3.11), supplying one to public schools erecting a flagpole.[22] The change in the South Australian salute in 1916 also saw a new addition: 'I salute her flag (the Union Jack)'. Why were these changes made?

THE 'THREAT' WITHIN

They were introduced by a Labor government determined to teach children that they were British – a war-time reaction to South Australia's German-speaking minority. Across the whole of Australia less than 2 per cent of the population was of German descent, but in South Australia the figure was almost 7 per cent. Most of this minority lived in largely self-contained communities stretching from the Adelaide Hills through the Barossa Valley to the mid-north and the Murray Mallee. Lutheran schools and churches guaranteed the survival of the German language. South Australia had 49 Lutheran primary schools, Victoria only 11 and New South Wales three.[23] With anti-German feeling growing, Lutheran schools became targets.

The Labor government reluctantly responded in July 1915 to pressure for a daily, rather than weekly, national salute in public schools. Crawford Vaughan, premier and minister of education, a quietly spoken Australian-born lawyer and Unitarian, feared that the measure would lead to indifference towards the ritual. But the director of education, Milton Maughan, was determined on the issue. The English-born son of a Methodist minister was a lay preacher and also a member of the Royal Society of St George, and believed there was 'no better means than the flag ceremony of … keeping alive the national spirit', especially as Australians came to terms with the mounting casualties at Gallipoli.[24]

As calls for the closure of Lutheran schools began, legislators argued that it was enough to require them to teach in English for at least four hours a day – the school day was four-and-a-half hours long. A former Labor premier, John Verran, a Methodist lay preacher, freemason and fiery miner from the Labor mining stronghold of Moonta, moved an amendment to ban German in the schools altogether. Having migrated from Cornwall as an infant, this self-styled 'Britisher under the British flag' called for Lutheran children to 'be taught pure English, and taught by those who are British, and taught what it is to be British' (adding later 'Our Empire today demands a British race and British loyalty'). Although the move failed on this occasion, only two members defended the Lutherans as Australians, a term that did not carry much weight with other speakers.[25]

A year later, as Australians prepared for the first referendum on conscription, the South Australian government ended the ambiguity in the words of the national salute: country meant the British Empire; its flag was the Union Jack. The next month it legislated to close Lutheran schools. Though reluctant, Vaughan acknowledged the practical difficulties of retaining Lutheran schools, especially in remote farming districts where some 'British' children had to attend 'German' schools because there were not enough children in the district to justify a public school. Inspectors had reported the absence in these schools of the Union Jack, the national anthem, royal portraits and of any reference to Empire Day. One inspector said that 'children should know under which flag they live'. Verran, strengthened by the All British League's petition of 49 000 signatures, gained enough support for his amendment this time to close Lutheran schools by the end of 1917 (see: Speaking in whispers).[26]

LOYALTY IN PRIVATE SCHOOLS

Directions to NSW public schools showed a similar concern with flag ritual as the war continued: first the insistence by the Labor government in November 1916 on the singing of the national anthem at the end of each day; then a year later, the Nationalist government's requirement of a daily salute. In Victoria, the Liberal minister of public instruction believed so strongly that the flag ceremony developed 'sound ideals of imperial and Australian citizenship' that he tried to impose it on all private schools.[27]

The response in Catholic schools was diffident and ambiguous. In Lutheran schools, where children had been saluting the flag every week since the department's instruction in 1914 (and some before that), the response was impeccable. By contrast, the well established Protestant schools of Wesley College (Methodist) and Trinity Grammar School (Anglican) were appalled at the minister's impertinence. These schools followed the tradition of their counterparts in England. As Trinity's English-born headmaster bluntly told the minister, patriotism did not need to be taught in private schools because it was 'in the air they breathe'. These schools were not the minister's concern: Lutheran schools were. As it was, the acquiescence of the Lutheran schools protected them from calls for their closure coming from the Council of Public Instruction, led by the xenophobic Dr Alexander Leeper, the Irish-born Anglican warden of Trinity College at the University of Melbourne.

> ### Speaking in whispers
>
> Lutheran children were apprehensive as they began attending the nearest public school, or saw their own school taken over by a strange teacher. 'For the first week I could not get them to speak above a whisper when saluting [the] flag', one teacher reported to the education director, Milton Maughan.
>
> More widely, Maughan was having second thoughts about the daily ceremony, given criticism that it was becoming 'commonplace and meaningless'. Inspectors favoured holding the full ceremony once a week, but there was a danger that requiring the salute less often might encourage debate about whether it was necessary at all, one of them warned.[28]

The SA government, unlike those in Victoria and New South Wales, had become less rather than more tolerant of the appearance of Australian flags in schools during the war. But even in those states which allowed an Australian flag to be used in schools, governments were careful not to prescribe it instead of the Union Jack. This caution was even more marked after the war ended and Australian flags became ambiguous markers in a volatile political landscape – so ambiguous that, unless accompanied by the Union Jack, they were seen as symbols of disloyalty.

AUSTRALIAN ENSIGNS
become
DISLOYAL SYMBOLS

THE 1920 ST PATRICK'S DAY
PROCESSION IN MELBOURNE

The choice of flags for Melbourne's St Patrick's Day procession on 20 March 1920 was the subject of much discussion between the St Patrick's Day Committee and the city's lord mayor. The previous year there had been no procession because the committee refused the lord mayor's condition that the Union Jack must be carried as well as an Australian flag. This followed the appearance of the Irish tricolour of Sinn Fein in the 1918 procession. Reassured that St Patrick's banner would carry the Union Jack, the lord mayor allowed the procession to go ahead. The Loyalist League's president, Dr Leeper, was suspicious.[29]

The procession was to be more than the usual gathering of Catholic schools and societies. Included were several thousand returned men, most of them in uniform, with a few hundred on horses. Preceding them was Archbishop Mannix with a guard of honour of Victoria Cross winners on white

figure 3.12 Organisers of the St Patrick's Day procession in Melbourne in March 1920 refused to carry the Union Jack because of the Anglo-Irish war, choosing instead to attach an Australian flag to St Patrick's banner.

chargers. He took the salute on the steps of Parliament House, still the seat of federal government. Melbourne businessman John Wren had spared no expense in organising the procession. A lapsed Catholic but an admirer of Mannix, Wren had made his Richmond racecourse available to the archbishop for his 5 November 1917 Home Rule demonstration. Melbourne's Protestant elite despised both men.

Eyes scrutinised St Patrick's banner: there was no Union Jack, except the one in the corner of an Australian flag (figure 3.12). As well, two officers carried Australian flags at the head of the returned men (figure 3.13). In this context Australian flags played an ambiguous role. The organisers, banned from displaying the Irish republican flag, refused to carry what they regarded as the symbol of English despotism in Ireland. They used Australian flags to make the procession appear both loyal and disloyal at the same time: loyal because Australian flags included the Union Jack in their design, disloyal because they carried no separate Union Jack. Australian flags were also less divisive symbols for Australians with Irish sympathies than the Irish tricolour. Since the 1916 Easter Uprising, the green, gold and white of the tricolour had symbolised the republic of the outlawed Sinn Fein. The green harp flag represented self-government within the empire for those who still believed in the pre-1916 goal.

figure 3.13 Australian flags led returned soldiers in the St Patrick's Day procession of 1920, the absence of the Union Jack infuriating Melbourne's militant Protestants.

Loyalist Melbourne was outraged by the calculated snub to the Union Jack and the empire. Leeper and his supporters saw in the procession an attempt to turn Australians against Britain over the worsening Anglo-Irish war. In Ireland, Britain was reacting to the rebels' systematic shooting of police by recruiting thousands of special armed police, the brutal Black and Tans and Auxiliaries. The silent film *Ireland Will Be Free* was to corroborate loyalist beliefs about the Melbourne procession.

PROJECTING THE MESSAGE

In honouring Mannix with this extraordinary procession, Wren had in mind a wider audience than Melbourne or even Victoria. The film of the procession would take its message of Australian support for Ireland against England around Australia and overseas. Included was a statement, made at Mannix's residence *Raheen* after the procession, by the Victoria Cross winners on behalf of the returned men, urging freedom for the Irish people. More than the press and intelligence reports, the film indicates the threat Mannix and Wren posed on behalf of Australia's Irish Catholic community and Australians generally. 'Australia and her Soldier Sons', Mannix said, were with the Irish 'in their final effort to shake off an alien oppressor'. Melbourne's lord mayor had assumed that the presence of returned soldiers in the procession would guarantee its loyalty, but they had quite the opposite effect.

Mannix took great care in Australia and overseas to blur the difference between independence and self-government for the Irish. In promoting their cause he encouraged Australians to see themselves as the Irish did – a nation apart from the British Empire. Why, he asked, must Australian children on Anzac Day salute 'some other flag' than 'the flag of the Australian nation'? The 'other flag', he insisted, must take second place. As during the conscription crisis, so now in 1920: putting Australia and its flag before the empire and the Union Jack became the critical issue for Mannix. His rhetoric made him sound like an Australian nationalist, as had Cardinal Moran before him. But it was rhetoric serving Irish and Catholic Irish-Australian interests against Protestant England and the Protestant Anglo-Australian elite. To Mannix's mind, Irish-Australians who supported the Irish cause were good Australians; they did not have 'British souls'. 'Irish-Australians who love Ireland most', he explained, 'love Australia best'. This was anathema to loyalists, especially the Anglo-Irish Australian Leeper, Mannix's main antagonist.[30]

Wherever the film *Ireland Will Be Free* was shown – Sydney, Adelaide, Brisbane and provincial centres in Queensland and New South Wales – it stirred up Irish Catholic feeling against the British. Loyalists were horrified that the Commonwealth government had no power under trade and customs law to prevent the film being shown. They determined to be not so easily outwitted by their enemies in future.

The following year Melbourne City Council insisted that the Union Jack be carried at the head of the St Patrick's Day procession. In protest, Catholic organisers paid an English-born derelict to do the job, but he had to be escorted to ensure the flag's safety. The deliberate humiliation of loyalists was even greater than in 1920 – as Dr Patrick Phelan, the Irish-born Bishop of Sale, exulted: 'We have spat back today the sham loyalty that was sought to be thrust down our throats ... We live ... under the Australian flag, and it is that flag that should be carried in front of the procession'.[31]

The irony of the situation was that Irish Catholic use of Australian flags in these circumstances made other Australians less rather than more likely to use them. For many, an Australian flag became a suspicious symbol: the Union Jack it featured was no guarantee of loyalty; it had to be accompanied by the real thing. That explains why Victoria's director of education refused to encourage schools to fly an Australian flag to mark Anzac Day as the 'nation's birthday'. While teachers could use either the Union Jack or an Australian flag, he feared that insisting on an Australian flag might reinforce 'the propaganda of disloyalists'.[32]

THE 1921 MAY DAY CELEBRATION IN SYDNEY

A dispute over flags – the Union Jack, Australian flags and the red flag (the flag of the international socialist movement) – occurred in Sydney in 1921, with similar results. On May Day about 4000 people gathered in the Domain under the red flag, no longer banned as it had been during the war, to hear speakers organised by the communist-controlled NSW Labor Council. During the meeting about 20 demonstrators, including returned soldiers, charged the platform, intending to replace the red flag with their Union Jack. In the struggle, the Union Jack was allegedly torn and burnt.

A week later the King and Empire Alliance and the Returned Sailors' and Soldiers' Imperial League of Australia (which became known as the RSL) organised a counter-demonstration of up to 150 000 people to show that 'the Union Jack is the flag for Australia, and that the red flag, or any other emblem of revolution, shall not be exhibited in Australia' (figure 3.14). No flag other than the Union Jack was safe. RSL men seized an Australian flag from the platform of their rivals, the Returned Sailors' and Soldiers' Political League (RSSPL), also known as the Returned Sailors' and Soldiers' League (ALP Section), and trampled it. Their argument was that the Australian flag had been used 'as a substitute for the red flag'. Then they burnt a red flag.[33]

SYDNEY DOMAIN—GOD BLESS IT!

figure 3.14
Percy Leason's battle
of the Union Jack and
the red flag, 'Sydney
Domain – God bless
it!' in The Bulletin,
19 May 1921. In
this ideological and
political dispute there
seemed no place for
an Australian flag.

With Labor in power at the state and Sydney municipal levels, but only by narrow margins, the Nationalists sensed the possibility of electoral success, especially if they could win the returned soldier vote at a time of significant unemployment. Working with the Protestant Federation, the RSL, the King and Empire Alliance and related groups, they made much of Labor's links to the two issues they believed threatened the unity of the British Empire and with it Australia's security – namely Irish republicanism and Bolshevism (see: Influence in the Labor Party).

Influence in the Labor Party

The growing strength of Irish Catholicism in the Labor Party had attracted increased criticism during the Anglo-Irish war: 61 per cent of the state Labor MLAs were Catholic, compared to 37 per cent before the war. But the focus of Nationalist attention was Bill Lambert, the lord mayor of Sydney and president of the NSW Labor Party. An Australian of Irish Catholic background, Lambert had persuaded the municipal council to support Ireland's cause against Britain in 1920.[34] A former shearer, he was secretary of the powerful Australian Workers' Union, which lay at the centre of NSW Labor politics. The pragmatism and moderation of the Labor premier, John Storey, marked the parliamentary wing of the party, but members of the Australian Communist Party, formed in late 1920, controlled its industrial wing, and were a reminder of the Communist International and Bolshevik Russia.

It's Our Flag!

Our Diggers Fought For It!
Our Women Worked For It!
Our Bolsheviks Would Haul It Down!

How much longer will the loyal citizens of Australia suffer this sneaking insidious conspiracy of revolution that is almost ripe in our midst?

In no other country in the world would these disloyalists be permitted openly to preach Bolshevism in a nation that is overwhelmingly loyal.

The Union Jack is befouled without a public protest. The red flag is brazenly paraded through our streets. The forces of disaffection, of disloyalty, of rebellion take courage by the silence of the patriots.

IT IS TIME!

It is time to take action.

It is time to clear the good name of Australia from this disloyal stain.

It is time for every patriot and every loyalist, every believer in The Flag, to make a public protest against this assiduously engineered Bolshevism.

It is time for the overwhelming majority of decent patriotic citizens to put these birds of evil omen in their proper place.

We have been complaisant too long. Our good name as a loyal nation has been besmirched. Our Flag has been insulted!

It is up to us!

PUBLIC MEETING AT TOWN HALL NEXT FRIDAY NIGHT.

A public meeting will be held in the main hall, at 8 o'clock, to which every loyal citizen, every patriot, every believer in Australia—man and woman—is invited to attend.

The meeting will be a public meeting, not a party meeting, not a sectarian meeting. The cause is too important to be in party hands. The only party will be the patriotic party, which should cover all parties.

All patriotic bodies are cordially invited to co-operate.

At the meeting resolutions will be proposed that promise to be the beginning of an Australia-wide campaign against the evil forces in our midst.

Every loyal and patriotic citizen, no matter of what party or what creed, is invited to attend.

RALLY ROUND THE FLAG---OUR FLAG!

Speakers and resolutions will be announced later. Roll up and defeat the disloyalists.

Mr. Ernest Truman, the City Organist, will render patriotic selections between 7 and 8 p.m.

Doors Open at 6.30 p.m. Patriotic Selections on the Grand Organ.

ADMISSION FREE.   Convener: W. Scott Fell, 251 George Street, Sydney.

figure 3.15 A loyalist advertisement in Sydney's Daily Telegraph of 4 May 1921 for a rally in the Town Hall drew on the words of a World War I recruitment poster from Britain: 'It's Our Flag. Fight for it. Work for it.'

DOMAIN POLITICS

Separate large rallies to publicise the opposing views represented in the Domain demonstrations were held at Sydney Town Hall. In the first meeting, organised by Scottish-born William Scott Fell, shipping merchant and president of the British Empire Union, some 25 000 people (most having to stand outside the hall) affirmed their attachment to the Union Jack and the empire (figure 3.15).

The influential group behind the organiser was the King and Empire Alliance, the front organisation for the Old Guard, a secret army dedicated to preventing the breakup of the empire in the face of the Bolshevik threat. Community singing warmed the crowd, the most popular songs being *Rule Britannia* and *Keep the Union Jack A-flyin'* with its chorus of 'There's no red flag for us'. The meeting condemned the May Day insult to their flag, pledged loyalty to the king and determined to crush disloyal sentiment in Australia.

The 'Australian Rally', mounted by the city's lord mayor, Bill Lambert, which almost filled the Town Hall two months later, saw Australian flags draped above the slogan, 'Australia First' to publicise the mayor's stand against 'the exploiters of the Union Jack for political purposes'. The president of the RSSPL presented him with a framed Australian flag, said to be the one trampled in the Domain. Harried externally by the Nationalists and internally by communists within the labour movement, Lambert had been using an Australian flag as the national symbol to steer a middle course between imperialism's Union Jack and communism's red flag.

The organisers of the rally were representatives of the Ratepayers' and Citizens' Committee, established for the purpose, and the Sons of Australia, which was linked to the RSSPL. Behind them were Labor Party stalwarts, most of them state and Commonwealth MPs, and the RSSPL, who were concerned about the effect the Nationalist Party and RSL campaign would have on the working-class vote in the approaching state election. Moderate Labor leaders, convinced that the burning of the Union Jack was 'a frame-up', were making a stand with Lambert for an Australian flag.[35]

They were right to be concerned about the effect of the Nationalist campaign on working-class opinion. In Geelong, Victoria, for example, the Trades Hall Council insisted on flying the Union Jack, believing 'that the time had come to choose between the red flag and that of the Empire'. It feared that an Australian flag was divisive: with it, a member suggested, 'the Party ... might be charged with favouring a Republic'. Many municipal and district councils seized on the May Day incident to urge the NSW government to introduce a daily flag ceremony in public schools to control 'the element responsible for the insult to our flag'. Most assumed the flag saluted would be the Union Jack, only one council mentioning an Australian flag.[36]

In this context, Labor's promotion of an Australian flag made it a suspicious symbol in the eyes of the wider public – unless it was accompanied by the Union Jack. On its own, it was seen as anti-British, which seemed to undermine not only Australians' sense of security but also their sense of identity. As *The Daily Telegraph* observed when deploring the introduction of the Union Jack and an Australian flag into 'Domain politics', to be loyal to Australia and disloyal to Britain was not possible. The two sentiments were 'incompatible'. Here the newspaper echoed the comment of the deputy prime minister, Sir Joseph Cook, made at a St George's Day dinner in Sydney: 'No man could be a true Australian who was not at the same time a true Britisher'.[37]

Divisions evident during the war over conscription had hardened in its aftermath as Irish republicanism and international communism challenged the pre-war certainty of the British Empire. Linked by ethnic, religious and ideological ties to both those movements, the Australian Labor Party sought cover behind an Australian flag and the nationality it represented. For the Nationalists, an Australian flag was not enough – commitment to the Union Jack was the true test of loyalty. An Australian flag on its own could not be the national flag.

Chapter four
The red and the blue

The antics over flags in the streets of Melbourne and Sydney revealed deep-seated divisions among Australians about their flags and what they represented. But there were two further problems which would continue to puzzle citizens and their governments for more than 20 years.

Two questions of PRECEDENCE

WHICH FLAG SHOULD FLY AT THE VIEWER'S LEFT?

If, as Nationalists and their allies so often insisted, the Union Jack should be used with an Australian flag, which flag should be given precedence? Australia, like Canada, New Zealand and South Africa, was not an independent country but a self-governing dominion of the British Empire – or British Commonwealth of Nations as it was becoming known. The use of the Union Jack as the national flag reflected that fact. It signified British rule, protection and nationality – a powerful symbol in an uncertain post-war world. Dominion flags, red and blue British ensigns – with the national flag in the most important first quarter – carried their own symbols, usually in the less important fly. Giving precedence to the Union Jack long seemed obligatory, even natural (figure 4.1). But at what point would Australians and their governments give an Australian flag, representing Australian nationality, precedence?

Official and public confusion reigns

The First World War prompted questions about which Australian flag could be used by state governments and the general public on flag days, questions that the prime minister's department – which had responsibility in this area – found difficult to answer. Advice provided to that department by the departments of the navy and defence varied over the years.

Many Australians assumed that they should fly the red ensign, as should state governments. 'Is it a fact', the stores officer in the NSW education department asked the minister for external affairs in 1916, 'that only Departments under the Federal Government are permitted to fly the Blue Ensign and that the Government Offices *under the States* should fly the Red Merchant Flag of the Commonwealth?' Simmering flag troubles in Sydney in 1921 raised the issue of precedence for the NSW Local Government Association: were councils right to fly the Union Jack and an Australian flag together on special days? If so, which flag should take precedence?[1]

WHICH FLAG COULD GOVERNMENT *AND* PEOPLE USE?

The second problem concerned the Australian red and blue ensigns. Devised for the use of ships, which of them would become the national flag for use on shore by government and people? While the Admiralty insisted that the two ensigns distinguished government (blue ensign) from merchant (red) vessels, most dominions had chosen one of them as their dominion flag on shore. New Zealand had legislated as early as 1901 for the blue; less formally, Canada and South Africa had adopted the red. The choice in Australia was not so simple.

On shore, flags had been primarily used to mark the celebration of special days, such as the monarch's birthday and coronation day. There had been much confusion about the use of Australian flags since they were gazetted in 1903, especially in relation to the states' blue ensigns and the Union Jack (see: Official and public confusion reigns). Evolving flag custom varied across the states. The Tasmanian government, for example, flew only the Union Jack on its buildings – as a sign of state sovereignty, jealously guarded since federation. Despite the surge in Australian patriotism during the war, states retained their provincial loyalties and the direct ties with Britain and the Crown. Even the Commonwealth government was not prepared to spend money on Australian flags for its post offices.[2]

Souvenir of AUSTRALIA'S Voluntary Effort in the Great War 1914-18

*figure 4.1
James Sanders' 1920
poster, Souvenir of
Australia's voluntary
effort in the Great War
1914–1918, gave the
Union Jack precedence
as the national flag over
an Australian ensign –
which was common
practice on honour rolls
after the war.*

Advice appearing to favour an Australian flag over the Union Jack encouraged the Labor lord mayor of Sydney, Bill Lambert, to insist that the Australian red ensign take precedence over the Union Jack on Sydney Town Hall to mark the death of the Labor premier, John Storey, in October 1921. Conservatives keen to make an issue of Lambert's preference for Australia over the empire professed outrage. A few days later the Nationalist prime minister, WM Hughes, who had just returned from the 1921 Imperial Conference in London, took advantage of the uproar to score political points against Lambert when returned soldiers took matters into their own hands and unfurled a Union Jack from the town hall balcony.[3]

But while Hughes turned the Union Jack against the Labor Party in Sydney, the head of his department in Melbourne was trying to draft guidelines which would promote the use on all public buildings of the Australian blue ensign without the Union Jack, so avoiding the awkward issue of precedence. After all, it was said, the Australian flag included the Union Jack. Making the blue ensign the flag for all governments, not just the Commonwealth, would be a significant step. Would it also be the flag for people to use? The prime minister's department thought not: the public should use the red ensign.[4] But the guidelines remained unpublished, and the questions continued (see: Confusion in Coleraine).

Confusion in Coleraine

In Coleraine, a developing soldier–settler area northwest of Hamilton in Victoria, the question of which ensign to fly on Anzac Day at the war memorial was the centre of a long dispute. The secretary of the committee organising the event had ordered the blue ensign, but the committee chairman argued that this was the navy's flag and that 'the National Flag of Australia ... should have a red ground'. By the time the committee received government advice favouring the red ensign it had already begun using the blue, and requested permission to continue doing so. The prime minister's department could hardly refuse, but its permission made a farce of the whole issue and underlined the confusion of both government and general public.[5]

Blue ensign for PUBLIC BUILDINGS

In the absence of legislation on the use of the blue ensign, the departments of the prime minister and defence looked to each other to answer inquiries. By the end of 1923, although they agreed that the red ensign was for the public's use, they differed on where the blue ensign could be flown: on all government buildings, said the prime minister's department; only on Commonwealth government buildings, said the defence department. A

prime minister's department circular to state premiers in January 1924, signed by Dr Earle Page, the acting prime minister, followed defence department opinion, causing even further confusion.[6]

'Which flag? Commonwealth intervenes. Right of states', trumpeted the headline in the 20 March 1924 edition of *The Sun*. Sydney's popular tabloid, which bore the motto 'Above all "for Australia"', was protesting at the Commonwealth's exclusive right to the blue ensign. The issue was taken up by the RSL and in parliament, some assuming that the Commonwealth was forcing the states to use the Union Jack. The Commonwealth government hastened to clarify the situation: if the state ensign was not available, then the Commonwealth blue ensign should be used, it said.[7]

By May 1924 the Commonwealth had grudgingly approved the use of the blue ensign on public buildings, but private businesses and individuals wanting to use an Australian flag had to use the red ensign. For universal use, there was only the Union Jack, which the prime minister's department circular regarded as the national flag: 'It should never be flown in a position inferior to any other flag', the circular advised. When flown with an Australian flag, a yardarm had to be used (figure 4.2). At least, after years of confusion, there was some clarification of when and where Australian ensigns could be flown, and which one was appropriate to the situation. However, bureaucrats and politicians were feeling their way on the issue. The uncertainty was epitomised in the uniform of Australia's team for the 1924 Olympics; on it, the Union Jack appeared beside the Australian coat of arms (figure 4.3).

The debate surrounding the choice of ensign for the RAAF also provided an insight into the times (see: A bumpy takeoff).

figure 4.2
The provision of a yardarm became standard practice during the inter-war years when flying the Union Jack (honoured on the left) and Australian blue ensign together on Armistice Day at Parliament House in Canberra – on this occasion in 1928.

figure 4.3
Britain's Union Jack and Australia's coat of arms on the uniform of Australian gold medallist Anthony 'Nick' Winter, the fireman from Manly, New South Wales, who set a triple jump world record at the 1924 Paris Olympics.

figure 4.4
In March 1922 the Royal Australian Air Force's Air Council had to discard its Australian design with the Commonwealth Star and Southern Cross, proposed in July 1921, in favour of the Royal Air Force ensign.

Security a PRIORITY

A bumpy takeoff

Underlining the role of the Union Jack as national flag, the Commonwealth government had agreed to forego an Australian ensign (figure 4.4) for its fledgling air force. The defence minister's approval of an Australian ensign for the newly established Australian Air Force in 1921 (soon to have the prefix Royal) meant little in the face of Air Ministry opposition in London. British control, symbolised by Australia's use of the ensigns of the Royal Navy and Royal Air Force (figure 4.4), was part of 'the price we pay for Empire', as the prime minister, WM Hughes, had put it at the Imperial Conference of 1921.[8]

Stanley Melbourne Bruce, who displaced Hughes as prime minister, accepted continuing dependence on Britain in the hope of influencing imperial policy in Australia's favour and ensuring national security. During the 1920s the more Canada, South Africa and the newly formed Irish Free State assumed the right to be independent as well as self-governing, the more vulnerable Australian governments felt. Believing that Australia was unable to defend itself, they continued to argue, as Bruce had at the 1923 Imperial Conference, for an empire that was 'one and indivisible'. When the more radical dominions succeeded in forcing the 1926 conference to issue the Balfour Report confirming dominion independence, Bruce's government hoped that Australians and the rest of the world would ignore it.[9]

Canada and South Africa were now making changes to their flags to reflect their more independent status. The Canadians, who had been using the Union Jack on their public buildings, replaced it with the Canadian red ensign – not in Canada but on Canadian buildings abroad. The South Africans went further, discarding their red ensign in favour of a version of the old Dutch flag – now bearing three small flags in its centre, the Union Jack and the flags of the two Boer republics. In Australia, the country's blue ensign was becoming more widely recognised as the flag of government, but it was not yet the national flag. How then would Australians dress their new Parliament House for its opening in 1927? Which flags would be used? Which would take precedence?

FLAGS FOR THE OPENING OF PARLIAMENT HOUSE

Canberra's cold and frosty night gave way to a sunny autumn day on 9 May 1927. There was barely a breath of wind to stir the huge flags hanging from buildings and decorating the streets. Union Jacks and Australian flags flew from the roof of Parliament House and hung from its dazzling white stuccoed walls, the Union Jack taking precedence, just as the British coat of arms took precedence over its Australian counterpart near the main entrance. Above was the Duke of York's standard, ready to be unfurled on his arrival. The architect John Murdoch's simple design of a long, low building, with a roof line which emphasised the two chambers, echoed the dual national symbolism.

But the use of British as well as Australian flags was a last-minute decision. A Federal Capital Commission sketch showing the position of flags for the opening ceremony suggested only Australian blue ensigns accompanying the duke's standard. The Royal Visit Cabinet Committee confirmed in March 1927 that the 'Commonwealth Flag', not the Union Jack, would fly with the duke's flag on Parliament House in the morning and at the armed forces review in the afternoon.[10]

Black and white photographs verify the different outcome – Australian *and* British flags were flying for the official opening of Parliament House. More difficult to establish from the photographs is whether blue rather than red ensigns were used. A commemorative lithograph with the duke's address and MPs' signatures shows blue ensigns (figure 4.5), but Septimus

*figure 4.5
A lithographer chose Australian blue ensigns, with precedence to the Union Jack as the national flag, in this commemorative picture of the official opening of Parliament House in Canberra on 9 May 1927.*

Power's commissioned painting of the event shows red ones (figure 4.6). Was the artist painting an accurate record or using artistic licence? Known for his ability to 'create a feeling of movement and drama', Power may have painted the ensigns red for dramatic effect – to highlight the St George crosses in the Union Jacks and the carpet leading from the duke's carriage to the main entrance.[11] Or perhaps he deliberately chose the flag the people had to use. Yet this was the opening of the Commonwealth's most important public building – surely an occasion for the Commonwealth's official flag.

Whichever ensign was flown, the appearance of the Union Jack late in the preparations and the precedence accorded it emphasised both its continuing role as the national flag and uncertainty about the use of Australian flags.

When steps were taken to change the flag of governors-general, the same uncertainty dogged Australia's response (see: Royal Crest or Commonwealth Star?).

Australians were not ready to confirm their independence from Britain, to recognise their flag as the national flag and give it precedence over the Union Jack. But some were prepared to solve the problem of the ensigns by insisting that the Australian flag to fly on land for people as well as government was the blue ensign (figure 4.8). The push for this came from Victoria in 1938.

figure 4.7
In 1936 Australia belatedly followed the other dominions in replacing the flag of governors-general. The Commonwealth Star, seen in its 1903 six-pointed version, was replaced with the Royal Crest; the Union Jack was replaced by a blue ground.

Royal Crest or Commonwealth Star?

The Union Jack was also the flag at Government House, replaced when the governor-general was in residence by his personal flag: the Union Jack with the Commonwealth Star in its centre, surmounted by the British crown (figure 4.7): symbols of the British government and monarchy. Well before the Balfour Report of 1926, the governor-general in practical terms had become the represen-tative of the Crown rather than the British state. Subsequently a new flag for domin-ion governors-general emphasised their changed role: they were to fly 'the King's own flag'.[12]

In 1928, King George V proposed changing the flag of governors-general to a plain blue flag bearing the Royal Crest in the centre with a scroll beneath carrying the name of the particular dominion. This was in response to the situation in South Africa, where the governor-general was continuing to use the royal standard after it had become the flag for the sovereign alone to use. In addition, there was growing desire to fly the South African flag over Government House in Pretoria. When consulted in 1930 about the king's proposal, the dominions preferred a design which included their arms as well as the Royal Crest. But the king was adamant. South Africa and Canada accepted the new flag immediately. What would Australia's decision be?[13]

The change posed a dilemma for Australia's prime minister, James Scullin. A devout Catholic with Irish parents, Scullin had opposed conscription in Australia during the war and enthusiasti-cally supported independence for Ireland. With such a background, he was unlikely to approve a design that replaced the Commonwealth Star with the Royal Crest, even if the Union Jack was replaced with a blue field. There was the additional

dilemma for Scullin that agreeing to the change would prompt the accusation that he was anti-British. The parliamentary opposition had already criticised Scullin for insisting that the king appoint an Australian, Sir Isaac Isaacs, as Australia's next governor-general. Some people were also pressing for the Australian flag to accompany or replace the Union Jack on Government House, including Richard Crouch, now a Labor MHR, who put a question to that effect in Parliament House on 21 July 1931. The *King's Regulations* would not allow it, Crouch was informed – and there the matter rested.[14]

After the Statute of Westminster formalised the independent status of the dominions in December 1931, Australia, now governed by the former Labor MHR Joseph Lyons and his United Australia Party (UAP), insisted the statute would apply only when the Australian parliament adopted it. Such reluctance reflected a sentiment which had long confused loyalty to the Crown with loyalty to the United Kingdom. It also disguised a long-held sense of defence insecurity and depend-ence on the Royal Navy.[15]

The form and substance of British power remained. The Admiralty insisted in 1932 that foreign ships visiting Australian ports should hoist the British white ensign, not Australia's blue ensign. In the same year the Union Jack covered the coffin at the state funeral of Bert Jacka VC, 'Australia's greatest front-line soldier', as it had the year before for the state funeral of Sir John Monash, widely regarded in the post-war years as the greatest living Australian. When Lyons finally agreed to the change in the governor-general's flag he did so cautiously (figure 4.7). State governors continued to use the Union Jack with the state badge in its centre.[16]

figure 4.8
The Commonwealth government advised private individuals and organisations to use the Australian red ensign.

The Sydney Mail *used it on 27 April 1938, with the Union Jack as the national flag, to commemorate Anzac Day.*

VICTORIA:
battleground for
THE BLUE

Victoria had been the first state to accept a school's right to fly an Australian flag instead of the Union Jack. By leaving the choice of flag to the school committee, governments in Victoria distanced themselves from the sensitivities associated with choosing between British and Australian flags. Even so, the flag and the ceremony continued to attract attention in the wider community, especially from soldier–settlers and the RSL, who favoured the Union Jack, and the ANA, which promoted an Australian flag.

figure 4.9
Most Australian public schools, such as Brighton-road State School (now St Kilda primary) – pictured here in 1938 – saluted the Union Jack as the national flag. Schools wanting to fly an Australian flag had to use the red ensign.

THE RSL AND THE ANA

The education department of Victoria found it difficult to ignore RSL complaints that 'flags were very seldom seen at local schools'. At issue was how often the department required schools to hold the flag ceremony: every week or only on 'national occasions'? Practice varied according to teachers' interpretation of the department's regulations. Amending them to include a weekly salute in 1932 renewed RSL pressure on teachers. The RSL had another victory when the department pulled into line schools which had been using a more secular form of the pledge – omitting references to God and obedience to parents, teachers and the laws. Labor had been in power for most of the period from 1927 to 1932. Its opposition to militarism in schools made the RSL distrustful, while in country areas especially, the White Army (a clandestine conservative organisation formed to respond to the unorthodox policies of the Depression) attracted ex-servicemen determined to see that public schools taught children to be patriotic and law-abiding.[17]

When in 1930 the ANA requested that all schools in Victoria fly 'the Australian Flag as the official School Flag', the education department had maintained its earlier stance.[18] Although more schools were choosing to fly an Australian flag, the department's director was not willing to insist that all public schools follow the practice: the decision, he said, should be left to local authorities (figure 4.9). But in October 1938 the *Education Gazette and Teachers' Aid* advised Victorian schools wishing to fly an Australian flag to choose the blue ensign, not the merchant flag. It was the beginning of a campaign by the state government that would eventually cause the federal government to declare the blue ensign the flag for people as well as governments.

figure 4.10
Albert Dunstan, Victoria's Country Party premier 1935–43 and 1943–45, recognised the Australian blue ensign as the Australian flag for people as well as government in 1938, and legislated accordingly in 1940. But the Commonwealth government was slow to respond.

PARTY POLITICS AND PATRIOTIC PURPOSES

From 1935 Victoria had a Country Party government led by the stocky, shrewd rural radical Albert Dunstan and supported by Labor (figure 4.10). The state minister of public instruction was Sir John Harris, an active member of the ANA – as was Ned Hogan, the minister of agriculture and mines. Hogan, a former Labor premier until he resigned over economic policy during the Depression and subsequently joined the Country Party, had been a determined opponent of attempts to remove Australian flags from schools in the early 1920s. Dunstan and Hogan were close associates of John Wren, who had helped to organise the St Patrick's Day procession of 1920 with its prominent display of Australian flags.[19]

The astute leader of the Labor Party, John Cain, was from an Irish Catholic background, as was Hogan. But while Cain had rejected his faith, Hogan was devout. Both had opposed conscription during the war. Aware of the competing communist and Catholic influences within the labour movement during the 1930s, Cain encouraged a moderate centre. Promoting an Australian flag, especially the blue ensign, served that cause, given the slur levelled by some that the red ensign stood in place of the red flag.

The colour blue had other associations: within the labour movement it was the colour of that early symbol of radicalism, the Eureka flag (figure 1.4), Lawson's 'rebel flag', the 'bonny blue'. For Australian Catholics,

blue – the colour of Mary, Queen of Heaven, the focus of their devotion – symbolised their religious identity.[20]

The *Education Gazette and Teachers' Aid* notice recommending the use of the blue ensign in schools placed school committees in an impossible situation. The refusal of flag suppliers to meet orders unless they were accompanied by 'special authority' (because suppliers assumed the blue ensign was for Commonwealth government use only) provided Dunstan with a reason to take up the issue with Canberra in February 1939.

Dunstan objected to using the state ensign for 'patriotic purposes' in schools: 'young Australians should be taught to associate themselves with Australian nationality as symbolised by the Australian flag', he said. The state premier urged the prime minister to end restrictions on the blue ensign's use in schools, or make 'a definite pronouncement' that Australians generally could fly that flag on shore in the same way that the British government acknowledged in 1908 the right of Britons to fly the Union Jack.[21]

THE RELUCTANT COMMONWEALTH

For nearly two years Dunstan waited for the Commonwealth to respond. It, however, was preoccupied with defence matters as war unfolded in Europe and Asia. There were also leadership problems within the UAP, whose coalition with the Country Party had collapsed. Following the death of Lyons, Robert Menzies had succeeded him as prime minister in April 1939, but without the support of Sir Earle Page's Country Party his minority government was vulnerable as Australia prepared for war.

Even so, the Commonwealth government did not ignore the issue. Lyons had asked Tom Collins, an energetic NSW Country Party MHR, to handle Dunstan's poser. Collins, a grazier and stock and station agent from Young, who had won Hume from Labor in 1932, was sympathetic to Menzies and was one of four Country Party members who dissociated themselves from Page's leadership and urged a return to the coalition. The son of Irish-born parents and a Catholic, Collins favoured Dunstan's suggestion of allowing the blue ensign to be used by all.[22] While the prime minister's department sought defence department approval for the proposed change and information from the British government, Collins looked to New Zealand and Canada for a comparative perspective.

A FALSE DAWN

The result in June 1939, the prime ministerial department paper Flying of Flags, was a watershed, recognising for the first time the need for an Australian national flag and recommending the blue ensign for that purpose. The defence department concurred, but the item remained on Cabinet's

agenda for more than a year, despite Dunstan's reminders. In July 1940 it was deleted with the terse comment, 'this question is not of moment at present'. Nazi Germany had turned on Britain after the fall of France. In Australia, Nazi sympathisers active in German clubs had already been interned (figure 4.11). The prime minister's department assumed that Dunstan would expect the issue to be resolved after the war. 'Presume we cannot tell *him* that matter has been taken off agenda', commented the head of the department. 'Probably better to let Premier revive the matter himself.'[23] Dunstan did revive the matter – not by further requests to the prime minister, but by legislating in 1940 to permit schools to fly the blue ensign.

BLUE ENSIGN FOR VICTORIA

Victorian legislators supported Dunstan's proposal that school committees buying a new flag should choose between the blue, not red, ensign and the Union Jack. Only William Beckett, veteran Labor leader in the Legislative Council, thought the government was not 'game enough' to decide which flag – Australian or British – should command children's loyalty. Beckett had been a long-time associate of John Wren. His UAP colleague Clifden Eager, a barrister and the unofficial leader of the Legislative Council, acknowledged that 'many people' objected to saluting the British flag after the *Statute of Westminster 1931* declared dominions were separate and independent nations. But he still thought that Australians who refused to acknowledge the Union Jack were being disloyal to their country 'because Australia is part of the British Commonwealth of Nations'.[24]

Meanwhile, giving preference to the blue ensign was overshadowed by the more controversial purpose of the legislation.

MAKING THE SALUTE COMPULSORY

The Education (Patriotic Ceremonies) Bill aimed to make the weekly salute compulsory in public schools in Victoria, and give the government the power to dismiss a teacher who refused to hold it. There had been complaints about 'subversive' teachers – though only two had justified investigation, and the findings had reported moral opposition to the war and nationalism rather than anti-British sentiment as the cause of dissension. More difficult were the complaints about children, especially those of Jehovah's Witnesses, who refused to participate in the salute. But when it was challenged on the issue in August 1940, the education department found it did not have the power to expel such pupils.[25]

In November 1940 the bill was passed and the Victorian government enshrined in legislation the salute its predecessor had introduced 40 years earlier. Proposed during the Boer War, renewed during World War I, and now with World War II raging, the legislation found almost unanimous support from the Country and United Australia parties.

This war gave conservative legislators the opportunity to settle once and for all the legitimacy of the flag ceremony: to teach children to 'be patriotic to the Constitution and the British Flag', 'to reverence the Empire and its flag'. Not far behind the rhetoric was the threat of a digger's boot to bring reluctant children into line, and of barbed wire to surround parents who put religious belief before patriotism. To no avail did the Victorian Teachers Union protest that the weekly ceremony made patriotism 'a mere matter of routine' and was much less effective than when reserved for special days. As to the 20 per cent of Victorian children who attended private schools, they were not the government's concern.[26] A year later the *Education Act 1941* gave the government the power to expel children attending public schools who refused to salute the flag.

Dunstan had succeeded in ensuring that from 1940 Victorian public schools buying an Australian flag could buy the blue ensign. He had given up expecting a reply to his February 1939 letter to the prime minister, but in January 1941, after the *Education (Patriotic Ceremonies) Act* had come into effect, he wrote again to report the right it gave public schools to use the blue ensign.[27] In Canberra, Tom Collins was still wrestling with the issue. There was not yet a decision on the promising paper of June 1939.

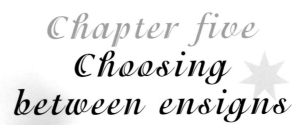

Chapter five
Choosing between ensigns

Australians had entered World War II in September 1939 with the Union Jack as their national flag, unsure about which Australian ensign they could use. They were just as unsure by the war's end. Their government was either unable or unwilling to act on the recommendation to make the blue ensign the national flag of Australia. Albert Dunstan had tried to force a decision on the Commonwealth and failed.

The most the government would do was to issue a press release in 1941 explaining that as both ensigns were official flags, Australians were allowed, even encouraged, to fly the blue ensign. Despite a similar statement in 1947, the Commonwealth had not resolved the issue by the time Australians prepared to celebrate its jubilee. Would the jubilee trigger a decision? It did – in December 1950.[1] But Cabinet's decision made no difference to the way Parliament House was dressed for the jubilee in June 1951. As in 1927, the Union Jack, flown with an Australian flag, took precedence as the national flag. When would an Australian flag have that role?

MOBILISING AUSTRALIA: *flags and World War II*

At the outbreak of World War II the Commonwealth government was wrestling with the Victorian premier, Albert Dunstan's plea to have the blue ensign declared the national flag. After the sudden escalation of the war in Europe in July 1940, there was growing pressure on the government to encourage shops and offices in city and country to fly flags every day.

Inevitably, questions about the Australian ensigns and the issue of precedence with the Union Jack arose again.

In Canberra, the NSW Country Party's Tom Collins, in the absence of a Cabinet ruling on the issue, tentatively adopted the pre-war view that the Union Jack should be given precedence, and that the red, not blue, Australian ensign should be used for non-Commonwealth buildings. The prime minister's department disagreed, seeing no reason why town halls should not fly the blue ensign which was 'really the national flag of Australia'.[2]

LIFT RESTRICTIONS OR PROCLAIM A NATIONAL FLAG?

Debate on Dunstan's legislation in Victoria was having an effect. It led the Sydney *Sun* to declare on 30 October 1940 that 'the red Australian flag, most often flown is not the real Australian flag'. Others, including a major supplier of flags, sought additional clarification (see: Guardian of custom).

Responding to these developments Collins recommended to Menzies in November 1940 that he publish a notice in the *Commonwealth of Australia Gazette*: 'That the Commonwealth Blue Ensign shall be regarded as the National Flag of Australia and that there shall be no restrictions on the flying of the Australian National Flag'. But, aware of sensitivities on the issue, especially in war time, Collins added: 'If it is not desired to proclaim the "existence" of a national Flag', then the *Gazette* could simply announce the lifting of restrictions on the use of the blue ensign on shore.[3] Menzies endorsed the latter. His department answered the Dunstan and Gair letters on that basis, but made no public statement. The press release Collins drafted in December 1940 had to wait.

Guardian of custom

The managing director of the Gair Manufacturing Company in Melbourne, a major supplier of flags and a guardian of the custom restricting the blue ensign to Commonwealth buildings, badgered the prime minister's department during November 1940. Was the education department of Victoria correct in saying 'that the State, and also the private individual could fly the Commonwealth Government Ensign, when the State Flag was not available?' the businessman asked. In his view 'the State Flags are not available at any time ... nobody wants to fly a State Flag'. 'Every day', he complained, 'we are being asked, what is the correct Flag to fly, and some Firms are now buying the Blue Commonwealth Ensign, and no doubt, their intention is to fly it whether they have the right or not'.

By the end of November, still without an answer, the flag maker and supplier concluded that 'the general opinion now is, that since the Victorian Government fly the Commonwealth Ensign, then the private individual is entitled to fly it.'[4]

Which flag for allies' days?

The government had opposed the daily display of 'The British and/or the Australian flag' – suggested in July 1940 by the NSW United Australia Party Council as a reminder of the seriousness of the threat facing Australia – saying it would detract from special flag days. But in 1941 it added the special days of its allies: first the United States of America's 4 July, then the Union of Soviet Socialist Republics' 7 November. Matters of precedence had to be considered, especially where there were few flagpoles. Sir Edward Lucas, the former agent-general for South Australia who had proposed flying the Stars and Stripes on 4 July, thought it should fly with the Union Jack. Menzies immediately agreed but over the next few days in drafts of a memorandum to Commonwealth departments, state premiers and the press, 'Union Jack' became 'Union Jack and/or Australian flag', then 'Union Jack or Australian flag', and finally simply 'Australian flag'.[5]

By the time the Soviet Union's day had come around, Labor's John Curtin had replaced Menzies, making instructions about flags a more sensitive matter. Curtin was careful to include the Union Jack. His close friend John Dedman, the minister for war organisation of industry, had sent a circular to premiers suggesting the display of Australian and Russian flags. But the next day Curtin telegraphed revised directions, advising that Commonwealth buildings would also fly the Union Jack and seeking the premiers' cooperation. In Sydney, Australian and Russian flags flew from the town hall's matching turrets with the Union Jack high above them on the tower – a reassuring sight to the director of the Commonwealth Investigation Bureau, who was alarmed at a communist flag in the heart of the city when the Australian Communist Party was still a banned organisation.[6]

It was impossible to declare the blue ensign the national flag when many Australians, especially Protestants, regarded the Union Jack as the national flag. For example: the United Protestant Association in Stanthorpe, on the edge of the Darling Downs in Queensland, still wanted the Union Jack to fly over the town's post office. Soldier–settlers from World War I and later Italian Catholic immigrants had stimulated the town's growth, prompting the association's complaint to the prime minister's department about the 'Roman Section … who never honours the Union Jack'. Like those Protestants in Melbourne in 1920, it saw the 'pretence of honour accorded the Australian flag in order that they may flout the Union Jack' as 'an insult'.[7]

MARCH 1941: 'A NATIONAL EMBLEM'

Questions about the blue ensign continued. 'A country has only one national flag', the external affairs department secretary protested, 'and the Australian flag is the blue ensign which the general public are not allowed to fly'. William Hodgson was among the first graduates of the Royal Military College, Duntroon, and a Gallipoli man. Mollified on hearing that restrictions had been lifted on the blue ensign, Hodgson wanted a statement to make the public aware of the change in policy. On 15 March 1941, while Menzies was in Britain to discuss war strategy, his department issued Collins' revised press release to explain the uses of the 'two official flags' – the two ensigns.

The 'official view' was that there were now no restrictions on the use of the blue ensign, provided it was flown properly as 'a national emblem', and that the government would appreciate the public flying it. But, as Collins noted, the statement 'received little or no publicity in the press'.[8]

The wartime celebration of the national days of Australia's allies added another layer of confusion for government and society (see: Which flag for allies' days?).

Subtle messages of nationality, even ideology, on city buildings continued throughout the war. Despite the belief of the head of the prime minister's department that the blue ensign was 'really the national flag of Australia', Curtin, as prime minister, took a more cautious view. As Japanese bombs brought the United States into the war and ended British naval power in the Pacific in December 1941, Curtin balanced his concern for the Union Jack as the symbol of British kinship with his appeal to the USA as the defender of Australia. By February 1943 the Union Jack still accompanied the Australian flag on Parliament House in Canberra, to the surprise of the Australian Natives Association (ANA). After all, the association pointed out to the attorney-general, Dr Evatt, parliament had acknowledged dominion independence in 1942 by adopting the 1931 *Statute of Westminster*.[9]

The ANA went on to pose further awkward questions to the government (see: Choice of pall).

Choice of pall

The ANA raised more awkward questions about flags with the prime minister in June 1943. Why was the Union Jack, not the Australian flag, used to drape the coffins of members of the Australian forces, both in Australia and overseas? Did regulations require the Union Jack to be used? The defence committee recommendation was diplomatic. The use of the Union Jack as a pall, 'a time-honoured custom', was an appropriate honour. But a request by the next of kin for an Australian flag alone or with the Union Jack should be met 'without question'.

By acknowledging the power of the British symbol but leaving the decision with relatives, the defence department avoided having to make a choice between the two flags and the conflict that might bring. But four years later army headquarters reversed the emphasis, advising its sections that the Australian flag would normally be used for military funerals, but that relatives' requests for the Union Jack, alone or with the Australian flag would be granted.[10]

*figure 5.1
People waved
Australian ensigns
and Union Jacks
when cheering
soldiers of the
Australian Army's
7th Division at a big
parade in Brisbane
in 1946.*

February 1947:
'*THE* NATIONAL EMBLEM'

Given the confusion about the Australian ensigns and the Union Jack during the war, renewed calls for clarification after the conflict ended were to be expected. The department of the navy warned the prime minister's department at the end of February 1946 that the public would continue asking questions until 'the national flag of Australia' was defined. Howard Beale, a former RAN officer and Liberal Member for Parramatta, agreed, complaining of 'the widespread ignorance' which led Australians to use the red rather than blue ensign, and calling for a public statement.[11] Ben Chifley, the Labor prime minister, obliged on 24 February 1947 with a statement similar to that of 1941.

There was, though, a subtle, significant difference: Chifley referred to the blue ensign not as 'a national emblem' but as 'the national emblem'. This time, at least, *The Sun* noticed the issue: 'We're not red, we're blue', its headline declared, playing on the opposing political standpoints associated with the two colours.

But general lack of interest by the press ensured that the people continued to be uninformed. However, the NSW United Protestant Association, with its motto of God – King – Empire, had noticed the change. Suspecting that the government was replacing the Union Jack with the blue ensign, its general manager asked Chifley 'just what was in [his] mind' in releasing the statement.[12]

JUBILEE
of federation

What role then would flags play in marking 50 years of the Commonwealth? The jubilee of federation was an ideal opportunity to clarify which flag was the national flag of Australia. After 50 years of confusion, there was now another surge in the demand for an answer. Bureaucrats had pushed their political masters as much as they could. Menzies had been cautious, Curtin even more so. Chifley moved on a little in 1947; now, in 1949, he encouraged two developments which suggested a way forward.

DEPARTMENTAL COMMITTEE RECOMMENDS THE BLUE

In October Chifley requested advice on a range of issues relating to flags in Australia, especially in determining the national flag. A committee was formed to represent the interested departments of defence, the armed services, civil aviation, shipping and fuel, trade and customs, and the prime minister's department. In November it put forward 14 recommendations. Three were of particular note: that the blue ensign 'be proclaimed as the Australian national flag'; that it be flown daily from Parliament House while parliament was sitting; and that it be used as a pall in state and service funerals, unless relatives preferred the Union Jack.[13]

The draft report revealed the long discussion leading to the first recommendation. It recognised that if the Australian blue ensign were regarded as an ensign normally was – a service or marine flag – then 'a new flag would be required as the national flag'. In a paper from the prime minister's department there was some support for a new flag. This argued that the design of the two ensigns was 'typically colonial' and perpetuated Australia's 'colonial status' – with the Union Jack in the corner, the flag could not be 'truly Australian'. 'It would appear', the unidentified writer concluded, 'that the grant to the Commonwealth of a flag had no greater significance than had that to say Tasmania in pre-federation days ... The Commonwealth was merely another Colonial unit and the flag was merely a Colonial Ensign.'[14]

The point was valid but unrealistic. Given that the Union Jack was still being used as Australia's national flag, the committee had to choose one of the ensigns. It justified its choice of the blue one because it had been the flag on the jackstaff of RAN ships since 1911 and the flag preferred in the 1941 Menzies government statement.

BLUE ENSIGN FOR SCHOOLS

The second development under Chifley was a proposal to present an Australian flag to every school to mark the jubilee of federation. This idea originated in October 1949 with the departmental committee planning the celebrations. Perhaps its chairman, the head of the prime minister's department, saw the occasion as a rare opportunity to establish the blue ensign as the Australian flag – especially since the press took so little notice of his department's attempts over the years to establish it as such. The Cabinet's sub-committee on the celebrations approved the proposal.[15]

One of its members, Arthur Calwell, was a strong advocate of the blue ensign. The Member for Melbourne since 1940 and the minister for information and immigration, he had known Wren since 1919, and, like him, was a great admirer of Archbishop Mannix, who had promoted Australian flags in the Irish cause since World War I. As then secretary of the Young Ireland Society, Calwell probably took part in the St Patrick's Day procession of 1920[16] (see Chapter 3: The 1920 St Patrick's Day procession in Melbourne).

BLUE ENSIGN FOR CITIZENSHIP CEREMONIES

As the minister for immigration, Calwell had introduced legislation to formalise Australians' existing status as British subjects and Australian citizens. Under the *Nationality and Citizenship Act 1948*, aliens becoming citizens were now required to do more than swear allegiance to the sovereign; they were also to swear to 'faithfully observe the laws of Australia and fulfil duties as an Australian citizen'.

Calwell saw a need for impressive citizenship ceremonies for the thousands of 'New Australians' brought to the country by his post-war immigration programs. Aware of the way Americans had used their flag 'to build up Americanism', he told parliament on 3 June 1949 he was 'sure that, if proper respect were shown for the Australian flag … a healthy Australianism would be promoted'. Calwell had Australian flags displayed at citizenship ceremonies and had plans to use only Australian flags to line the paths to the first Immigration Convention, due to be held at the Albert Hall, Canberra, on Australia Day in 1950.[17]

CROSSING THE COMMONWEALTH–STATE DIVIDE

With the change of government from Labor to the Liberal–Country Party Coalition in December 1949, there was some doubt that Menzies, the new prime minister, would support the proposal of an Australian flag for schools. But it had the backing of his department, which argued that while most schools might have flags, they were not always the same flag – the problem

Victoria's premier Albert Dunstan had tackled in Victoria before the war.

The proposal was high on the list of the Jubilee Education and Science Sub-committee, accounting for more than half its budget. Sub-committee chairman Professor RC Mills, director of the new Commonwealth Office of Education, hoped that the gift of the flag would encourage parents and schools to provide a flagpole and organise an appropriate ceremony. The use of an Australian flag in schools, he thought, would also influence New Australian children and their parents.[18]

The implementation of the proposal was to be complicated but it led to a historic Cabinet decision (see: Cabinet's historic decision: 4 December 1950).

figure 5.2
As a prelude to making it the national flag in the Flags Act 1953, the Commonwealth government presented an Australian blue ensign to every school in 1951. Note how the certificate's graphics honoured the Union Jack as the national flag.

THE FLAG CERTIFICATE

The Commonwealth government presented blue ensigns to more than 10 000 public and private schools across the country, in individual school ceremonies organised as close as possible to 9 May. With the flag went a

Cabinet's historic decision: 4 December 1950

The proposal to present an Australian flag to every school, which was approved in July 1950, immediately ran into difficulties. Representatives of the Victorian and NSW premiers' departments had already made clear that the jubilee celebrations would 'need a lot of flogging' (lots of publicity and a large budget) if left to the states to organise. The states' loss of income-taxing powers during the war had increased their financial dependence on the Commonwealth.

The flag initiative required the co-operation of the states, which controlled public schools. Mills, the director of the Commonwealth Office of Education, needed the premiers' permission to approach his state counterparts about numbers of schools and the distribution of flags. Responses were slow and sometimes discouraging, with some states at first refusing to distribute flags to private schools.[19]

The intention of Mills to distribute flags in September for presentation by

9 May 1951 was optimistic, especially given the government's response to the problem he had raised in May 1950: which ensign should be presented to schools – the red or the blue? South Australia's director of education thought the red was 'more appropriate for non-Commonwealth organisations'. Later that month Menzies took to Cabinet the November 1949 recommendation on the blue ensign. But as in 1939, Cabinet had more pressing business; it was implementing the new Liberal–Country Party government's anti-communist policies after eight years in opposition. It was going to war against North Korea under the United Nations banner. Mills was still waiting for an answer in late November.

Finally, after the director-general of the Commonwealth Jubilee Celebrations intervened, Cabinet decided on 4 December 1950 that the blue ensign 'be proclaimed as the Australian National Flag'.[20] It was a significant moment in the history of the blue ensign.

COMMONWEALTH OF AUSTRALIA

Jubilee

1901   1951

CELEBRATIONS

To mark the fiftieth anniversary of Federation the Commonwealth of Australia is pleased to present an Australian flag to .... school. It is fitting that, on the occasion of this Jubilee, each of our schools should receive and display this symbol of our unity and nationhood.

On 1st January, 1901, the Australian Commonwealth was born. Our people, till then six separate colonies, became one Nation. It was then that the Australian flag came into existence.

Its design includes the Union Jack, to show Australia's link with Britain and the other countries of the British Commonwealth of Nations; the Southern Cross as the symbol of our great south land; and a seven-pointed star, representing the six States and the Commonwealth Territories.

For fifty years, in prosperity and adversity, in peace and war, this flag has flown over the Australian people as they have progressed to an honoured position among the peoples of the world.

May it long wave over our free and peace-loving nation.

Robert Menzies.
PRIME MINISTER.

certificate drafted by the Commonwealth Office of Education with assistance from Charles Bean, official historian of Australia's role in World War I and member of the Jubilee Education and Science Sub-committee, and signed by Menzies (figure 5.2).[21] What history would they give the Australian flag? How would schools interpret the Commonwealth's gift?

Pedalling for patriotism

School flag ceremonies were not the centre of attention in May 1951 as they had been 50 years before. That place was taken by the Loyalty Despatch Bicycle Relay, an Australia-wide project involving thousands of people, including children. The relay had three starting points – Darwin, Cairns and Launceston – and ended in Canberra, where three truck-loads of loyalty messages were delivered to Menzies on the steps of Parliament House on 8 May. Some expressed loyalty to the king, some to the Commonwealth, and some to Menzies. A condition of participating in the relay was the display of loyal greetings to the prime minister on a plaque on the front of each bicycle.[22]

The extraordinary rally took place against a background of a bitter election campaign, leading to Menzies gaining control of both houses on 28 April. As he stood on that cold day in May to welcome the cyclists, *The Canberra Times* reported the prime minister's reflections on the first 50 years of federation: 'In those years Australia became a really well-knit nation, and we became Australians ... We are Australians and we must thank God for that. In our 50 years there has never been argument about whether we are British or not. We are British.' Australians' dual nationality continued.

Drafts of the certificate reveal how hard it was to explain the story of the blue ensign in relation to the red ensign and the Union Jack. Bean discarded the education office's mention of the red ensign and the blue, 'now recognised as the official Australian flag'. In essence, the certificate presented the flag, 'this symbol of nationhood and unity', which had 'flown over the Australian people' 'for fifty years', with a status it had not had for most of that period. At the same time, the certificate's graphics gave the Union Jack precedence as the national flag when displayed with the Australian ensign (figure 5.2).

That was not surprising, for the Union Jack was still the national flag. Mills had hoped that Menzies would have the blue ensign proclaimed on 1 January 1951 to mark the 50th anniversary of the Commonwealth's inauguration in 1901. But the prime minister was awaiting advice from the attorney-general on whether the proclamation of the blue ensign as the Australian national flag should be by legislation or the approval of the king or governor-general. The prime minister's department was uneasy about issuing the certificate, but its head was philosophical: the certificate was 'embarrassing' in preceding the proclamation; however, it '[did] not contain any really damaging statement' and 'could have been worse'.[23]

Fifty years before, Sir Frederick Sargood had put the Union Jack into public schools, ostensibly to celebrate federation but really to nurture the ties with Britain. The Commonwealth government now put an Australian flag into all schools, not simply to mark the jubilee of federation but to ease the

*figure 5.3
Union Jacks (on the left) took precedence as the national flag when paired with Australian ensigns on Parliament House at the military parade held to mark the Jubilee opening of the 20th federal parliament in Canberra on 12 June 1951.*

transition from British to Australian nationality. In 1951, as in 1901, Australia was at war, only this time the threat was seen as much greater – combining fears of China and communism. Seeking closer defence ties with America, the government was reaching across the states with the flag and its certificate to re-shape the loyalties of Australian children and their parents. In the context of the Cold War, the Commonwealth wanted to be sure of its citizens' allegiance, especially with Australia's growing proportion of non-British immigrants.

However, what really caught the public's imagination was not the gift of the blue ensign to schools, but the Loyalty Despatch Bicycle Relay (see: Pedalling for patriotism).

THE FLAGS ACT
of 1953

There had been talk of 'an appropriate ceremony' to publicise the Cabinet's decision of December 1950. Anzac Day was suggested as an appropriate date, but Menzies was still waiting for legal advice. On receiving it the prime minister chose legislation, but was preoccupied with defence issues and dealing with the Communist Party now that the High Court had declared the *Communist Party Dissolution Act* invalid.[24]

IVOR EVANS: THE MYTH OF
THE SOLE COMPETITION WINNER

The Commonwealth continued to give flags to new schools after 1951. New words appeared in the certificate to assert the flag's status. The education office wanted to add that the winning flag design, selected in 1901 from more than 30 000 entries in a world-wide competition, was by Ivor Evans, an Australian schoolboy. Since 1918, Evans, as partner and then managing director of his father's canvas goods and flag manufacturing business, had promoted himself as the designer of the Australian flag in a booklet, *The History of the Australian Flag*, which tended to give the impression that he was the sole designer. He issued the history to schools, scouts and girl guides. During the jubilee year, Evans suggested that the government provide not only Australian flags to schools but also Union Jacks, and smaller flags for children. He offered copies of his flag booklet at cost price.[25]

The education office's proposal to use the idea of a 14-year-old boy winning the flag design competition in a flag certificate for schools was appealing. But it was potentially misleading: Evans was one of five winners of the competition. There were complaints to the prime minister about his claim, including a question in parliament in August 1952 and, in 1953, a letter from another of the winners, EJ Nuttall, then aged 86. Concerned to 'allay the Ivor Evans legend', the prime minister's department insisted that all five winners' names be included in the new certificate.[26]

FLAG OF TRANSITION

The addition promoted the legitimacy of the blue ensign as Australia's flag: the public competition; the winners; the consistency of design since 1908; and its use since 1901. The prime minister's department went further, adding to the draft of the revised certificate the conviction that schools would give the flag 'a place of honour', teaching children 'to know and cherish' it. Its design linked past and present: 'a constant reminder of our lasting ties with the United Kingdom'; and also 'the symbol of our own free and peace-loving nation'. As in 1951 two flags were shown on the certificate: the Union Jack – in the place of honour – and the Australian flag. This was a document which could please supporters of both emblems.[27]

The Commonwealth government's presentation of the Australian flag to schools posed an issue for state governments. Accepting Australian flags for their schools to celebrate the jubilee of federation in 1951 was one thing. It was quite another if that flag were to replace the Union Jack. As South Australia's director of education reported to his minister in early 1953, 'there may be an implied suggestion that it should be used in preference to the Union Flag in our schools'. South Australia chose to continue with the Union Jack, though it did update the words of the 'Declaration of Loyalty':

> I am an Australian [no longer optional].
> I love my country, the British Commonwealth.
> I honour her Queen, Queen Elizabeth the Second.
> I salute her flag, the Union Jack.
> I promise cheerfully to obey her laws.[28]

Only on special Australian days was the Australian flag to be used in South Australia. How much longer would the state government insist on the Union Jack as the school flag?

Although Menzies had chosen legislation to designate the blue ensign as the Australian national flag (see: The colour of anti-communism?), he ultimately found it necessary to issue a proclamation as well. As in late 1940, when he had cautiously lifted restrictions on the use of the blue ensign instead of declaring it to be the national flag, so now on 20 November 1953 Menzies presented the Flags Bill as legislation that would make 'no change'. It was simply formalising established practice – at least 'almost the established practice'.

There was general agreement on 2 December with Menzies' view. Arthur Calwell, the main spokesman for the opposition, differed only in the interpretation placed on the use of Australian ensigns since federation. He insisted that until 1953 the red and blue ensigns had equal significance. But he went further, claiming a link between the Eureka flag and the national flag in the blue background they shared. Calwell knew very well the struggle Dunstan had in Victoria in trying to persuade the Commonwealth to allow the blue ensign to be widely used.[29]

BOWING TO TRADITION

When introducing the bill, Menzies took care not to alienate those Australians who still regarded the Union Jack as the national flag. He made the point that the 'common practice in Australia' of displaying the Union Jack and the Australian national flag together would continue, and drew attention to section 8 of the proposed legislation, which guaranteed Australians' 'right or privilege … to fly the Union Jack'. (The minister for immigration had already added the Union Jack to Calwell's Australian flag at citizenship ceremonies.) Use of the term 'Australian national flag', rather than national flag of Australia, was useful in that it allowed those still attached to the Union Jack to regard it as the national flag, as *God Save the Queen* was the national anthem of Australia. Only Calwell remarked on

Menzies' desire to include section 8, interpreting it as an attempt 'to allay the fears' some Australians might have that defining the Australian flag would diminish the standing of the Union Jack.

QUEEN ELIZABETH II'S ASSENT

Menzies, 'That master of sentiments and symbols' as Don Watson has called him,[30] was aware of the emotional significance of the transition in flags, as the carefully worded legislation indicated. To make quite sure that Australians accepted the change without question, he arranged for the proposed law to be reserved for the Queen's assent when she visited Australia early in 1954. She gave it on 14 February. The next day Elizabeth II opened the third session of the 20th federal parliament. Which flag would be given precedence as the national flag at the opening? For the first time the Australian blue ensign, now designated the Australian national flag, took precedence over the Union Jack as the national flag (figure 5.4). (Note that the Australian flag now has the position of honour on the left, in contrast to its position in 1951 – figure 5.3.) Some doubt as to whether notifying parliament was sufficient to bring the Act into force (due to an inconsistency between Section 60 of the

The colour of anti-communism?

Some have suggested that Menzies chose to legislate for the blue rather than red ensign as the Australian national flag because the colour red was now indelibly associated with communism.[31] But it is clear that if one of the Australian ensigns was to be selected in 1953 as the Australian flag, it would be the blue one. In 1904, parliament recognised the blue ensign as the flag of the Commonwealth government. Twenty years later, it could also be flown by state and local governments. Dunstan extended the right to fly it to state schools in Victoria in 1940. Commonwealth governments, both non-Labor in 1941 and Labor in 1947, allowed and encouraged Australians to use it. Cabinet in 1950 declared it should be proclaimed as the Australian national flag.

While the newspapers had not taken much notice of these developments, they had clearly given the blue ensign precedence over the red. That was convenient for Menzies and the Liberal Party in pursuing their campaign against the communists. The red ensign had been more widely used as the people's flag, largely because the Commonwealth government and flag suppliers had prevented Australians from using the blue. The blue ensign also suited Calwell in the Labor Party because the Eureka flag was the same colour. It was also the colour favoured by the Catholic Church in its own struggle against communism. But Calwell, unlike Menzies and Beale, the Liberal member for Parramatta, recognised the role the red ensign had played. It would not be the last time Labor and Liberal gave a different history of the use of the two ensigns.

Constitution and Section 5 (2) of the *Acts Interpretation Act*) led the government to have the governor-general proclaim the royal assent in the *Commonwealth of Australia Gazette* of 14 April 1954.[32]

Menzies hoped that his legislation would not attract attention and comment. But Calwell, like Dunstan, had been waiting for this moment for years. There had been times since 1901 when non-Labor parties had used the Union Jack against the Labor Party for political purposes. Now the tide seemed to be turning with the choosing of an Australian national flag. The Union Jack and Australian flag might still be displayed together, but perhaps the Union Jack on the Australian flag would eventually suffice to ensure its legitimacy.

figure 5.4
Queen Elizabeth II, with Australia's prime minister, Robert Menzies, opened the 20th federal parliament's third session in Canberra on 15 February 1954. For the first time the Australian flag took precedence as the national flag over the Union Jack.

Chapter six
Searching for Australian symbols

As part of blurring the change from a British to an Australian national flag, Menzies decided against promulgating the sort of rules the USA had to control the use of the national flag. The first of these drafted but unpublicised conditions was unequivocal: 'The Australian National Flag should never be hoisted in a position inferior to any other Flag or Ensign …' it said. But prosecuting those who continued to give precedence to the Union Jack, as many did, would not do; Menzies adopted the softer option of publishing a prime ministerial department booklet, *The Australian National Flag*, with guidelines on the use of Australia's national flag. This was largely ignored by the press, but schools and some national organisations welcomed it.[1]

Gradually Australians learned to treat the blue ensign as their national flag. In 1971 the booklet no longer needed to assure them of their right to fly it. But it was not until 1985 that illustrations showing how to correctly fly or display the Australian national flag and Union Jack together were deleted from editions of the booklet. And by this time the issue had changed: many Australians were now questioning the place of the Union Jack on the Australian flag.

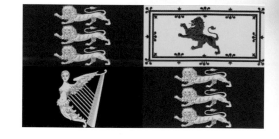

figure 6.1
The British monarch's royal standard features English, Scottish and Irish symbols – seen here in its 1901 version. In 1962 the Queen's personal flag for Australia replaced it, using the symbols of the states, Commonwealth and Crown.

PROMOTING THE
Australian Flag

WRITING THE FLAG'S HISTORY

Menzies' foreword to the first edition of *The Australian National Flag*, in 1956, essentially a copy of the flag certificate of 1953, sketched the flag's history. But slight rewording showed how the reconstruction of the flag's history was proceeding: 'For over fifty years ... the flag has been the symbol of a united Australian people', it said. Strange, then, that among the rules there was reassurance that Australians were allowed to use it. Also reassuring to some was the acknowledgment, until 1977, of Australians' right to fly the Union Jack. But given that the Australian flag as national flag now had precedence, the booklet's foreword emphasised the Union Jack 'in the place of honour in the design'. Now that the Australian flag was an acceptable symbol on its own, the Union Jack within it had become more important in maintaining the British link.

A MATTER OF PERSUASION

By the time the booklet was published, the South Australian government had once again revised the 'Loyal Affirmation' for its schools:

> I am an Australian.
> I love my country.
> I salute her flag.
> I honour her Queen.
> I promise to obey her laws.[2]

The deletion of 'Union Jack' from the words left the choice of flag to the individual school principal. Depending on the flag used, 'country' could refer to either the Commonwealth of Nations (formerly the British Empire or the British Commonwealth) or Australia. The ambiguity continued.

In Canberra, Government House flew the Union Jack on flag days, together with the governor-general's flag when he was in residence. This was despite the *Flags Act 1953* proclaiming the Australian national flag. Even after the prime minister's department forwarded a copy of its booklet in August 1956, Government House continued to fly the Union Jack until finally making the change in December 1958.[3] The flag for Australia's head of state, the Queen, also changed soon afterwards. Traditionally the flag of the British monarch was the royal standard which from the early 20th century was to be flown only when the monarch was present. In 1962 the Queen approved a new flag for her use when visiting Australia (figure 6.1).

PARLIAMENT HOUSE: LEADING BY EXAMPLE

From 1964 the flag, once flown on special days only, became a daily sight above the entrance to Parliament House, and with the provision of lighting a few years later, it flew continuously. Menzies also expected the Australian flag to fly from government buildings on working days (figure 6.5).[4]

In Canberra generally the Australian flag became more visible. The National Capital Development Commission, created by the Menzies government in 1958, erected two huge flagpoles for Australian flags on Capital Hill and City Hill. Together with the Australian–American memorial at Russell, they marked the triangle at Canberra's heart (figure 6.5).

In 1963 the Commonwealth Office of Education prepared a new flag certificate to serve not only new schools but also youth groups – which were now eligible to receive a free flag. It was the symbols, rather than the words, that changed. The Commonwealth Coat of Arms now stood alone, pushing the state symbols to the sides. The Australian flag was on its own. The prime minister's department considered that there was 'no need to include the Union Jack at all'.[5]

AN AUSTRALIAN ENSIGN FOR THE NAVY

In 1948 the RAAF followed the example of Canada and India by seeking its own ensign to realise the 1921 ambition (figure 4.4) of adding the Southern Cross and Commonwealth Star to the RAF ensign (figure 6.2). The RAN continued to use the white ensign of the Royal Navy, signifying the continuing close relationship. With one exception, British officers headed the RAN until 1948.[6] However, as more Australian warships visited South-East Asian ports in joint operations with allies, their British ensign caused growing confusion. Were they Australian or British ships? Australian involvement in the Vietnam War made the British ensign an impossible symbol for Australian warships as Britain had stayed out of the conflict. The white ensign compromised Australian independence.

With questions being asked in parliament, the chief of naval staff decided late in 1965 to initiate the change to an Australian flag before it was imposed on him. He proposed adding the stars of the Australian flag to the white ensign. '[I]t would be an unthinkable break with tradition to part with the White Ensign altogether', he said, while assuring naval staff that the small St George cross in the Union flag in the upper hoist and not the large one in the ensign was the oldest, most important feature of the flag (figure 1.2).

Senior staff were almost equally divided in their support for the two variations proposed: one with the Australian national flag, not the Union Jack, in the upper hoist, and quartered by the red St George cross; the other

with the Union flag, but with the blue Australian stars replacing the St George cross (figure 6.3).[7]

figure 6.2
In 1949 the Royal Australian Air Force gained an Australian ensign but retained the roundel from the Royal Air Force ensign (figure 4.4). The new ensign included the Commonwealth Star and the Southern Cross but differed from the 1921 proposal (figure 4.4).

figure 6.3
In 1911 Britain insisted that the Royal Australian Navy fly the Royal Navy's white ensign (figure 1.2) without an Australian badge in the fly. Not until 1967 did Australian warships fly an Australian white ensign.

The navy chose the latter and, together with a range of issues relating to the Vietnam War and the American alliance, the Cabinet approved the change in October 1966. Special ceremonies around Australia marked the hoisting of the new ensign on 1 March 1967. At HMAS Harman outside Canberra the new ensign was marched on to the tune of *Advance Australia Fair* and raised to the national anthem, *God Save the Queen,* with the white ensign being marched off to *Auld Lang Syne.*[8]

Off the coast of Vietnam, RAN destroyers with the new ensign operated with the US Seventh Fleet from 1967 to 1971.

POLITICAL PARTY LOGOS

Starting in 1961, some political candidates began using the Australian flag in their election material. By the late 1960s the Australian flag had particular appeal for Labor candidates, drawing attention to the dangers of growing foreign investment from Britain, the United States and Japan. The logo linking the Australian flag and the ALP (figure 6.4), which appeared in the 1970 federal election, was used consistently in federal elections after 1980. The Liberal Party in 1966 and 1969 used orange Southern Cross stars on a blue ground. But a symbol using the Australian flag, devised in 1977, served as the party's logo after 1980 (figure 6.4).

figure 6.4
During the 1970s the Australian Labor Party began to use a logo featuring the Australian national flag. The Liberal Party soon followed suit. Both parties consistently used the logos in federal elections from 1980.

AUSTRALIAN ICON

By 1977 the prime minister's department was more willing to explain the history of the flag, now moved from the foreword to a separate section of its booklet *The Australian National Flag.* For the first time the department acknowledged the early restrictions on the blue ensign, the attempts by governments from 1941 to encourage Australians to use it, and the need for the 1953 legislation.

But there was no acknowledgement that until 1954 Australia's national

figure 6.5
The Australian flag dominates the new Parliament House in 1993. By contrast, on the Capital Hill flagpole and on the provisional Parliament House the flags are barely visible in the photograph from around 1970.

'The visual climax required'

A joint select committee in 1970 had called for a building which would be 'an impressive symbol of Australian unity'. A joint sitting of parliament in 1974 determined that its site would be Capital Hill. Design entrants in 1979 were made aware that the Australian flag was important to the project and the site. The covers of the two volumes of the brief featured the Australian flag.

Accompanying drawings and slides of the 'parliamentary triangle' recorded the 36-metre flagpole at its apex on Capital Hill.[9] Two of the five winning design teams in stage one of the competition responded to the symbol: Denton Corker and Marshall of Melbourne displayed the flag inside a dome crowning the building. The winners of the competition, Mitchell Giurgola and Thorp Architects of New York, put the flag at the top of a shining, almost transparent mast thrusting 81 metres above their building, which was buried in the hill (figure 6.5).

In explaining their concepts at the end of stage one, the winners described the flag above the curved walls on the hilltop as 'the unifying symbol of the nation'. For the competition assessors in 1980 the mast structure with the national flag was 'a simple and imaginative solution to achieve the visual climax required'.[10] As the designers intended, the image became an Australian icon.

flag was the Union Jack. Indeed the history implied that after federation Australia no longer used the Union Jack and its British ensigns: 'Prior to Federation the Australian colonies made use of the flags of Great Britain – the Union Flag and the Red, White and Blue Ensigns', the booklet said. According to this version of history, with federation had come the flag competition and the two ensigns; those living in Australia between 1901 and 1954 would not have recognised such a version of events.

It was against this background of promoting the Australian flag that parliament began preparing for the new Parliament House in Canberra (see: 'The visual climax required').

ONE NATIONAL FLAG OR TWO ENSIGNS?

For all its efforts to promote the national flag, the Commonwealth government found British tradition too strong when it attempted to replace the red ensign with the blue on merchant ships in 1980. The move was part of the Shipping Registration Bill, which was intended to end a long-standing anachronism, namely that Australia had no way of granting Australian nationality to its ships because they were registered as British ships under Britain's *Merchant Shipping Act 1894.*

A British Commonwealth agreement of 1931 had permitted member countries to set up their own shipping registers, and the 1958 Geneva Convention on the High Seas, of which Australia was a signatory, had emphasised that ships must be registered in the state whose flag they flew. By 1978 Australia was the only independent member of the Commonwealth of Nations, apart from Britain, which had still not established its own shipping register.[11]

Cabinet had decided in July 1971 to prepare legislation to establish a register and require ships to fly the national flag. But the issue was complicated and change was difficult. The departments of transport and administrative services revived the one flag policy in 1979, though there were signs of opposition to dropping the red duster, as the red ensign was affectionately known.[12] Growing opposition forced the government to table the bill in May 1980. The men of Australia's merchant navy would not give up the colours they had served under in peace and war without a fight.

By the time the transport minister presented the revised bill on 26 February 1981, he had conceded the right of commercial ships to continue to fly the Australian red ensign. Other ships under the terms of the proposed legislation could fly the red ensign or the national flag. The minister declared that the bill was 'an important step forward in the development of Australia's status as an independent nation'.[13] But the fact remained that, when the *Shipping Registration Act 1981* came into force on Australia Day 1982, Australian ships on the high seas would not be flying the national flag.

THE ARMED SERVICES
favour Australian symbols

With the promotion of the Australian flag from 1954, not only by govern-ments but also by the community, it became evident that most Australians (63 per cent in a 1982 survey) accepted it as their national symbol. Although relinquishing their former national flag, the Union Jack, they still had it in the place of honour on the Australian flag. The design of the Australian blue ensign smoothed the transition from British to Australian flag, so cleverly managed by Menzies. The same survey reported that 69 per cent of Australians thought the Union Jack should remain on the Australian national flag.[14]

But how secure was its standing when merchant seamen were not prepared to give up their red ensign for a 'government' flag, nor the navy to surrender its white ensign? Yet there were signs, even within the ser-vices, of a search for symbols less British and more Australian.

STAR, CROWN AND KANGAROO

From penny to plane

Before gaining its own ensign in 1949, the RAAF during World War II had adapted the RAF roundel on its aircraft to include an Australian symbol – a kangaroo in motion – copied by aircrews based in Britain from the Australian penny. After the war, Australian airmen, aware of the recognition earned by South Africa's springbok and Canada's maple leaf roundels, pressed for a national symbol to distinguish Australian from British aircraft.[15]

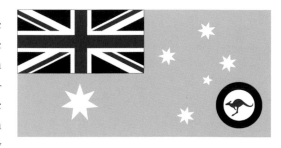

In June 1955, the kangaroo – rather than the Southern Cross, a spray of wattle, or a boomerang – was approved on a trial basis. A year later all RAAF ranks voted overwhelmingly for a red kangaroo in motion (over the RAF roundel or an upright kangaroo), a choice the Air Board cautiously endorsed for the fuselage only. The unmodified RAF roundel remained on the wings until international confusion forced the RAAF to complete the change in 1965.[16]

At the time the kangaroo became the symbol on RAAF (and RAN) aircraft, there was a suggestion that it might also be used on the force's ensign. But the Southern Cross seemed to serve that purpose, and opinions within the RAAF varied. Those pushing the idea hoped the RAAF's jubilee year of 1971 might bring success, but they had to wait another ten years before the change to the force's ensign was gazetted in May 1982 (figure 6.6).[17]

figure 6.6
The Australian ensign of 1949 (figure 6.2) was not Australian enough for some in 1971 who hoped to add a kangaroo in motion to the roundel to mark the Royal Australian Air Force's 50th anniversary. Ten years later they succeeded.

Skippy and the rising sun

The kangaroo, again taken from the penny, also became an important symbol in the Australian Army from 1954 when, combined with the crossed swords and crown of the British Army badge, it replaced the rising sun badge on the cover of the *Australian Army Journal*. Soldiers later referred to it as the Skippy badge (figure 6.7), named after the kangaroo in the popular 1960s Australian children's TV series *Skippy the Bush Kangaroo*. The director of military training, who made the decision, saw the rising sun badge as 'more the emblem of the Australian Expeditionary Forces rather than representative of the Australian Army' (see: Rich heraldic heritage).[18]

Rich heraldic heritage

The rising sun had been the basis of the general service badge for Australians serving overseas since February 1902 (figure 6.7). It had a rich heraldic heritage as a crest on unofficial Australian arms going back to at least 1850 (figures 1.9, 2.4–2.6). Australia's earliest rising sun badge represented the sun as a star. Perhaps the designer had copied the Commonwealth Star from the Australian ensigns. The semi-circular rising sun, placed above the wreath, symbolised the Commonwealth protecting Australia and the Crown, not just the Crown as in the 1904 badge (figure 6.7). That more martial version suggested the trophy of arms above the office of the first head of the Australian Commonwealth Military Forces: two kinds of bayonets protecting the Crown.[19]

A request from the Australian military attaché in Washington in March 1963 for an official army insignia to use on allied documents set off a debate as to whether it should be based on the kangaroo or the rising sun. The Military Board chose the rising sun, confirming it in 1969 as the general service badge. In returning to the symbolism of the 1902 badge, the board added to the centre the crest of the Commonwealth Coat of Arms – the Commonwealth Star on the wreath – to represent Australia, with the crown superimposed (figure 6.7). But the board also retained the Skippy badge as the army's emblem because of its clarity when used on stationery (figure 6.7).[20] The Commonwealth Star had gained a new significance within the army. Earlier reluctance about using the kangaroo had disappeared in the search for a distinctively Australian symbol.

Commonwealth Star

At the highest level of the defence force, the Chiefs of Staff Committee (COSC) was also discussing the Commonwealth Star in relation to a joint service flag for Australian forces serving in Vietnam. The committee chairman, General Sir John Wilton, believed that none of the components of his badge (anchor, crossed swords and Australian wedge-tailed eagle

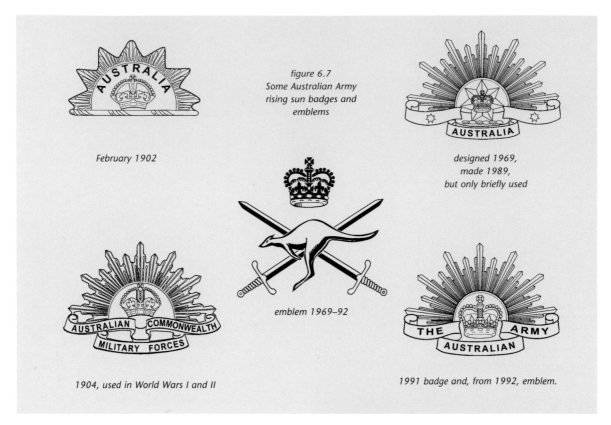

figure 6.7
Some Australian Army
rising sun badges and
emblems

February 1902

designed 1969,
made 1989,
but only briefly used

emblem 1969–92

1904, used in World Wars I and II

1991 badge and, from 1992, emblem.

surmounted by the crown) was 'readily identifiable as Australian'. In fact, the badge had been adapted in 1958 from that of his British counterpart, the United Kingdom Unified Commanders-in-Chief. The sketches General Wilton sought suggested replacing the crown with the Commonwealth Star, a move opposed by those wanting to continue to symbolise the services' 'traditional loyalty to the Sovereign'. But in June 1968 COSC endorsed a design along the suggested lines (figure 6.8), and the minister approved it the next year.[21] With the Commonwealth Crest, not the crown, above the joint symbol of the three services and the boomerang beneath it, the defence chiefs had taken a bold step.

figure 6.8
The joint service flag of 1969 for Australian forces in Vietnam became the Australian Defence Force Ensign when gazetted in 2000. The decision to use Australia's Commonwealth Star, rather than Britain's crown, indicated a growing Australian nationalism.

figure 6.9
The Australian Republican Party, formed in Victoria in 1956, suggested a simple solution to Molnar's question about the Australian flag (figure 6.10): the Commonwealth Star.

figure 6.10
George Molnar,
reflecting in The
Sydney Morning
Herald, *26 August
1967, on Australia's
closer ties with the
USA, wondered what
would replace the
Union Jack.*

Watch
THIS SPACE

The Union Jack on the Australian flag seemed safe enough in 1967, according to a Morgan poll. But some wondered how long it would remain on the flag when closer ties with the USA suggested another alternative (figure 6.10). Political parties made points with their own flag designs. The Australian Republican Party had replaced the Union Jack with the Commonwealth Star in the flag (figure 6.9) on its 1961 election material. Formed in Victoria in 1956 in reaction to the playing of *God Save the Queen* as Australia's national anthem at the Melbourne Olympics, the party had branches in New South Wales and Queensland by 1970, but members were few.[22]

figure 6.11
*Ulrich Ellis, the driving force behind
the new state movement established
in Armidale in 1949, suggested a
'lion combatant' to symbolise the
movement's determination.*

figure 6.12
*This early 1960s
Daily Mirror
photograph shows
New England New
State Movement
members in Sydney.
A 54 per cent 'no'
vote in northern
NSW's 1967
referendum rejected
the creation of a
new state.*

The push for a new state in the north of New South Wales, evident at sporadic intervals since 1915, revived again after World War II and became strong enough for a referendum to be held in 1967.[23] Not republican, the New England New State Movement simply chose a lion 'to symbolise our British connection' as the basis of a flag to publicise its cause (figures 6.11, 6.12).

When the Northern Territory gained self-government in 1978, its flag featured the Southern Cross instead of the Union Jack, an example the Australian Capital Territory followed in 1993. Quite different was the Aboriginal flag.

THE ABORIGINAL FLAG

Harold Thomas, a Luritja man from central Australia working as a survey artist at the South Australian Museum, designed the flag for Aboriginal people to use at the National Aborigines Day celebration held in Adelaide's Victoria Square in July 1971. The previous year Thomas had been concerned to see that of several groups marking the day only the Aboriginal one was without a banner. He chose red and yellow ochre, dominant colours in Aboriginal art, to represent the land (and Indigenous people's spiritual relationship to it), and the sun, giver of life. Black, the colour of his

*figure 6.13
Harold Thomas, a
Luritja man from
central Australia
working at the SA
Museum, designed
this flag – red for
the land, black for
the people, and
yellow for the
sun – in 1971 for
Aboriginal people to
use in publicising
their cause.*

people, from the fringe-dwellers of outback towns to those in metropolitan suburbs, 'had to be used', he later explained, 'because we were talking in terms of black consciousness, black awareness, black power'. His design was stunning in its power and simplicity (figure 6.13).[24]

Thomas was born in Alice Springs in 1947, sent at the age of seven to St Francis House at Semaphore near Adelaide, fostered at 12, and educated at Willunga High School, then Pulteney Grammar School in Adelaide. By 1969, when he completed his diploma at the South Australian School of Art, the movement to end discrimination against Aborigines was gaining ground. South Australia's *Prohibition of Discrimination Act 1966* had set an example the Commonwealth government could follow after a federal referendum the following year gave it the right to legislate on Aboriginal issues.

In 1972 the Tent Embassy in Canberra selected Thomas's flag as its symbol. When first established opposite Parliament House on Australia Day in 1972 to symbolise Aborigines' feeling of being 'foreigners in their own country', the embassy had two flags. One was the red, black and green Afro-American tricolour; the other a black and orange-brown flag with Aboriginal emblems in white surrounding a barbed spearhead, symbolising a meeting of people from all parts of the continent.[25] Subsequently Aboriginal groups of all kinds across Australia used Thomas's flag to publicise their causes and agencies (figure 6.14).

QUESTS FOR AN AUSTRALIAN FLAG AND ANTHEM

In the same month that Thomas's flag appeared in Adelaide, an energetic John Lavett in Sydney established a committee to organise quests for 'a truly Australian anthem and a true Australian flag' (without the Union Jack) by the time the Queen opened the Sydney Opera House in October 1973.[26] Launched on 1 August 1971, the twin quests invited entries by the following Australia Day.

Lavett intended, after Australians voted on the ten best entries selected by judges, to forward the results to the Commonwealth government for consideration. His flag quest was especially ambitious, since more than 70 per cent of Australians thought that the Union Jack should stay on the flag; by comparison, only 21 per cent supported *God Save the Queen*.[27] The ten designs, chosen from some 2000 submitted, were made into flags and exhibited by major stores in capital cities and larger towns during 1972. Publicising the words and music of the anthems had to wait for WH Paling's album.

It was an Olympic Games year and once again *God Save the Queen* would be played as Australia's national anthem for its gold medallists, even though it had long ago been replaced by *Advance Australia Fair* for the

figure 6.14
About 2000 people carrying Aboriginal flags and banners protested in Adelaide on 15 March 1980 against change to the Pitjantjatjara Land Rights Bill. Passed in 1981, the Act gave Aboriginal peoples of north-western South Australia control of their land.

Commonwealth Games. Leaders of both major parties before the December 1972 election acknowledged the need for change, with Gough Whitlam, Labor's leader, promising if elected to make one in time for the 1976 Montreal Olympics.[28] As prime minister, he launched an official quest for a new Australian national anthem on Australia Day 1973. Later, when judges ruled that none of the submitted words or music compared with the traditional songs *Waltzing Matilda*, *Advance Australia Fair* or *Song of Australia*, these three became the options. In February and March 1974 the Bureau of Census and Statistics conducted a national poll of 60 000 people on the issue. The winning choice was *Advance Australia Fair*. Some had fought a rearguard action to have *God Save the Queen* included as one of the choices (despite support for it having dropped from 57 per cent in 1965 to 19 per cent in 1973), and for the issue to be put to all Australians.[29]

Whitlam did not intend to change the flag, only the anthem – that would be difficult enough. Labor had more urgent priorities after 23 years in opposition, especially when it did not have control of the Senate. To reassure conservative critics, the tourism and recreation minister announced in March 1974 that the government would extend its program of issuing free Australian flags to national sporting bodies for display at international events at home and overseas. Lavett disbanded his committee.[30]

ENTER AUSFLAG AND THE AUSTRALIAN NATIONAL FLAG ASSOCIATION

The change begun by Whitlam led to the emergence of two organisations – one dedicated to promoting change to the flag, the other opposing change – and shaped the tactics they adopted. To conservative opponents of change, the apparent ease with which Whitlam had changed the anthem in little more than a year was shocking. He had simply endorsed the poll result – the least obtrusive of the six options offered by the department of the special minister of state. Ten days later the prime minister's press statement announced that *Advance Australia Fair* would be played as the 'Australian national anthem' at the official Anzac Day ceremony in Canberra, and, Whitlam hoped, at all other ceremonies 'in recognition of the people's wishes'. With only a week to go until Anzac Day, the result was confusion, especially surrounding the vice-regal musical salute.[31] But by the time of Whitlam's dismissal from office in November 1975 *Advance Australia Fair* had become the national anthem and shared the vice-regal salute with *God Save the Queen*.

The government of Malcolm Fraser tried to reinstate *God Save the Queen* as the national anthem in 1976, but public opposition forced a change of tack. A national poll in May 1977, which offered three traditional Australian songs (the tunes not the words) and the anthem *God Save the Queen*, resulted in the choice of *Advance Australia Fair*. It was then used, except for regal, vice-regal and defence force occasions, until further pressure forced the government to concede in March 1979 that an Australian national tune was not an appropriate alternative for *God Save the Queen*. Some occasions needed words as well as a tune.[32]

Some people watching the government grudgingly give way over the anthem were encouraged to press for changes to the flag. Harold Scruby, a Sydney consultant in management and marketing, was one of them. Born in Singapore of British and Norwegian parents, he longed to replace the Australian flag stickers on his overseas travel bags with emblems which could not be mistaken as British. In 1981 Scruby and others established Ausflag, which had the aim of finding and promoting 'a flag which clearly and unequivocally proclaims our identity to other nations ... and a flag which unites the Australian nation in all its diversity'.[33]

Incorporated in Sydney as a non-profit company in January 1983, Ausflag 1988 Limited drew its directors from across Australia and the political spectrum. With Scruby as the company's executive director, the organisation hoped to have a new flag by the bicentenary of 1988, as well as an Australian anthem and officially recognised national colours. Finding the right design for the flag became the centre of its campaign.

Ausflag's campaign, Labor's 1982 platform of encouraging support for an Australian flag and national anthem, and the party's resounding success under Bob Hawke in the March 1983 federal election, provoked a reaction by the NSW branch of the RSL. Within a week of the election, Sir Colin Hines, RSL president (and deputy national president) had formed a steering committee to establish the Australian National Flag Association (ANFA). State RSL officers for research and public relations were prominent members. Other members had strong links with the Australian Heritage Society (a division of the Australian League of Rights), the Royal Commonwealth Society and the American Legion – the US veterans' organisation. The RSL also established Queensland and Victorian branches at about the same time.[34] The association's aim was to promote the existing flag and oppose changes to it.

The NSW steering committee's flag expert was Sydney-born John Vaughan, then a regional marketing representative of Westpac Banking Corporation, who worked with schools. His hobby was flags, especially old Australian flags, developed as a business since 1973. Vaughan was the founder in 1974 of the Willoughby District Historical Society and its first president for 11 years. At the launch of the ANFA on 5 October 1983 at Anzac House in Sydney's Darlinghurst, Vaughan began a campaign to establish 3 September as National Flag Day.[35] Curiously, he had been a member of Lavett's Committee organising a new Australian flag. Now he was at the centre of another committee determined to preserve the old one (see: Boxing for the yachties).

By the end of 1983 the lines were clearly drawn between Ausflag and the ANFA, two organisations which would shape the debate about the Australian flag, especially its Union Jack. One wanted to change this element of the flag; the other to retain it. Of their spokesmen, both were from Sydney marketing backgrounds and so highly aware of the power of images in moulding public opinion. Ausflag saw the flag essentially as a British ensign, chosen to reflect the Admiralty's requirements. Only in 1953 had it become Australia's national flag. By 1983, Ausflag said, its Union Jack was inappropriate for an independent country. The ANFA believed the flag had been Australia's national flag since 1901, a role the *Flags Act* simply confirmed in 1953. As for the Union Jack, to the ANFA it was 'the primary symbol of our foundation, kinship and inheritance'. To the association the Union Jack on the flag represented the British core of the Australian nation.[36]

Boxing for the yachties

Coincidentally – or perhaps deliberately because the association hoped Alan Bond, owner of *Australia II*, would be its patron – the ANFA launch was on the very day that the yacht's triumphant crew flew into Sydney. (They were the first to defeat the Americans in the 132-year history of the America's Cup.) But the flag the public wanted to wave to celebrate *Australia II*'s win on 26 September 1983 was the victorious crew's boxing kangaroo flag (figure 6.15), which Qantas had painted on the aircraft carrying them home. Manufacturers rushed to meet the demand, despite uncertainty as to the exact design.[37]

During the late 1980s the Australian Olympic Committee bought the rights to the image, while the Western Australian Museum holds the *Australia II* flag.

figure 6.15
Australia II's triumph in the America's Cup in 1983 popularised its boxing kangaroo flag. The WA Maritime Museum at Fremantle now displays the boat, the WA Museum the flag. A boxing kangaroo was Australia's mascot at the Athens Olympics, 2004.

Chapter seven
British or Australian?

For many Australians, so used to regarding the two strands of their nationality – British and Australian – as inextricable, changing the national anthem and flag was difficult. Party politics made it more so, especially when Labor governments initiated and non-Labor oppositions resisted change. Advisers briefing prime ministers Malcolm Fraser and Bob Hawke warned them of the sensitivities surrounding the symbols. But by 1983 the anthem needed to be resolved: Australians had chosen the tune of *Advance Australia Fair* in 1977; they needed words. The National Australia Day Committee in 1980 selected two verses, with amendment, of the original song written by Peter McCormick around 1878.[1] The only question was how to make the change.

Establishing consensus on the flag was more complicated because there was no ready alternative. Ostensibly the transition in national flag from Union Jack to Australian flag had occurred in 1954 – though the Union Jack continued to be used, and there were still two ensigns, with one of them designated the national flag. More importantly, the Australian national flag featured the British national flag in the place of honour, an emblematic acknowledgment of British nationality. More and more Australians saw the Union Jack element as the flag of another country on the Australian flag. Yet others were loath to let go of a flag they had regarded as their own. Governments and teachers had told generations of Australians that they were British, that the Union Jack was their flag. When the *Flags Act 1953* replaced it with an Australian ensign, they could, and did, still point to its Union Jack. For all their Australian citizenship, Australians were still British subjects until 1984.[2] But for how long would Australians want that British badge to affirm their Australian nationality?

Questions of
CONSENSUS AND CHANGE

NATIONAL ANTHEM, ROYAL ANTHEM

Within a few months of Hawke's election as prime minister in 1983, Kim Beazley, as special minister of state, put forward twin approaches to the anthem and flag issues – one long-term, the other more immediate. One was a joint parliamentary committee of inquiry to find a consensus on the flag, anthem and national colours; the other was to seek the governor-general's agreement to revert to the Whitlam government's practice of recognising *God Save the Queen* and *Advance Australia Fair*.[3]

An inquiry offered the possibility of consensus, perhaps by the 1988 bicentenary. But there was widespread expectation that there would be immediate resolution of the national anthem problem. Following departmental advice, Hawke sought the governor-general's concurrence on the use of *Advance Australia Fair* for all except royal occasions. But Sir Ninian Stephen, fearing disunity on the issue, was reluctant to make any changes before a review had been completed. In December 1983 the government called for a report on possible mechanisms for a review of national symbols but decided on 9 April 1984 to proceed with *Advance Australia Fair*.[4] Ten days later, Sir Ninian proclaimed *Advance Australia Fair* (tune and words) as the national anthem, for use on all occasions except official royal visits when the *royal* anthem *God Save the Queen* would be played.

Announcement of the change on Australia Day had not been possible. Now Anzac Day was only a few days away. However, Hawke had kept the RSL and the premiers informed of developments. While acknowledging the difficulties the recent change in anthem caused for organisers of Anzac Day, he took the high patriotic ground in pointing out how 'unfortunate' it would be if the national anthem, *Advance Australia Fair*, were not used 'on such a significant day for the nation as Anzac Day'. Even so, the Commonwealth government had to recognise, as the *Gazette* made clear, that it could not prescribe *Advance Australia Fair* as the vice-regal salute for state governors. As it was, all states except Queensland and Tasmania readily followed the Commonwealth's lead.[5]

The transition in national anthem, from *God Save the Queen* to *Advance Australia Fair*, had taken ten years from 1974. Hawke's apparent ease in finally changing the anthem provoked the first of the parliamentary opposition's attempts to amend the *Flags Act* by making it more difficult to change the flag.

FINDING THE RIGHT DESIGN

Ausflag executive director Harold Scruby, encouraged by the government's decision on the anthem, was not surprised by the flag's absence from the 1984 proclamation. 'We knew Bob Hawke probably was very keen on a new flag but didn't think the electorate was ready for it', Scruby said. Ausflag pursued its search for a design to capture the public's imagination, launching its first competition in 1985 with the help of *The Bulletin*. Scruby hoped that preparations for the bicentenary would stimulate interest in and support for a new flag. A second competition followed in 1993, this time in the pages of *The Australian* and after Sydney had won the rights to host the 2000 Olympic Games. The winners, Wayne Stokes in 1986, whose original design Ausflag modified, and Mark Tucker in 1993, both of Sydney, submitted designs that retained the colours of the existing flag and featured the same defining symbol (figure 7.1).[6]

figure 7.1
In Ausflag's competitions of 1985 and 1993, winning designs by Wayne Stokes (above) and Mark Tucker (below), both of Sydney, honoured the Southern Cross constellation, the red band or arc representing the continent.

Morgan opinion polls during Ausflag's first ten years indicated a significant change in thinking on the flag issue, with the proportion of Australians wanting a new flag design increasing from 32 per cent to 42 per cent, and the proportion opposed to change dropping from 63 per cent to 52 per cent (figure 7.2).[7]

Meanwhile, the campaign over service emblems continued (see: Crown, rising sun and Commonwealth Star).

figure 7.2
'Go on! Be a devil!' urged Geoff Pryor's cartoon in The Canberra Times on 13 March 1986: Australia, wrapped in the Union Jack, should cut the umbilical cord to Britain and support a new flag of its own.

Crown, rising sun and Commonwealth Star

While the kangaroo with crossed swords and crown of 1969 (figure 6.7) quickly became established as the army's emblem, development of the 1969 rising sun badge with the crown and Commonwealth Star (figure 6.7) proceeded slowly. By late 1988, when the army ordered badges of the 1969 design for the first time, the RSL was well into a campaign against it. The league, thinking of the traditions of the Australian Imperial Force as it prepared to mark the 75th anniversary of Gallipoli, wanted two changes: the return of the rising sun badge to its traditional design, and its use as the army badge; and the replacement of the army emblem by the rising sun badge.[8]

At first both the army and the government resisted RSL pressure on the grounds of cost and the emblem's acceptance within the army. But eventually, in September 1990, the army agreed to remove the Commonwealth Star, acknowledging that in time it might be 'appropriate' to replace the crown with the Commonwealth Star but to use both now was 'inappropriate'.[9]

What had been accepted in the country's renewed sense of Australian nationalism during the 1960s was rejected in the conservative resurgence of 1985–90. The army also agreed to use the amended rising sun badge more widely, but insisted on retaining the crossed swords and kangaroo emblem for use, especially in UN or other multi-national forces, because the kangaroo gave 'an unambiguous Australian identification' – a significant admission. Australian UN observers in some Middle

figure 7.3
From Royal Crest on the flag of the chief of the general staff to Australian badge on that of his 1990s counterpart, the chief of army – merging 1969 and 1992 emblems (figure 6.7) but without the kangaroo.

East countries had advised 'that the kangaroo is more widely identified with Australia than the national flag, this especially being the case where the Union Jack in the Australian flag may mistakenly be identified with the UK'.[10]

The chief of the general staff, reassured that he was 'not going to be ambushed by the RSL' over the army's response to its request, advised the minister that the badge would now be used as 'the principal emblem of the Australian Army'. Launched on 19 February 1991, the new badge had become within a year the army's emblem (figure 6.7). The crossed swords with crown and kangaroo were now to be used only on the army button and with UN forces. Within a further year Australian soldiers were wearing the badge on the side brim of the slouch hat (now to be used more widely), displacing corps and regimental badges to its front.[11] The crown had won out over the Commonwealth Star.

The Commonwealth Star nevertheless survived on the joint service flag. With reforms in the 1970s and 1980s emphasising joint rather than separate service capability, this flag was becoming increasingly important. However, it had not been proclaimed and so could not be given precedence over navy and air force ensigns. (The army did not have an ensign, but came to be seen as the protector of the national flag.) This increasingly embarrassing anomaly for defence force headquarters led to the flag's proclamation as the Australian Defence Force Ensign in April 2000 (figure 6.8).[12]

The flag in THE CORNER

By December 1991 when Paul Keating replaced Hawke as prime minister changing the flag was no longer part of Labor's platform. The issue had dropped off the agenda during the bicentenary preparations when it became clear that there could be no resolution of the matter in time for the celebrations. But since its federal conference in June 1991, Labor supported Australia becoming a republic by 2001. Keating championed both issues. For a prime minister keen to restructure the economy and make Australia more competitive globally, especially in the fast-growing Asia-Pacific region, new symbols of nationhood that were unambiguously Australian were needed to project to the world the image of an independent dynamic multicultural society.

'I don't think the Australian flag should have the flag of another country in the corner of it', Keating told an ABC radio interviewer early in 1992. 'It suggests that we're still in some kind of colonial relationship with Britain.' 'We can fly two symbols of our nationhood no longer', he said in March. Similar statements followed in April in Indonesia, and in Papua New Guinea on Anzac Day, where Keating reinterpreted the Anzac legend for his generation by dwelling on the battle of Kokoda in 1942 as an event in the defence of Australia. In parliament the opposition, their desks sprouting little Australian flags, thundered against Keating as unpatriotic. Yet research indicated that Australians were warming to his leadership. By early May there was talk that Cabinet was considering a process for selecting a new flag, then flying it as an alternative flag beside the national flag as a way of winning acceptance. But press reports indicated that some Cabinet members also worried about the possibility of 'irrational fear campaigns' promoted by extreme right-wing groups, especially in country areas.[13] Keating's political vision also extended to the Aboriginal community (see: Addressing inequalities).

REPUBLICANISM *gains ground*

While Keating's desire to change the Australian flag won supporters among the intelligentsia, the arts community, and the media, his language and style alienated some people. The parliamentary opposition, whose electoral policy after 1987–88 did not include protection of the flag, saw votes to be won in pushing the government on the issue. Especially when baited, Keating sometimes went over the top in criticising Britain and those Australians who

Addressing inequalities

Part of Keating's vision for the new Australia was to recognise and address the inequalities of indigenous Australians. His speech given in the Aboriginal heart of Sydney on 10 December 1992 to launch the Year of the World's Indigenous People reached out to white Australians with a passionate call for a change in attitude to past black–white relations.

Coming after the High Court's Mabo decision of June 1992, which recognised Torres Strait Islander and by implication Aboriginal land rights, Keating's speech signalled a new era in black–white relations. Also in June,

figure 7.4
The Torres Strait Islander flag, designed in 1992 by the late Bernard Namok, of Thursday Island, has green for land, blue for sea, black for indigenous peoples and white for peace; the dhari *(headdress) and star represent Torres Strait Islanders.*

the Aboriginal and Torres Strait Islander Commission had recognised the Torres Strait Islander flag after a competition held as part of a cultural revival workshop organised by the Islands Co-ordinating Council in January 1992. The flag's colours were green for the land, blue for the sea, black for the indigenous peoples and white for peace. Its central symbols, the *dhari* and five-pointed star, represented the Torres Strait Islanders and their five major island groups (figure 7.4). The star was also a reminder of the importance of navigation to the seafaring people.[14]

defended her symbols. Coming to the Labor Party from an Irish Catholic background, he brought to the issue the assumptions and prejudices of an earlier era. The opposition, however, failed to recognise that almost half the nation wanted to see the flag change, and more than a third wanted a flag without the Union Jack.[15]

When Keating began campaigning for a republic early in 1993, it was not clear whether seeking this and a flag change at the same time would compromise the success of either or both causes. The emergence of the Australian Republican Movement (ARM) in July 1991 had provoked its antithesis a year later – Australians for Constitutional Monarchy (ACM). Both organisations were concerned more with constitutional issues than the flag, leaving the latter to Ausflag and the ANFA to fight over. But there were links between the two sets of organisations and their policies. Malcolm Turnbull, chairman of ARM and also an Ausflag director, believed that 'Just as Australians deserve a head of State who is exclusively their own, so do they deserve a national flag which unambiguously symbolises Australia and its unique destiny as an independent nation.'[16]

The ACM, like the Australian Monarchist League, had an interest in opposing change to the flag, especially its Union Jack (figure 7.5). With poll figures showing fewer wanting to remove the Union Jack than change the flag, monarchists had more reason than their opponents to enter the flag debate.[17]

figure 7.5
With Australians more likely to approve a republic than change the flag in 1993, the monarchist organisation Australians for Constitutional Monarchy made a point of using the flag in recruiting drives and appeals for funds in campaigning against a republic. The Charter signatories mentioned are: Sir John Atwill, Neville Bonner AO, The Rt Hon Sir Harry Gibbs GCMG AC KBE, Gareth Grainger, Stephen Hall AM, Angelo Hatsatouris OAM, The Hon Michael Kirby AC CMG, Dame Leonie Kramer AC DBE, Vahoi Naufahu, The Hon Barry O'Keefe AM QC, Margaret Olley AO, The Hon Helen Sham-Ho MLC, Ald Doug Sutherland AM, Margaret Valadian AO, Lloyd Waddy RFD QC.

When
Republicans
see this...

They think of England.
We think of Australia.

Australians for Constitutional Monarchy.

Inserted on behalf of the Charter Signatories: Sir John Atwill, Neville Bonner AO, The Rt Hon Sir Harry Gibbs GCMG AC KBE, Gareth Grainger, Stephen Hall AM, Angelo Hatsellouris OAM, The Hon Michael Kirby AC CMG, Dame Leonie Kramer AC DBE, Vaiusi Naulaita, The Hon Barry O'Keefe AM QC, Margaret Olley AO, The Hon Helen Sham-Ho MLC, Ald Doug Sutherland AM, Margaret Valadian AO, Lloyd Waddy RFD QC.

QUESTION OF PRIORITIES

In parliament the opposition's baiting of Keating became more intense in 1994, with an insistence that Australians had fought and died under the current flag in both world wars. The implication was that an emblem made sacred by sacrifice could and should not be changed. This was false history. The Union Jack and both Australian ensigns were used in both wars. While Alexander Downer wrapped himself in the current flag, Keating struggled without an alternative. With opinion polls indicating greater support for a republic than change to the flag, the ARM and Cabinet members advised Keating to drop the idea of changing the latter in the hope of gaining consensus on the former (see: Flags and logos). For Barry Jones, president of the ALP, changing the flag should follow rather than precede becoming a republic.[18] The flag issue became a cartoonist's delight (figures 7.6–7.8).

figure 7.6
Sturt Krygsman's cartoon from The Australian Financial Review *of 1 April 1993 presented the Labor prime minister Paul Keating cutting the Union Jack out of the national flag. Keating believed the British flag compromised Australia's status as an independent nation.*

figure 7.7
A Geoff Pryor cartoon from The Canberra Times *on 4 June 1994 showed the new Liberal opposition leader Alexander Downer wrapped in the Australian flag while Paul Keating waited for an alternative.*

figure 7.8
Labor prime minister Paul Keating followed his colleagues' advice to drop the flag issue, as drawn by Cathy Wilcox in The Sydney Morning Herald *of 9 June 1994, to avoid compromising his government's campaign for a republic.*

Flags and logos

A poll commissioned in June 1994 by the library of the administrative services department found that 60.5 per cent of Australian voters wanted to keep the current flag and 34.6 per cent wanted a new one. Opponents of change tended to be older, less well educated, live in rural and regional Queensland, South Australia and Western Australia, and were more likely to be Coalition supporters.[19] Despite the government's decision to put on hold its plans to change the flag, a variety of flag-using organisations decided to change their logos at this time (figures 7.9–7.11). Ansett had used the Commonwealth Star and stars of the Southern Cross on the tails of its aircraft from 1981. In 1990 the airline became Ansett Australia and adopted the flag as its logo to emphasise its Australian identity. In 1994, it removed the Union Jack from its logo (figure 7.10).

NATIONAL AUSTRALIA DAY COUNCIL

NATIONAL AUSTRALIA DAY COUNCIL

australia day

NATIONAL AUSTRALIA DAY COUNCIL

A Star is born! Our new look takes us into a new era.

figure 7.9
In its search for an appropriate logo to unite all Australians, the National Australia Day Council moved away from the Australian flag to the Commonwealth Star in 1993 to, in 1998, colours representing Australia's diverse peoples in a united nation.

AUSTRALIAN LABOR PARTY

figure 7.10
Ansett, one of Australia's two major airlines, used the Commonwealth Star and Southern Cross on its aircraft from 1981. After a brief fling with the Australian flag from 1990 to 1994, Ansett Australia returned to the idea of its previous logo.

figure 7.11
The Australian Labor Party on 14 June 1994 followed the 1993 lead of its NSW and SA branches in removing the Union Jack from the party's logo, retaining the Commonwealth Star, Southern Cross constellation and colours of the Australian flag.

*figure 7.12
Athlete Cathy
Freeman carried the
Aboriginal flag with
determination and
pride, later adding
the Australian flag,
after winning the
400 metres final at
the 1994 Common-
wealth Games in
Victoria, Canada.
It was a defining
moment for the
Australian nation.*

Athlete's SYMBOLIC STATEMENT

Few Australians could have imagined that the flag debate was about to enter a new phase when Cathy Freeman won the 400 metres race at the Commonwealth Games in August 1994. In a victory salute she carried the Aboriginal flag 50 metres around the track before accepting an Australian flag from the crowd (figure 7.12).[20] After her 200 metres win she carried both flags. Despite some criticism, her symbolic statement was received with widespread delight.

Many letters to the press drew lessons from the incident. 'Why should anyone', asked one writer, 'be expected to carry a flag that carries the symbol of the decimation of their race?' Sol Bellear, a respected Aboriginal spokesman, formerly on the Council for Aboriginal Reconciliation, had made the same point some days before Freeman's win. 'Aboriginal reconciliation can never be achieved unless there is a new Australian flag without the Union Jack', Bellear said. Knowledgeable about flag design as one of the judges in the recent Ausflag competition, he saw the British symbol on the Australian flag as signifying 'a note of racial superiority'. Indigenous Australians, he thought, could never accept reconciliation 'with the Union Jack hovering over us'.[21]

CENTENARY AND THE OLYMPICS FOCUS MINDS

Official moves to endorse the Aboriginal and Torres Strait Islander flags had begun in February 1994 in response to approaches from representative Aboriginal organisations. Robert Tickner, minister for Aboriginal and Torres Strait Islander affairs, and Frank Walker, administrative services minister, were considering the development of an indigenous national symbol and the proclamation of both flags as official flags under the *Flags Act*. The Aboriginal and Torres Strait Islander Commission encouraged Australia's formal recognition of the two flags, as symbols of the 'unity' and 'identity' of the two peoples, in the 'spirit of Reconciliation'. Tickner went further, defining the flags as symbols of those peoples' 'struggle' for justice, a struggle which would become a focus for world attention during the centenary of federation and at the Sydney Olympics.[22] The UN, moreover, had declared 1995–2004 as the International Decade of the World's Indigenous People as a means of addressing their inequality.

Two reports in March 1995, commissioned by the Australian government following the High Court's granting of native title in 1992, recommended official recognition of the two flags. They were the Council for Aboriginal

Reconciliation's *Going Forward: Social Justice for the First Australians*; and ATSIC's *Recognition, Rights and Reform: A Report to Government on Native Title Social Justice Measures*. The latter saw Freeman's display of the Aboriginal and Australian flags as 'a cause of great pride for the indigenous community' and 'a highly symbolic act supported by the vast majority of Australians'. It was time for the government to do the same. Keating did. But before the proclamation took effect on 14 July 1995, it became the centre of 'a furious row as to the legal and symbolic significance of the government move'. On 4 July John Howard, the leader of the opposition, accused the prime minister in a news release of 'Playing politics with flags'. Giving the two flags official status 'would rightly be seen by many in the community not as an act of reconciliation but as a divisive gesture', Howard said.[23]

For Howard, the government's decision was further evidence of 'yet another move by the Prime Minister to diminish the status of the Australian flag'; for the ANFA, it was part 'of a covert plan to change the Australian flag'. Yet there was some bipartisan support for the proclamation. Ian Viner, deputy chairman of the Council for Aboriginal Reconciliation and a former Liberal Aboriginal affairs minister, saw it as 'one of the great acts of reconciliation'. Keating made much of the fact that his government had acted on the unanimous recommendation of the council, on which the opposition was represented. But he also insisted that the national flag would continue to fly in the position of honour.[24]

The words of the two proclamations had been chosen with care to affirm that the flags of the Aboriginal peoples and the Torres Strait Islander people of Australia were 'of significance to the Australian nation generally'. Here was another symbolic step, drawing together indigenous and non-indigenous Australians. The great majority of voters approved.[25] The government planned to encourage schools, churches and other community organisations to fly the new flags by making them available free through Members of Parliament.

One person who did not approve the proclamations was the designer of the Aboriginal flag, Harold Thomas, who believed it 'would lose its potency as a symbol of the struggle of Aborigines' if it became an official flag. Before the proclamation, the government had checked intellectual property rights issues with ATSIC staff, who were not aware of any claim. Only after the government contacted Thomas about the use of the Aboriginal flag in its booklet, *Australian Flags*, was his claim of copyright made, tested, and confirmed in 1997. By then Australians had taken to the Aboriginal flag with enthusiasm, a decisive majority supporting the use of elements of that flag in a new Australian flag. Even more remarkable was the significant minority who wanted to see the Aboriginal flag as the national flag.[26]

THE CONSERVATIVE
response

DEBATING LEGISLATION

In opposition since 1983, the Coalition had supported more than ten private members' bills – all unsuccessful – which attempted to amend the *Flags Act* in ways that would make future changes to the flag more difficult. Howard led the Coalition into the March 1996 election against Keating and the Labor Party, with the flag as the symbol of his promise to govern 'for all of us'. Declaring that the Liberals spoke for mainstream Australia against Labor's 'sectional' policies, Howard emphasised the need 'to reassert a unifying national spirit'.[27] The Coalition would protect the nation's symbol by legislation. His decisive victory enabled Howard to keep that promise.

Howard chose Anzac Day to announce the introduction of legislation requiring 'a referendum or plebiscite' before the flag could be changed. Some editorial writers were sceptical. The move was 'far too reactionary' said *The Australian Financial Review*, which found protection of the Australian flag with its Union Jack 'hard to believe', and thought a national symbol should 'reflect Australia's new complexity, not its old conformity'. *The Australian*, citing constitutional opinion, doubted that Howard could legislate to bind a future government on the issue and questioned 'the real value of his move'. *The Age* was uneasy about the announcement being made on Anzac Day.[28]

How to protect the flag became a matter of debate within the government. Trying to entrench it in the constitution was ruled out: that could be seen as 'an act of weakness, an admission that [the flag] has lost the respect of those it was designed to represent', speechwriter Gareth Hall pointed out to the minister for administrative services. The likely failure to win the referendum for constitutional change (a majority of the people and a majority of the states) would embarrass the government: a poll showed 43 per cent of Australians supported change to the flag, as against 53 per cent who opposed it.[29]

Even without entrenchment there were differences within government: for example, whether changing the flag should require a simple majority vote or a double majority vote as for constitutional change; and whether the existing flag should be one of the choices in any change. Having whipped up feeling about the flag while in opposition, Howard now wanted to keep the proposed legislation as simple as possible. The outcome, a bill introduced on 26 June 1996, required a simple majority vote with electors choosing between a new flag or flags and the existing flag. Parliament would determine the details of how to implement the result. 'Pointless grandstanding', said *The Canberra Times*; 'an empty gesture', said *The Sydney Morning Herald*. To really protect the flag, critics argued, the constitution would have to be amended. The bill became law in March 1998.[30]

A SPECIAL DAY FOR THE FLAG

Coalition governments accepted several opportunities presented by the ANFA to embed the current flag in Australian hearts and minds. The association had adopted the American idea of a special day to honour the flag. It chose 3 September, the day the blue ensign was hoisted above Melbourne's Royal Exhibition Building in 1901 to announce the result of the design competition for two ensigns. The ANFA was unlucky with its first celebration of the day in Sydney: strong winds forced organisers to deflate a giant balloon decorated with the flag.[31]

Well connected to the RSL and wishing to emphasise the Australian Army's role as 'Protector' of the flag, some branches of the association requested the use of defence force resources – especially bands and guards of honour – for their Flag Day ceremonies.[32] But the chief of the Australian Defence Force (ADF) observed to the national president of the RSL on 6 November 1992 after a dispute in Brisbane that the ANFA as a private organisation had 'no automatic entitlement to an ADF presence at its functions'.[33]

The ANFA in Queensland described itself as 'simply a community and service body' (and its ceremony as 'an occasion simply concerned with our history and heritage in a celebratory spirit which unites all Australians'). It was also opposed to changing the flag. The way that the ANFA used a Brisbane Defence Centre (DC-B) letter in its protest at being denied resources for Flag Day in 1992 was seen as 'anti-Government propaganda' by the DC-B head. Queensland's opposition leaders gave the ANFA their support, criticising both the federal and state Labor governments.[34]

In 1995 the administrative services department adopted John Vaughan's suggestion and listed 3 September as Australian National Flag Day in its booklet *Australian Flags*. The next year Vaughan, president of the NSW branch of the flag association since 1991, lobbied the new Coalition government to have 3 September proclaimed as Flag Day. He also sought 'a Prime Ministerial Flag Day message' for the ANFA to circulate to its members and the media – a request Vaughan would make to both government and opposition in succeeding years. Howard agreed to proceed with Flag Day.[35] His administrative services minister announced the proclamation of Australian National Flag Day at an ANFA ceremony in Sydney.

figure 7.13
Since its foundation in 1981, Ausflag has consistently campaigned, through flag competitions and the media, for a distinctively Australian flag that can unite Australians. This poster was one of a series in the mid-1990s presenting Australia's 'identity crisis'.

GROWING UP

UNITED STATES

Colonised 1607   Grew Up 1776

INDIA

Colonised 1611   Grew Up 1947

MALAYSIA

Colonised 1786   Grew Up 1957

CANADA

Colonised 1583   Grew Up 1965

SOLOMON ISLANDS

Colonised 1893   Grew Up 1978

IRELAND

Colonised 1170   Grew Up 1921

GHANA

Colonised 1662   Grew Up 1957

NIGERIA

Colonised 1861   Grew Up 1960

PAPUA NEW GUINEA

Colonised 1884   Grew Up 1975

SOUTH AFRICA

Colonised 1795   Grew Up 1994

AUSTRALIA

Colonised 1788   Grew Up ?

OVER 50 BRITISH COLONIES HAVE GROWN UP. SHOULDN'T WE?

OUR OWN FLAG FOR THE 2000 OLYMPICS

SUPPORT AUSFLAG - PO BOX 500 NEUTRAL BAY NSW 2089 FAX (02) 9953 9400 TEL (02) 9953 9444

Internet: http://www.ausflag.com.au

A call for informed debate

While the ANFA made the most of a Coalition government sympathetic to its aims, Ausflag called without success for the government to promote informed debate about changing the flag, for funds to encourage the professional design of alternatives, and for the appointment of a multi-party parliamentary committee to consider a new flag.[36] Supported by polls suggesting the Australian flag was no longer a symbol of national unity, Ausflag portrayed Australia's 'identity crisis' in a series of posters (figure 7.13).

Meanwhile, Howard's position was being undermined by a new political force to the right of the Coalition (see: One Nation).

Ausflag pressed ahead with its search for a flag for a new Australia, launching in July 1997 a competition aimed at professional designers. Judges selected 100 designs to tour the country in 1998, reminiscent of Lavett's 1971 scheme. It helped to spur renewed interest in the flag, and for the first time Morgan polls indicated that a majority of Australians wanted a new flag.[37] Ausflag announced the winners of the judges' and people's

One Nation

figure 7.14
Bill Leak's cartoon from The Weekend Australian of 26–27 April 1997 characterised the challenge Pauline Hanson, leader of One Nation, posed to the prime minister, John Howard, who saw the flag as a symbol of unity.

The Australian flag, especially its Union Jack, was serving other purposes in the hands of Pauline Hanson, the new independent Member for Oxley of 1996 in the Australian Parliament (figure 7.14). Launched in April 1997, Pauline Hanson's One Nation Party (as it was called from June) sought to speak for disaffected people who felt neglected by the major parties. For Howard – who realised One Nation could not be ignored because of its early success, especially in Queensland – the Australian flag with its Union Jack became even more important in reaching old Australia.

figure 7.15
In Ausflag's professional design competition of 1997–2000, the Commonwealth Star appeared in the selections of both judges (above) and people (below): unlike George Margaritis's design from Melbourne, Frank Gentil's from Sydney gave it the place of honour.

choices on Australia Day 2000 (figures 7.15). The judges' choice was very similar to the 1961 flag of the Australian Republican Party (figure 6.10), with the Commonwealth Star replacing the Union Jack in the place of honour.

RE-ENACTING AND REWRITING HISTORY

While Ausflag pursued a new design for the flag, the ANFA presented its view of the history and design of the existing one to Australians, especially through the approaching centenary of the 1901 competition for the two ensigns. Vaughan's list of suggestions for the government in 2000 was comprehensive, backed by the reminder that he spoke for 20 000 members (some were part of corporate memberships).

He wanted all schools to have an Australian flag so that they could participate in a simultaneous flag-raising on 3 September 2001 (reminiscent of Sargood's Union Jack on 14 May 1901). The association also wanted commemorative stickers, booklets and posters distributed to schools. Every classroom should permanently display an Australian flag, and the ANFA's video about the flag should be distributed to all schools and youth groups.

Vaughan also proposed an Australian national flag website, and encouraging the public to fly the flag from homes, boats, and offices. Re-enactments of 1901 flag-raisings in Melbourne and Townsville followed by the signing of special flags for placing in the state parliaments would complete the Flag Day celebrations.[38]

At first non-committal, Howard later agreed to the Melbourne ceremony re-enactment. Arrangements became a diplomatic minefield for the Commonwealth and Victorian governments, and centenary of federation organisations (state and federal) as ANFA state presidents in Sydney and Melbourne tried to shape proceedings.[39] The proposed re-enactment in Melbourne in fact mixed two different events in Australian history: the 3 September 1901 raising of the blue ensign in the presence of Edmund Barton, the prime minister; and the Duchess of Cornwall and York's raising of the Union Jack on 14 May 1901, copied in schools around Australia. The Commonwealth government was interested in the first, the Victorian government in the second for Victorian schools, but with the Australian flag not the Union Jack (see: A new myth begins?).

A special flag for the day

Concerned that 'a national focus' had been sidelined through control of arrangements by the Centenary of Federation Victoria, Howard considered withdrawing from a ceremony he now saw as 'a State show'. His department, directed to put 'a federal stamp' on the event, proposed a special 'Centenary Flag', which the ANFA could present to the prime minister during the ceremony. With the first flag of 1901 long gone without trace, the department adopted the ANFA's idea of a new flag – an Australian national flag specially made of fine material with stars inset. The association arranged to make and in part donate the flag, which after the ceremony would then be flown in the six states and two territories before being displayed in Canberra. It would be used as a flag of state for special occasions.[40] After extensive negotiations, the ceremony went ahead.

Despite the expected emphasis on the flag's centenary *as the national flag*, Howard's speech mentioned a very different view: 'It is true that it took a long time before there was unambiguous acceptance of the flag chosen as one central undeniable emblem of Australia.' This rare acknowledgment of the flag's more complex history from 1901 to the early 1980s was significant. But the speech did not acknowledge the growing percentage of Australians since then – more than 50 per cent by 1998 – who wanted to change the flag. The prime minister simply emphasised the flag (and anthem) as 'great unifying symbols of all of the Australian people'.[41]

In accepting the Centenary Flag Howard did not refer to the red line running the full length of its white headband (figure 7.16). What was it for? The departmental letter confirming discussion of the special flag with Vaughan suggested the line was to represent 'the crimson thread of kinship of all peoples of Australia'. Vaughan saw the Australian flag as 'the icon representing continuity of customs, traditions and values like the crimson thread of kinship'. The phrase 'the crimson thread of kinship' comes from Henry Parkes, who used it in 1890 to refer to British kinship in urging the separate Australian colonies to federate.[42]

The Centenary Flag was a useful device for both prime minister and flag association: giving the former a national role in the Victorian ceremony; and reinforcing for the latter the legitimacy of the national flag. The flag's red line subsequently served – somewhat ambiguously – 'to represent the thread of kinship that stands at the heart of the federation' in the *Flag Facts* leaflet published by the department of the prime minister and cabinet.

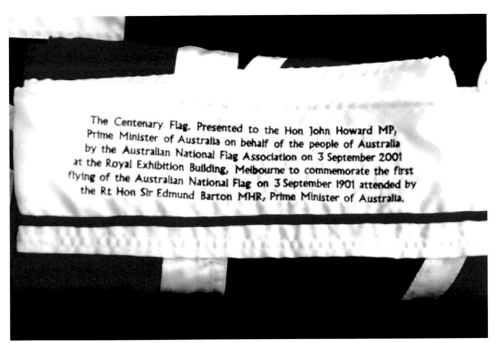

The Centenary Flag. Presented to the Hon John Howard MP, Prime Minister of Australia on behalf of the people of Australia by the Australian National Flag Association on 3 September 2001 at the Royal Exhibition Building, Melbourne to commemorate the first flying of the Australian National Flag on 3 September 1901 attended by the Rt Hon Sir Edmund Barton MHR, Prime Minister of Australia.

figure 7.16
The red line on the headband of the special Australian national flag, the Centenary Flag, presented to the Commonwealth government in 2001 by the ANFA, symbolised 'the crimson thread of kinship' – a reminder of Henry Parkes' 1890 reference to British kinship.

A new myth begins?

On the ANFA website in the schools section appeared the feature 'Important Facts: National Flag Day Facts'. Two questions and their answers are of particular interest.

What happened on National Flag Day in 1901?
The first National Flag Day was held on 3 September 1901 at the Royal Exhibition Building, Melbourne. As the flag was raised all schools were requested via telegraph to raise their Australian flag at the school assembly being held at the same time.
What happened on 3 September 2001?
On National Flag Day of 3 September 2001 the ceremony was re-enacted.[43]

The first question and answer, taken from Victorian education department studies of society and environment material, appears to confuse two ceremonies, both occurring at the exhibition building but four months apart.

On 3 September 1901 an Australian blue ensign was raised, but not in schools and there was no coordinating telegraphic message. The ceremony marked the selection of a design for two ensigns, blue and red, and the announcement of the five separate winning entrants (pp. 16–21).

On 14 May 1901 the Union Jack – not an Australian flag – was raised in many schools around Australia, coordinated by a telegraphic message. They were celebrating the opening of the first Australian parliament five days before (pp. 26–29). (It should also be noted that Australian National Flag Day was not proclaimed until 1996.)

The answer to the second website question compounds the confusion. The ceremony at the exhibition building on 3 September 2001 had two aspects: the presentation of the Centenary Flag to mark the selection of a design for two Australian ensigns 100 years before; and the flying of the Australian flag there and in Victorian schools, invited a few days before by electronic message to participate.

THE CAMPAIGN FOR YOUNG MINDS

The ANFA, led by Vaughan, had achieved several of its aims. But it could not persuade the government to have Vaughan's Australian flag promise proclaimed: 'I promise allegiance to our National flag of "Stars and Crosses"; to serve my country and all its people faithfully, and to uphold Australia's laws, customs, values and traditions to the best of my ability'. Vaughan had wanted this promise to be 'the focal point for school flag ceremonies across Australia' on 3 September 2001 and beyond. Finding no support within the Awards and National Symbols branch of the Department of the Prime Minister and Cabinet, he took the proposal to the prime minister's office in his attempt to revive what he saw as the 'once popular, but since lapsed, tradition'. Vaughan also approached Brendan Nelson, Member for Bradfield, a federal constituency in Sydney. Nelson, recently appointed education minister, had been a guest at the association's Flag Day ceremony in Sydney.[44]

What Vaughan described as Nelson's 'kind offer to circulate our video kit … to all schools and youth groups across Australia' provided another opportunity to consider the flag promise. The ANFA's video *Making Our Flag* had been part of its long-term strategy for promoting the current flag among the young. Launched by NSWs Liberal minister for education in August 1992 at the multicultural Five Dock Primary School in Sydney, it was, according to Ausflag's Harold Scruby, 'a very clever advertisement for one side of the story'. The video's second edition in 2000, with the assertive title, *Our National Flag…Since 1901*, included the now proclaimed Flag Day. Even with state RSL assistance, the ANFA had had only moderate success getting its video and teacher's notes into schools.[45] Now Vaughan hoped that with Nelson's help both would be in schools by February 2002.

Despite the RSL national president's personal support for the flag promise, the office and department of the prime minister remained opposed to the ANFA's request. They advised the association to seek community support for its promise rather than expect the Commonwealth government to impose it, given that this was a matter for school authorities, states and territories to decide. Recognising that 'the Association had an agenda beyond the promotion of the flag' – protecting its current design, they also thought it should 'remove the reference to "stars and crosses"'. However, the ANFA was determined to retain its 'stars and crosses'. (Its later modification read: 'I promise allegiance to Australia and our flag of "Stars and Crosses"…')[46]

An opportunity missed
Nelson permitted his department 'to wrap the flag video distribution up in the DD [Discovering Democracy] communication strategy'. The minister was not persuaded by advice from the chairman of his Civics Education

Group that the video gave only one side of the debate. However, he accepted that it was unsuitable for secondary schools. Nelson also agreed that the ANFA's notes for teachers would have to be rewritten. What history of the flag would the notes record?[47]

Hotly contested by the ANFA and two historians, the final outcome of several drafts finalised by the education department's languages and civics education section and the Curriculum Corporation was ambiguous, especially for the period 1903–53. The notes acknowledged the Union Jack as the 'official' rather than national flag till 1953, the Commonwealth red ensign as the flag for merchant ships, and the blue for 'other' use. But in fact the red ensign was for other, that is, general use – the flag people could fly – as well as for merchant ships, and the blue was for Commonwealth official and naval use.[48] The opportunity to redress this misinformation about the history of the flag had been missed, and the notes also revived a myth (see: 'Ivor's key values').

Nowhere in the notes was the debate about the Australian flag acknowledged, an omission noted by two of four teachers invited to comment, as well as the chairman of the Civics Education Group and the senior project manager at Curriculum Corporation. The ANFA opposed mention of Ausflag's website in Discovering Democracy resources and the department removed it from the notes 'to avoid some angst'. On some related matters the department appeared to rely on the association's advice.[49]

'Ivor's key values'

The Curriculum Corporation had the difficult task of writing notes to link the ANFA's video to the Discovery Democracy Programme, whose funds were making its reproduction and distribution to schools possible. Written in little more than a month, the planned two-page brochure of information and activities became four, then six pages in length. In the process the notes revived and extended the myth surrounding the schoolboy flag designer Ivor Evans (see p. 104).[50]

Following the ANFA's lead in the video, which highlighted Evans above the four other entrants, the notes emphasised his use, at 14, of Dante's idea of the four main stars of the Southern Cross representing four virtues. The evidence for this link appears to rest on a statement made by Evans just before he died, which is now held in the Mitchell Library. His promotional booklets on the flag, describing the Southern Cross during his decades as a flag manufacturer, made no mention of Dante's idea.

'Ivor's key values' then became the basis for a classroom activity about Anzac Day, extended at the ANFA's insistence, to link the flag with World War I and the Anzac tradition through the boy soldier Alec Campbell, the last of the Gallipoli Anzacs, who died in May 2002. The ANFA wanted the notes to emphasise the symbolism of the aged Campbell handing the current flag to a young cadet, 'passing our flag traditions from the old to the younger generations'.[51]

The department was nevertheless steadfast in refusing to include the flag promise (figure 7.17). Nor would it allow mention of the daily raising of the flag or weekly flag ceremonies, because these activities were seen to be matters for the states and territories. But the department was willing to refer teachers to the ANFA website for details of holding a ceremony on Flag Day (and in 2004 agreed to the association's flag promise being posted on the department's *Discovering Democracy* website). The video with notes was despatched to schools in July 2002 without launch or press release. Nelson introduced it to principals as 'an associated activity of the *Discovering Democracy* programme' in reminding them of the coming Celebrating Democracy Week.[52]

FUNDS AND FLAGPOLES

During Celebrating Democracy Week in October 2002, shortly after many Australians died in the Bali bombing, Nelson promoted flag ceremonies in schools – public and private – as 'a means of raising the standard of civics education'. John Howard gave 'emphatic endorsement', but public opinion was divided. *The Australian* thought 'a little tempered patriotism can do a lot of good in a nation as disparate as ours'. *The Canberra Times*, suspicious of politicians 'skulking around flagpoles', thought it was 'a silly idea'. It was less than ten years since *The Sydney Morning Herald* reported the Victorian government's re-introduction of daily flag-raising in schools (figure 7.18), having 'slashed $145 million from the education budget, closed 231 schools and cut 8100 jobs'.[53]

figure 7.17
John Vaughan (with microphone) led Australian National Flag Association supporters in reciting their flag promise at Sydney's Martin Place on 3 September 2004, Australian National Flag Day. Brendan Nelson, Liberal education minister (fourth from left) represented the Commonwealth government.

*figure 7.18
Peter Nicholson's
cartoon in* The Age
*on 27 January
1994 lampooned
the Victorian Liberal
government's re-
introduction of the
flag ceremony in
public schools,
showing the state
premier Jeff Kennett
conducting the
'national anthem'
while cutting the
education budget.*

Nelson opposed changing the flag, arguing that it was 'not a noticeboard to which we attach evidence of the latest fad sweeping the country'. Foreshadowing future policy, he declared that while schools 'should not be forced to introduce flag raising ceremonies … they should present a convincing argument as to why they should not'. An estimated 40 per cent of non-government schools did not have a flagpole.[54] Writing to his state counterparts and to independent school organisations seeking details of their flag ceremonies, Nelson offered funds under the Commonwealth's Capital Grants Programme for flagpoles in schools that did not have one (figure 7.19). At the same time he asked Coalition MPs whether schools – public and private – in their electorates had a flagpole and held 'regular' ceremonies, believing that they were 'a way of reaffirming our national identity'.[55]

State Labor education ministers thought ceremonies were a matter for schools to determine, though most did hold them weekly or on special occasions. (Only Victoria legally required them – a relic of Dunstan's 1940 Act.) The state ministers appeared more concerned to develop children's civic values as part of the local community than to promote national pride. Some principals responded through their MPs to warn of the dangers of people 'wrapping themselves in flags'. But another welcomed the minister's support in reaffirming the flag ceremony in schools.[56]

As requests for the flagpole subsidy of $1500 came in from schools, the department forwarded application forms through the appropriate Coalition MP or duty senator (with responsibility for a group of electorates), outlining the conditions of a grant. These included the installation of a plaque on or near the flagpole acknowledging the Commonwealth government's gift.

figure 7.19
Education minister
Brendan Nelson with
Sussan Ley, MP for
Farrer, launching his
flagpole subsidy
scheme at Trinity
Anglican College,
Albury-Wodonga, May
2003 – the prelude to
the decision in June
2004 to make
funding of schools
dependent on flying
the flag.

The scheme proved to be the prelude to a joint initiative by the prime minister and education minister on 22 June 2004 to make federal funding for all schools dependent on their having a functioning flagpole and flying the Australian flag. (The move had been foreshadowed in advice to the minister in October 2002.) The announcement dominated the evening news, and by the following midday, readers of *The Sydney Morning Herald* had registered their disapproval of the policy at the rate of almost 2:1 on its website. Letters inundated the papers and the education department. Some welcomed the initiative as long overdue. Writers on both sides referred to the American school ceremony in arguing their views of the government's policy. The government announcement revived the flag debate in many minds. 'First, get a flag that represents a modern, independent nation, then talk about running it up the flagpole,' said one letter. Cartoonists made the most of the opportunity (figures 7.20, 7.21).[57]

figure 7.20
In The Canberra
Times of 25 June
2004 Geoff Pryor's
cartoon questioned
the validity of the
Howard government's
insistence that schools
fly the Australian flag
and display the values
education framework
when its actions
belied those values.

Melbourne's *Age* believed that the policy was 'election-driven' rather than 'parent driven', as the prime minister said when interviewed by the press. *The Sydney Morning Herald* wondered about its effect on Commonwealth-state powers: 'To nibble away at policies touching state schools…looks like interference or grandstanding on populist issues for which the Federal Government ultimately does not have a responsibility'. Questioning of departmental officials in a Senate committee revealed that the government did not intend to check whether schools accepting federal funds flew the flag. The Schools Assistance Bill, unamended, became law in December 2004, approving specific-purpose funding for schools for the period 2005–2008, and giving the minister power for the first time to include additional conditions for that funding. A flagpole was one such condition – mentioned not in the Act but in the agreement school authorities must sign to receive Commonwealth funds.[58]

The Commonwealth government's move in 2004 to require the flying of the flag in all schools receiving federal funds had no precedent. Until then displays of patriotism in schools had been the concern of state governments or the administrators of private schools. During World War I the Victorian government had questioned the patriotism of private schools. When pressed to display the Union Jack, Lutheran schools complied, Catholic schools were diffident. But some large Protestant schools objected, defending their patriotism. Now the Commonwealth government was taking an interest in the promotion of patriotism at a time when schools with access to Commonwealth funds since 1964 were becoming dependent on them.

figure 7.21 *In* The Australian *of 28 June 2004 cartoonist Bill Leak portrayed Coalition ministers, criticised for their treatment of asylum seekers, taking refuge in the Australian flag and the nationalism it represented.*

Coalition policies, especially since 2001, had encouraged growth in the numbers and size of private schools. By 2004 the Commonwealth provided 41 per cent of total expenditure on private schools (compared with 11 per cent of public expenditure on public schools, largely funded by state and territory governments). These had become more diverse as the percentage of Australia's immigrants from the British Isles dropped – from 42.5 per cent in 1959 to 8.4 per cent in 2000.[59] Australia now had not only Christian and Jewish schools but also Islamic ones.

Placing the flag in schools of the increasingly diverse private sector occurred in the midst of the war in Iraq, heightening the power of the national symbol, despite divisions in the community over Australia's involvement. Linking flags and funds, especially for private schools, could be seen as patriotic and likely to gain support for the Coalition in the coming election, where school funding was an issue. This promotion of the flag in schools reflected the Howard government's hope that Australians, despite their deep division over the flag's design – especially its British badge, would come to accept it.

However, the Union Jack on their flag continued to divide Australians, as was seen in Sydney's shocking incidents of December 2005 (see: Whose beach, whose flag?). Anglo-Australians' use of the flag to control Cronulla Beach underlined its British symbolism. Their opponents' burning of the flag symbolised their rejection of this Anglo-ethnicity. These events caused one writer to *The Sydney Morning Herald* on 15 December, who saw the flag as 'a pretty Anglo symbol', to ask, 'Does it really represent Australia anymore?' Lecturer in anthropology at Monash University, Peter Maddock featured a similar view in Melbourne's *Age* on 27 December. That the flag had been used 'to demarcate belonging and exclusion' led him to question whether 'modern, progressive Australians [can] continue to be proud of the ethnic chauvinism all too easily read from its iconography'. On the same day in Sydney's *Herald*, associate professor in human geography at Macquarie University, Jim Forrest, one of a team who mapped the tolerance levels of Sydney's suburbs, made a plea for 'tolerance-building among Anglo and non-Anglo groups' and for a nation of Australians, 'not Anglo and hyphenated Australians'. Which flag design would best represent their nation?

Whose beach, whose flag?

On Sunday, 11 December, more than 5000 'Aussies' (used as code for 'Anglos', that is, Anglo-Australians) gathered at Cronulla Beach in Sydney's south, primed by text messages, talkback radio, ultra-nationalist groups and alcohol. Many were wearing or carrying the Australian flag. In regaining control of 'their' beach after the alleged bashing of two lifesavers the previous Sunday by men of Middle Eastern appearance (used as code for 'Lebs', that is, Lebanese–Australians), the gathering degenerated into a riot. Some 200 ringleaders set upon the few assumed to be from a Middle Eastern background with bottles, sticks and flags, hounding them from the beach. Those who went to the victims' aid, including police and ambulance officers, were also attacked. On that and the next night up to 200 youths from western Sydney in a convoy of cars retaliated in beachside suburbs, smashing cars, shops and people with baseball bats and metal bars. At Brighton le Sands RSL Club they pulled down the Australian flag and burnt it.

Conclusion

ANSWER
to a dispute

This book began with a heated exchange between Paul Keating and John Howard in April 1992.

The answer to their dispute about the history of the Australian blue ensign is both simple and complex. It is true, as Howard said, that the blue ensign 'was gazetted before World War I', but not as the national flag. The entry in the *Commonwealth of Australia Gazette* in February 1903 was for two ensigns: the blue ensign for official and naval use; and the red ensign for merchant ships (figure 1.16). These were ensigns of the Union Jack, the symbol of British rule (figure 1.1). It is also true, as Keating said, that 'In 1953, the *Flags Act* for the first time formally established [the Australian blue ensign] as the national flag', though some Australians still treated the Union Jack as the national flag. Only after the Act received royal assent did the Commonwealth government regard the Australian blue ensign as the national flag by giving it precedence over the Union Jack and expecting its citizens to do the same.

TWO ENSIGNS, NOT A NATIONAL FLAG

Until the *Flags Act* received royal assent in 1954 most Australians accepted the Union Jack as their national flag. This was not surprising; they saw themselves as British as well as Australian. Their ethnic background might be English, Irish, Welsh or Scots, and they might identify with Australia or one of its states, regions or localities. But as Britons they shared the symbol of Britons throughout the British Empire, which became the British Commonwealth of Nations, and later the Commonwealth of Nations.

The blue and red ensigns, approved by the British Admiralty in 1902 for the new Commonwealth of Australia, were for flying from ships according to British tradition. Only very slowly did the Commonwealth government, encouraged by Richard Crouch MHR (figure 1.22), take up the blue ensign for use on land: in 1908 on forts; and in 1911 as the saluting flag in the Commonwealth Military Forces and the Royal Australian Navy. Even so, later in 1911 there was a further regulation requiring the Union Jack to be also used when vice-regal representatives were present. From February 1922, when Section 406 of the *Navigation Act 1920* took effect, the red ensign became the prescribed flag for merchant ships registered in Australia.

BRITISH ENSIGNS FOR AUSTRALIA'S NAVY AND AIR FORCE

The adoption of the British white ensign by the newly formed Royal Australian Navy in 1911, despite Australia's wish to fly an Australian white ensign, illustrated the fact of British rule (figure 1.2). Similarly, Britain rejected Australia's proposed air force ensign in 1921 showing the Commonwealth Star and stars of the Southern Cross: the fledgling RAAF was required to adopt the Royal Air Force ensign instead (figure 4.4). It was not until 1949 that the RAAF gained an Australian ensign, further adapted with the addition of the kangaroo in 1982 (figures 6.2, 6.6). Not until 1967 did Australian warships fly their own white ensign (figure 6.3).

TRANSITION 1903–53:
three contenders for the national flag

The first 50 years of federation were a time of transition for Australians accustomed to regard the Union Jack as their national flag. Their two ensigns by law, custom and tradition were ensigns of the Union Jack, which Australians naturally gave precedence.

DOUBTING THE ENSIGNS' DESIGN

At first Australians took some time to accept the design of their ensigns. There was criticism especially in New South Wales, where people saw it as too representative of Victoria – not the Commonwealth. Some

Commonwealth ministers, including Australia's first prime minister, Edmund Barton, wanted to fly the flag of the federation campaign (figure 1.3), but adapting it to the Admiralty's requirements would be difficult. Governments continued to be critical of the 1901 flag competition's winning design, including the Labor administrations of prime ministers Chris Watson in 1904 and Andrew Fisher in 1910. Fisher, a Scottish immigrant, having succeeded in replacing the English St George cross on the Commonwealth's first coat of arms, also wanted to change the design of the flag.

CONFUSING GOVERNMENTS AND PEOPLE

With wider use of the two Australian ensigns during World War I came confusion. The blue ensign, at first restricted to the Commonwealth government, in 1924 became the ensign for other levels of government. State schools, however, had to use the red ensign, the merchant shipping flag – as did individuals and private organisations. For this reason, the red ensign was more widely used than the blue. The only flag governments and people had in common was the national flag, the Union Jack.

VALIDATING THE ENSIGNS

There was a further problem: on its own, an Australian ensign became an ambiguous symbol because of the way some sectional groups used it for ethnic, sectarian or ideological purposes against Britain and the empire – as in Sydney in 1911 and 1921, and Melbourne in 1920. To be a valid symbol, an Australian ensign had to be accompanied by the Union Jack, which took precedence as the national flag. Party politics played a significant role in shaping this development. Reacting to Labor's 1905 goal of a socialist, self-reliant Australia, other parties looked to individualism and the British Empire to bind them together in combating Labor's growing success in elections. When the conscription crisis of World War I split the Labor Party, the re-grouped parties aligned even more closely than before along sectarian and ethnic lines. Nationalists and militant British Protestants were on one side with the Union Jack; Labor and Irish Catholics were on the other with an Australian ensign. The RSL favoured the Union Jack; the Australian Natives Association, an Australian ensign.

DEFINING THE AUSTRALIAN NATIONAL FLAG

It was the government of Victoria rather than Commonwealth government that moved in 1938 to resolve the confusion about the Australian ensigns. This was despite the prime minister's department, responsible for advice on the use of the two ensigns, being bombarded by the public for years about the issue. Albert Dunstan's Country Party government, supported by the Labor Party, extended to public schools – and by implication the public generally – the right of Commonwealth, state and local governments to fly the blue ensign as Australia's national flag.

The prime minister's department was keen to follow the Victorian lead. But Robert Menzies would approve only the lifting of restrictions on the use of the blue ensign. Preoccupied with the war, he was unwilling to declare it the national flag. Ben Chifley, as prime minister in 1947, issued a similar statement in response to the continuing confusion. Only in December 1950 did the pressing issue of which ensign to present to schools early in 1951 to mark 50 years of federation force the Cabinet to make a decision. Its members chose the blue ensign as the Australian national flag, a decision confirmed by the *Flags Act 1953*, and given assent by Queen Elizabeth II in February 1954. Menzies assured Australians that the Union Jack would continue to fly with the Australian flag.

USING SCHOOLS AS AGENTS OF CHANGE
IN TIME OF WAR

Presenting an Australian blue ensign to all schools in 1951 echoed Sir Frederick Sargood's scheme during the Boer War to place Union Jacks into public schools in 1901 (figure 1.17). Under cover of federation celebrations, and before the selection of Australian ensigns in which he was involved, Sargood intended the Union Jacks to remind future generations of children that they were British. Promoted by the British Empire League/League of Empire through Empire Day from 1905, the Union Jack became firmly established as the flag for Australian public schools.

The Commonwealth government's gift of an Australian blue ensign to all schools might appear to be simply part of the jubilee of federation celebrations. But, as the government intended, it was a more effective statement to the Australian people than the press releases of 1941, 1947 and 1950 in ending the confusion about the two ensigns. The Australian flag for government *and* people to use was the blue ensign. Further, in the context of the Korean war, the government was reminding Australians that their prime allegiance was to Australia rather than to Britain. Its action sent a message to state governments and the nation generally in preparing the way for the change in the national flag in 1953 – from Union Jack to Australian blue ensign. In effect, the Menzies government was weaning Australians off the Union Jack.

Even so, some schools continued to fly the Union Jack, as in South Australia. After the 1953 Act, some Australians still flew the Union Jack, or if flying both flags, gave the Union Jack precedence. The fact that the *Flags*

Act designated the blue ensign as 'the Australian national flag' encouraged many to continue to regard the Union Jack as 'the national flag' in the same way that *God Save the Queen* was the national anthem, but gradually they conformed to the change. By 1971 the government's booklet, first published in 1956, no longer needed to tell Australians that they were allowed to fly the blue ensign, and by 1977 the booklet had dropped the reminder of people's right to fly the Union Jack. Once required as a separate flag to validate an Australian ensign, the Union Jack on the ensign now served the same purpose.

THE SEARCH
for a national flag

Australians had let go of the Union Jack as their national flag in favour of one of its ensigns, the Australian blue ensign. But mariners' refusal in 1980 to accept the blue 'government' flag instead of their red ensign placed its role as the national flag at sea in doubt. The British tradition remained: essentially Australia still had two ensigns with Britain's flag in the place of honour.

By this time the percentage of Australians wanting a new flag had become significant, growing from 27 per cent in 1979 to 52 per cent in 1998.[1] There had been several attempts to find a new flag following John Lavett's Australian National Anthem and Flag Quests Committee in 1971. But the design competitions run by Ausflag in 1985–86, 1993 and 1997–2000 were more determined, attracting wide media interest and offering substantial prize money. Between 1992 and 1994 the Commonwealth government led by Paul Keating also supported the call for change.

In the period from 1979 to 1998 the size of the majority wanting to keep the Union Jack on the Australian flag decreased from 67 per cent to 53 per cent. In the circumstances, it is reasonable to ask what kind of country would be so divided over its national symbol as it approached the centenary of its federation: a country whose people are divided over their former national symbol.

EVOLVING NATIONHOOD

The federation of the Australian colonies in 1901 had been a triumph of Australian sentiment over colonial rivalry. But it was anchored in the kinship linking them to the people and power of Britain: the crimson thread of kinship. This sense of kinship was reflected in the evolution of an egalitarian society based on the exclusion of non-Europeans and an assumption of protection from larger powers operating in the Asia-Pacific region. When welcoming the new Commonwealth in 1901, the British poet Rudyard Kipling posed the challenge it faced: to make Australians love their country, as they had loved Britain.[2] Australian prime ministers met that challenge by pursuing Australian interests but expecting British support for them.

To many Australians of British Protestant descent, 'true Australians' were British, the very opposite to what some Australians of Irish Catholic descent believed – as reflected in the two groups' different use of the Union Jack and Australian ensigns. There was uncertainty about the term Australian. For some it described the first people of the country, the Aborigines, the 'real Australians'. For others shaped by World War I suspicions, the description hid a range of nationalities. 'New Australian' was yet another term, revived in 1949 to replace the derogatory names used by some to describe the large numbers of immigrants from the European mainland.[3]

Australia acknowledged its independence from Britain in 1942, but not until 1968 and 1986 did further legislation finally cut Australia's legal ties to Britain's Privy Council. As Britain gained entry to the European Economic Community and withdrew from most of its defence commitments east of Suez, trade, investment and defence ties with the United States and Japan became more important to Australia. Its citizens found their traditional easy access to Britain increasingly difficult after restrictive British laws in 1962 and 1968. From the 1970s the Australian government gradually removed privileges enjoyed by British immigrants. If they wished to become Australian citizens, they had to be naturalised in the same way as other immigrants. From 1984 new British immigrants had no right to vote in Australian elections without becoming Australian citizens.[4] In the same year Australians ceased to be British subjects. But they retained the British monarch as their head of state.

Australia's immigrants from 1947 came increasingly from mainland Europe and, especially after 1975, from non-European countries (though people born in Britain remained the largest immigrant group). The decline in British immigrants coincided with Britain's turning away from the Commonwealth of Nations to Europe and her withdrawal from defence commitments in South-East Asia at a time of increased volatility in that region. For Australians, used to seeing Britain as the source of immigrants and security, these events had a profound effect.[5]

The change signalled an acceleration of Australians' 'long journey out of Britishness', as they learned to accept Australians of indigenous, non-British and non-European descent as equal members of the Australian nation. Some took longer to learn than others. One young woman, for example, could tell another at a social gathering in Sydney as recently as 1997, 'You're not Australian. You're not pure-bred. You're Malaysian.' The insult was to an Australian-born citizen, the daughter of two Australian citizens: one of British descent, born in Australia; the other of Chinese descent, born in British North Borneo and naturalised in Australia before marriage. Other examples can be found in sport and employment. Racial abuse on the football field led the Australian Football League in 1995 to establish a racial vilification policy after a pioneering campaign by Essendon's indigenous champion, Michael Long. Victoria Police's first Asian-born recruit, who endured years of racial abuse before leaving the force, welcomed its Multi-Faith Advisory Council initiative of 2005 for reaching out to the community.[6]

From the 1960s Australian leaders struggled to find the right balance in re-defining the nation and its symbols. Historian James Curran's careful analysis of their responses to this issue revealed John Howard as 'the least at ease with the "new Australia"', and the only one who 'has retained an affection for and acceptance of the British heritage as the indispensable ingredient of national cohesion'.[7]

THE SEARCH FOR UNIFYING SYMBOLS

Aware of Australians' division over the flag, in particular its Union Jack, Howard governments were determined to promote it as the symbol of national unity, especially to the young. The Australian National Flag Association (ANFA), established by the RSL, provided several opportunities. One of them, the Centenary Flag, revealed a subtle emphasis on the British connection: the crimson thread of kinship (figure 7.16). It was a reminder of the importance to the association of the Union Jack. Yet the association had denied that flag's role as the national flag after 1901. To have recognised such a role would have detracted from the importance of the Australian blue ensign, which the association insisted was the national flag from 1901. Similarly the association understated the wider role of the Australian red ensign.

The flag association's successes – getting Australian National Flag Day proclaimed in 1996, lobbying for 1998 legislation that made changing the flag more difficult and seeing the re-enactment of the 1901 raising of the blue ensign and the Centenary Flag adopted in 2001 – showed how influential the association had become. But its prime focus was the young Australian, as it had been for Sir Frederick Sargood 100 years before. Although unable to have its flag promise proclaimed, the ANFA succeeded in 2002 in persuading Brendan Nelson, the education minister, to reproduce and distribute its promotional video on the flag to all primary schools.

For Sargood in 1901 the Union Jack represented the British Empire and the security its navy ensured. John Vaughan, the flag association's national spokesman in 2002, could no longer employ such symbolism. Instead the Union Jack on the Australian flag was to symbolise the principles of parliamentary democracy, though as Britain's national flag it inevitably represented that country. For both Sargood and Vaughan, pressing governments to put flags in schools was an attempt to reinforce the British core of the Australian nation at a time when it was changing.

In 2004 the Coalition government made flying the flag a condition for schools – both public and private – if they were to receive federal funds. Confirming its earlier promotion of the national symbol, the government's move was likely to be popular with Australians about to go to the polls. Australia was at war in Iraq. Flag sales had increased.[8] The Menzies government had put Australian flags into schools in 1951 during the Korean War. Now the Howard government insisted that schools fly them. Already, in 2003, the education minister had established a scheme for providing a flagpole to schools that lacked one.

Significantly both John Howard and Brendan Nelson were from Sydney, the centre of the debate about the flag and the home of Ausflag and the most influential branch of the ANFA. Division over the flag there can to some extent be seen as a feature of Sydney's post-war immigrant settlement pattern. Unlike Melbourne, Sydney's western working-class suburbs had not experienced a first wave of immigrants from southern Europe, leaving them unprepared for taking most of the second larger wave of immigrants from Asia and the Middle East. For Bankstown, 'the tabloid and talkback radio hearth of old Australia', it was 'a culture shock'. By 2002 a national study ranked western Sydney as Australia's 'least tolerant area'.[9] Here the Australian flag's Union Jack would have its greatest appeal.

By contrast, the judges of Ausflag's competitions for a new Australian flag were searching for a new symbol to unite all Australians in a way the current flag no longer could. In 1986 and 1993 they replaced the Union Jack with the Southern Cross constellation in the place of honour (figure 7.1). But significantly in 2000 they chose to honour the Commonwealth Star while retaining the Southern Cross in the fly (figure 7.15). The colours of the flag were the blue and white of the Commonwealth coat of arms of 1908 (figure 2.8) and the blue and gold of the 1912 coat of arms (figure 2.9).

For all the importance of the stars of the Southern Cross in Australian flags since the 1820s (figures 1.3, 1.4), the more recent Commonwealth Star from 1901 is the distinctive symbol of Australian federation. It was the federation symbol on the two Commonwealth ensigns of 1903 (figure 1.16). Both Commonwealth arms used it as a crest (figures 2.8, 2.9). In a real sense the

Commonwealth Star honours the men (and women of South and Western Australia, where they had the right) who voted for federation in 1899–1900. These were the people John Hirst remembered in his history of the making of the Commonwealth as 'the 422 788 Yes voters who have no other memorial'.[10] In recent times, particularly in its 150th anniversary year of 2004, some Australians have promoted the Eureka flag of 1854 as a replacement for the national flag, but it has no symbol for federation (figure 8.1).

figure 8.1
To mark the 150th anniversary of the famous 'stockade', Eureka flags flew above Canberra's Commonwealth Avenue and City Hill in the first week of December 2004 and over other cities. Some see it as an alternative national flag.

Despite Australians' deep division over their national symbol since 1982, no Australian government has been willing to inquire into the issue beyond a commissioned national survey in 1994. In the history of Australia's national flags, this unwillingness to inquire is not unusual, as can be seen by the decades it took governments to resolve the confusion over the use of the two ensigns. Wars and other issues intervened. But more importantly governments were unsure about how best to negotiate the transition from British to Australian symbols. They still are. Into that void stepped the flag association.

The Commonwealth that Australians created in 1901 nurtured a unique nation in its first 100 years, one that was no longer British but Australian, one which accepted immigrants not just from Britain but from around the world, one whose citizenship pledge is not to a British monarch but to 'Australia and its people', their 'democratic beliefs', 'rights and liberties', and 'laws'. But Australians, while rightly insisting that the Australian flag takes precedence over the flags of its immigrants, still privilege British immigrants by maintaining their national flag on the Australian flag. At the same time, that Union Jack is a constant reminder to indigenous Australians of their dispossession and exclusion from the Australian nation until the referendum of 1967.

For much of Australia's history, British Protestantism and loyalty provided the 'ethnic core' of the emerging nation and informed its dominant political party, the early Liberal Party and its successors: the

Nationalist Party, United Australia Party, and new Liberal Party. This core challenged the Australian Labor Party and its objective of a self-reliant Australia with a socialist framework. Non-Labor appeared to assume that its parties should negotiate the nature and pace of the transition from British to Australian nationality and symbols. During World War II Robert Menzies allowed an Australian flag to fly alone with the American or Soviet flag, but not John Curtin, his Labor successor. He made sure that the Union Jack accompanied the Australian flag, knowing how readily non-Labor used the anti-British stick against his party.

In some ways the dispute over the Australian flag between John Howard and Paul Keating in April 1992 typified the old Liberal–Labor divide: Howard, British and Protestant in background, berating Keating, whose background is Irish Catholic, for daring to suggest removing the Union Jack from Australia's flag. Both were from Sydney where the political and cultural divide had been greatest. Keating's support for flag change, following Labor's success under Gough Whitlam and Bob Hawke in changing Australia's national anthem, strengthened the Howard governments' stance against flag change, a strategy reinforced by the rise of Pauline Hanson's One Nation.

In promoting the existing flag, the Coalition discouraged the debate that had been kept alive in the 1980s and 1990s by the hope of many Australians for a new flag to mark the bicentenary in 1988, the Sydney Olympics in 2000, or the centenary of federation in 2001. Roy Morgan Research has not tested opinion on the issue since February 1998.

Some think that the debate is now over. The flag association was quick to claim victory against its rival when former Ausflag director Malcolm Turnbull, the aspiring Liberal member for Wentworth in Sydney, joined the ANFA in March 2004 at the invitation of association member John Howard. Vaughan called on Ausflag's executive director to close Ausflag's website and consider donating its funds to the association's program in schools. Harold Scruby, aware of the broader issues, not only in Australia but also in New Zealand and Canada, declined the advice.[11]

The real debate – a *well-informed* debate – has only just begun. To understand why Australians are divided over their national flag, especially its Union Jack, is to understand the transition Australians made in national flags from the Union Jack in 1901 to the Australian national flag in 1954. Further, that transition has continued to the present as Australians question the appropriateness of Britain's national flag in the place of honour on their country's national flag. *Is* the British Union Jack more important to Australians than their Commonwealth Star, the symbol of their nation?

APPENDICES

APPENDIX 1

Changes in the words of the
'National Salute': South Australia, 1911–1956:[1]

AUGUST 1911
I love my country.
I honour her King.
I will cheerfully obey her laws.

OCTOBER 1916
I love my country (the British Empire);
I honour her King (George V);
I salute her flag (the Union Jack);
I promise to cheerfully obey her laws.

MAY 1939
Optional addition [according to the principal]:
'I am an Australian.'

I love my country, the British Empire.
I honour her King: King George the Sixth.
I salute her flag: the Union Jack.
I promise cheerfully to obey her laws.

APRIL 1953
I am an Australian.
I love my country, the British Commonwealth.
I honour her Queen, Queen Elizabeth the Second.
I salute her flag, the Union Jack.
I promise cheerfully to obey her laws.

FEBRUARY 1956
I am an Australian.
I love my country.
I honour her Queen.
I salute her flag.
I promise to obey her laws.

APPENDIX 2

The words of the 'National Salute'
when first formally introduced into
Australian public schools:[1]

VICTORIA 1901
I love God and my country;
I honour the flag;
I will serve the King, and
Cheerfully obey my parents, teachers and the laws.[2]

SOUTH AUSTRALIA 1911
I love my country.
I honour her King.
I will cheerfully obey her laws.[3]

NEW SOUTH WALES 1917
I honour my God.
I serve the King.
I salute my flag.[4]

QUEENSLAND 1919
I honour my flag,
I love my country, and
I will always obey her laws.[5]

In 1933 Victoria's Education Department rejected its
Curriculum Committee's revised declaration:

I will serve the King;
I will be true to my country;
I will honour the flag.[6]

Western Australia and Tasmania used other words for
civics training:

WESTERN AUSTRALIA
I tender you my service,
Such as it is, being tender, raw, and young,
Which elder days shall ripen and confirm
To more approved service and desert.[7]

TASMANIA
Our debt to the community resembles our debt to
our parents. Very much is done for us. Most of our
comforts are provided by the community. We must
do our best to repay. We can do this best by our
behaviour, by the way we keep the rules, by the
way we do our work, by the way we help others, by
our courtesy, and by our speech.[8]

NOTES

Special access, abbreviated as (sa) indicates those records less than 30 years old that were made available to the author under the special access provisions of the *Archives Act 1983*.

Biographical information, unless otherwise sourced, is from the *Australian Dictionary of Biography*.

INTRODUCTION

1 *Commonwealth Parliamentary Debates (CPD)*, 28 Feb. 1992, pp. 1834, 1836, 1827, 1844.
2 Elizabeth Kwan, Exhibition Review. Flying the Flag: Australian Flags and Their Controversies, *Australian Historical Studies*, no. 103, Oct. 1994.
3 *CPD*, 2 Dec. 1953, p. 368; *Commonwealth of Australia Gazette*, 20 Feb. 1903, p. 93, 29 Apr. 1901, p. 89.
4 Appendix 1; Elizabeth Kwan, Making 'Good Australians', *Journal of Australian Studies, 29,* June 1991.
5 Appendix 2.
6 Published by Lions International, Brisbane.
7 Joint submission on the proposed 1995 draft, 27 Feb. 1995, HON94/00301/02, Department of Administrative Services, special access.
8 Transcript of speech, 17 Sept. 1995, *Crux Australis*, vol. 11/3, no. 47, July/Sept. 1995, p. 114.
9 Ralph Kelly, The 1901 Australian Flag Competition: Facts Behind the Myths, *Crux Australis*, vol, 10/1 no. 41, Jan/Mar. 1994.
10 Elizabeth Kwan, The Australian Flag: Ambiguous Symbol of Nationality in Melbourne and Sydney, 1920–21, *Australian Historical Studies*, no. 103, Oct. 1994; Elizabeth Kwan, Blue Over the Red: Australia's Victorian Flag Legacy and Menzies' Decision, *Crux Australis*, vol. 13/4 no. 56, Feb. 2000. Both were based on the author's Which Flag? Which Country? An Australian Dilemma, 1901–1951, PhD thesis, Australian National University, 1995.
11 *The Australian Flag: Colonial Relic or Contemporary Icon?* Federation Press, Sydney, 1996, pp. 56–73.
12 Philip L Gibson, Woollahra, to Ray O'Farrell, Oxford University Press, 27 June 2000.
13 52 per cent favoured a new design, 44 per cent wanted to retain the current design, Morgan Poll Finding No. 3055, 17 Feb. 1998; Deborah Keeley, Communications Strategy Adviser, National Council for the Centenary of Federation, comment to author, 6 May 1999.
14 41 per cent wanted to remove the Union Jack, 53 per cent wanted to retain it, Morgan Poll Finding No. 3055.

CHAPTER 1
AUSTRALIAN FEDERATION, BRITISH FLAG

1 AC Burton, Australia's Forgotten Flag, *Crux Australis*, vol. 8/4, no. 36, Oct./Dec. 1992; *We Swear by the Southern Cross: Investigations of Eureka and Its Legacy to Australia's Democracy*, Curriculum Corporation, Melbourne, 2004.
2 Ralph D Kelly, Australian State Flags (1865–1904: A British Admiralty Legacy, *Crux Australis*, vol. 8/4, no. 36, Oct./Dec. 1992.
3 *The Review of Reviews for Australasia (RRA)* (Melb.), 20 Sept. 1901, p. 240 (F Barlow Cumberland, author, *History of the Union Jack: How It Grew and What It Is*

(1897), Ward, Lock & Co., 1901).
4 *The Herald Standard (HS)* (Melb.), 4, 25 Sept. 1900; *RRA*, 20 Oct. 1900, pp. 442–443.
5 Colonial Secretary to Governor-General, 29 Nov. 1900, National Archives of Australia (NAA): A461, B336/1/1 part 1; Atlee Hunt, Federal Memories. The Commonwealth Flag, *The Sydney Morning Herald (SMH)*, 18 June 1932; M. Tudor, Sydney, to Barton, 19 Jan. 1901, NAA: A6, 1901/133.
6 Barton, minute, 13 Apr. 1901, NAA: A6, 1901/133; *Commonwealth of Australia Gazette (CAG)* No. 27, 29 Apr. 1901, p. 89.
7 Judges to Atlee Hunt, Secretary, Department of External Affairs, 31 Aug. 1901, I Evans and J Mitchell, Judges' Report, 2 Sept. 1901, to Barton, NAA: A461, B336/1/1 part 1.
8 CT Burfitt, later president of the Royal Australian Historical Society, to editor, *The Daily Telegraph (DT)* (Syd.), 13 Sept. 1901 NAA: A8, 1901/208/8; ANA (NSW), to Barton, 25 Feb. 1902, NAA: A8, 1902/135/13; Hunt, Federal Memories; John Hirst, *The Sentimental Nation: The Making of the Australian Commonwealth*, OUP, Melbourne, 2000, p. 247; *SMH*, 24 May 1898.
9 Hunt to Barton, 22 Nov. 1901, NAA: A461, B336/1/1 part 1.
10 Barton to Governor-General, 8 Feb. 1902, NAA: A461, B336/1/1 part 1.
11 WA Glue, *The New Zealand Ensign*, Government Printer, Wellington, 1965, pp. 16–20; gazetted in June 1902.
12 Elizabeth Kwan, Which Flag? Which Country? An Australian dilemma, 1901–1951, PhD thesis, Australian National University, 1995, pp. 83–85, 105–110; Letters, *The Times*, 23 June–23 Sept. 1902, editorial, 18 Sept. 1902.
13 Colonial Secretary to Governor-General, 29 Dec. 1902, NAA: A461, B336/1/1 part 1; *CAG*, 20 Feb. 1903, p. 93; Necessity of an Australian National Flag, n.d. but c. 1949, NAA: A462, 828/1/1 part 1.
14 *HS*, 4 Sept. 1900, also 8–24 Sept.
15 Sir Frederick's son to Minister of Public Instruction, 19 Oct. 1900, VPRS 794 Box 963 1900/39931 Public Record Office Victoria (PROV).
16 Jamish Furzer to HB Higgins, 29 Mar. 1901, and Higgins' reply, 17 Apr. 1901, Higgins Papers, MS 1057 items 78, 81, National Library of Australia (NLA).
17 *HS*, 4, 8 Sept. 1900; *The Advance Australia* (Melb.), the ANA journal, 14 Dec. 1909, p. 275.
18 'The Grand Old Flag', *The School Paper* (Melb.), Class IV, Dec. 1900, pp. 109–110.
19 *RRA*, 20 Oct. 1900, p. 413; *Education Gazette and Teachers' Aid (EGTA)*, Nov. 1900, p. 80; Education Department to Alfred Champion, flagmaker, 19 Apr. 1901, VPRS 794, Box 963, 1900/39931, PROV; *SMH*, 15 May 1901; *The Age* (Melb.), 15 May 1901.
20 Kwan, Which Flag?, p. 82; *EGTA*, Nov. 1900, p. 80.
21 *The Argus* (Melb.), 15 May 1901; Janet McCalman, *Journeyings: The Biography of a Middle-class Generation 1920–1990*, MUP, Melbourne, 1993, p. 136.
22 *SMH, The Age, The Advertiser* (Adel.), 15 May 1901.

23 *The Age*, 15 May 1901; HO Arnold-Forster, *The Citizen Reader for the Use of Schools* (1886), adapted for Australian children (1906) by CR Long, Cassell, London, 1910, pp. 128–145; *EGTA*, Nov. 1901, p. 67.

24 Balmain and Newtown in Sydney, and Warialda, New England, *SMH*, *DT*, 15 May 1901; *Echoes from St Stanislaus*, Apr. 1918, p. 18.

25 Kwan, Which Flag?, pp. 56–74; Scot M Guenter, *The American Flag, 1777–1924: Cultural Shifts from Creation to Codification*, Associated University Presses, Cranbury NJ, 1990, pp. 117, 130–131; *The Canadian Teacher* (Toronto), 15 May 1902, p. 1230, 2 May 1910, p. 1008, 1 May 1912, p. 1064 and 1 May 1914, pp. 1079–1080.

26 *EGTA*, Supplement, Oct. 1901.

27 William Gillies, *Simple Studies in English History for Young Australians* (n.d.), Whitcombe & Tombs, Melbourne, revd edn, n.d. (c. 1901–09), p. 246.

28 Correspondence between Naval Commandant, Defence Minister, Defence Secretary, External Affairs Secretary, 11–26 Mar. 1903, NAA: A461, A336/1/1 part 1.

29 Crouch to Barton, 16 Apr. 1903, and response, 24 Apr. 1903, Defence Minister's comment of 28 May 1903 on Commandant's letter, NAA: A461, A336/1/1 Pt 1; *CAG*, no. 18, 25 Apr. 1903, p. 253.

30 Capt. Robert Collins to Secretary, External Affairs Department, 22 Sept. 1903, NAA: A461, A336/1/1 part 1.

31 *Commonwealth Parliamentary Debates (CPD)*, 26 May 1904, p. 1605, 2 June 1904, p. 1914, 28 June 1904, pp. 2695–6.

32 *CPD*, 26 May 1904, p. 1609, 28 June 1904, p. 2696.

33 Hirst, *The Sentimental Nation*, pp. 246–247, 270–271; Henry Parkes, *The Federal Government of Australasia: Speeches Delivered on Various Occasions (November 1889–May 1890)*, Turner and Henderson, Sydney, 1890, p. 75.

34 'The Young Queen', *RRA*, Nov. 1900, p. 577.

35 *CAG*, no. 76, 29 Sept. 1921, p. 1377.

CHAPTER 2
EMPIRE DAY AND AUSTRALIA DAY

1 Maurice French, 'One People, One Destiny' – A Question of Loyalty: The Origins of Empire Day in New South Wales, 1900–1905, *Journal of the Royal Australian Historical Society*, vol. 61 Pt 4, Dec. 1975, pp. 238–44, The Ambiguity of Empire Day in New South Wales 1901–21: Imperial Consensus or National Division, *Australian Journal of Politics and History*, no. 1, Apr. 1978, pp. 63–5; FB Boyce, *Empire Day*, Sydney 1905, p. 4, in *Boyce Pamphlets 1892–1920*, ML.

2 FB Boyce, *Four Score Years and Seven*, Sydney 1934, p. 119.

3 John Rickard, *Class and Politics: New South Wales, Victoria and the Early Commonwealth, 1890–1910*, ANU Press, Canberra 1976, pp. 167–203.

4 *The Worker* (Syd.), 11 Feb. 1905, pp. 6–7.

5 AE Cahill, Catholicism and Socialism – The 1905 Controversy in Australia, *Journal of Religious History*, no. 2, Dec. 1960, pp. 89, 93–4; Judith Brett, *Australian Liberals and the Moral Middle Class: From Alfred Deakin to John Howard*, CUP, Cambridge, 2003, pp. 20–27.

6 *Education Gazette (EG)*, Apr. pp. 59, 67, May 1905, p. 71; *Education Gazette and Teachers' Aid (EGTA)*, Apr., May 1905, pp. 160, 162; *The Geelong Advertiser*, 9, 16 May 1905.

7 *The National Advocate (NA)* (Bathurst), 11, 12, 19, 26 May 1905; *The Bathurst Daily Argus (BDA)*, 13, 18, 22, 23 May 1905.

8 *NA*, 17, 18, 20, 22, 24 May 1905; David Cressy, *Bonfires & Bells: National Memory and the Protestant Calendar in Elizabethan and Stuart England*, Weidenfeld and Nicolson, London 1989, p. xi; *The Sydney Morning Herald (SMH)*, 24 May 1905; *EG*, Apr. 1905, p. 71; Victoria. Education Department, *Regulations and Instructions*, 1905, no. 571.

9 *EG*, Apr. 1905, p. 71; Victoria, *Regulations*; Elizabeth Kwan, Making 'Good Australians', *Journal of Australian Studies*, no. 29, June 1991; The National Flower of Australia, *The Children's Hour*, Class IV, Sept. 1904, p. 130.

10 *The Age, The Argus* (Melb.), *The Ballarat Courier, The Geelong Advertiser, The Daily Telegraph (DT)* (Syd.), *SMH*, *Newcastle Morning Herald & Miners' Advocate*, BDA (also 24 May), *NA*, 25 May 1905.

11 *SMH, Argus* 25 May 1905.

12 Editorials, *BDA, NA*, 25 May 1905.

13 *NSW Parliamentary Debates (NSWPD)*, 24 Oct. 1905, p. 3087.

14 Prefect of Studies Journal, Xavier College Archives, Kew; *The Age*, 25 May 1905.

15 Editorial, *The Bulletin*, 18 May 1905, p. 8; *DT*, 25 May 1905.

16 *DT, SMH*, 25 May 1905.

17 ALP, *Third Commonwealth Labour Conference Official Report*, 8–11 July 1905, p. 10.

18 *EGTA*, Sept. 1905, p. 42; *SMH*, 25 May 1905.

19 *Commonwealth of Australia Gazette (CAG)*, 7 Mar. 1908, p. 589.

20 *Commonwealth Parliamentary Debates (CPD)*, 18 Mar., 2 Apr., 7 May, 30 Oct. 1908, pp. 9192, 10 119–20, 10 969, 1791; *SMH*, 2 May 1908; National Archives of Australia (NAA): MP620/3, whole series, p. 223.

21 *CPD*, 13 Dec. 1907, pp. 7515, 7535; WJ Hudson and MP Sharp, *Australian Independence: Colony to Reluctant Kingdom*, MUP, Melbourne, 1988, p. 45.

22 Report of Proceedings of the Annual conference, Victorian Branches, 25–26 Mar. 1908, p. 17, ANA (Vic.) *Conference and Board of Directors Reports*, vol. 8; *The Advance Australia*, Apr. 1908, p. 85.

23 R Muirhead Collins, Commonwealth officer, to Atlee Hunt, Secretary, External Affairs Department (DEA), 14 June 1907, E Wilson Dobbs, heraldic expert, Toorak, to Hunt, 30 Sept. 1907, NAA: A462, 828/3/8 part 1.

24 Correspondence 14 June 1907–25 Mar. 1908, NAA: A462, 828/3/8 part 1.

25 ML Shepherd, Secretary, Prime Minister's Department (DPM) to Hunt, 20 June 1910, WA Gullick, Government Printer, to Hunt, 24 June 1910, PM to Governor-General, 27 Mar. 1911, NAA: A462, 828/3/8 part 1; *The Herald* (Melb.), 17 Sept. 1910.

26 *Public Instruction Gazette (PIG)*, Mar. 1908, p. 262; *EG*, Apr. 1910, p. 114.

27 *PIG*, Apr. 1906, p. 78, Apr. 1907, p. 377; *Reports of Proceedings of Annual Conferences of West Australian Branches, 16–17 Apr. 1906, 1–2 Apr. 1907*, in ANA (Vic.), *Conference … Reports*, vols 7, 8.

28 *Report … Annual Conference WA Branch, 1 and 2 Apr. 1907*, in ANA (Vic.), *Conference … Reports*, vol. 8; *Report and Proceedings of the Annual Session of the ANA (New South Wales)*, 1909; Official Report of the Proceedings of the Interstate Conference, Melbourne, 1–3 Feb. 1910, supplement *The Advance Australia*, Feb. 1910.

29 Pearce to Secretary, Defence Department (DD), 1 Apr. 1911, NAA: MP84/1, 1874/1/28; *Commonwealth Forces Military Orders 1911*, no. 135, 11 Apr. 1911; Military

Secretary, Governor-General, to Defence Minister, 28 Apr. 1911 and response from Acting Secretary, DD, 18 May 1911, NAA: MP84/1, 1874/1/28; Private Secretary, Governor-General, to Lionel Earle, Colonial Office, 19 May 1911, NAA: A11085, B7/5.

30 The Status of Dominion Ships of War: Memorandum by the Admiralty, Aug. 1910, NAA: A5954, 1185/4; J Menear, Registrar, The White Ensign and the RAN, to Secretary, 1st Naval Member, 9 Nov. 1965, File 295N, Naval History Section, DD.

31 *The Freeman's Journal (FJ)* (Syd.), 19 May 1906, p. 13, *St Joseph's College Annual* (Syd.), 1906, p. 44.

32 *FJ*, 28 May 1908, p. 17.

33 *Catholic Education Conference of New South Wales, 17–20 January 1911: Statement, Resolutions, Proceedings*, Sydney, 1911, pp. 16, 23, 30, 38.

34 Cardinal's Ultimatum, *SMH*, 31 Dec. 1910.

35 *SMH*, 26 Jan., 22 May 1911; *NA, DT*, 23 May 1911; *FJ*, 11, 18 May 1911.

36 *SMH*, 25 May, *DT*, 27 May 1911; *Echoes from St Stanislaus*, Dec. 1911, p. 43; Rev. FD King, *Memories of Maurice O'Reilly CM*, St Stanislaus' College, Bathurst NSW, 1953, p. 6.

37 *NSWPD*, 23 May 1911, p. 9.

38 *The Bathurst Times, DT*, 25 May 1911; *The Advocate* (Melb.), 20 May 1911, p. 26; *The Southern Cross* (Adel.), 19 May 1911, p. 402; Catholic Church, Archbishops of Australasia, Report of Conference held at Archbishop's House, Raheen, Melbourne, on 24 and 25 Oct. 1922, typescript, Melbourne Diocesan Historical Commission.

39 *DT, SMH*, 25 May 1911.

40 Monsignor O'Riordan to Moran, original emphasis, 1 Aug. 1911, Moran Papers, SC: M223 Corr. 1911/82, Sydney Archdiocesan Archives.

41 Memorandum of Conferences between the British Admiralty and Representatives of the Dominions of Canada and Australia, 29 June 1911, NAA: MP178/2, 2115/1/57; Commonwealth Forces Navy Orders, nos 77, 78, 5 Oct. 1911 in File 295N; Secretary, DD to Secretary, DPM, 16 June 1913, NAA: A461, A336/1/1 part 1.

42 *Commonwealth Forces Navy Orders*, no. 48, 27 July 1911, *Military Orders*, no. 391, 26 Sept. 1911.

CHAPTER 3
WAR AND THE QUESTION OF LOYALTY

1 ANA (WA) to Fisher, 11 Apr. 1913, Secretary, Defence Department (DD), to Secretary, Prime Minister's Department (DPM), 16 June 1913, National Archives of Australia (NAA): A461, A336/1/1 part 1; Naval Secretary to Secretary, DD, 7 May 1913, NAA: MP472/1, 1/13/4322.

2 LL Robson, *The First AIF: A Study of Its Recruitment 1914–1918*, MUP, Melbourne, 1970, pp. 24, 34–5.

3 Robson, *The First AIF*, pp. 57–8.

4 RELAWM08019.001, REL22338, REL18550, P02194.009, RELAWM15689, Australian War Memorial (AWM); George Watson and John Alexander McKay, personal dossiers, NAA: B2455, Watson GH, B2455, McKay JA.

5 RELAWM15650, RELAWM15057, RELAWM15062, RELAWM15595, RELAWM01068, J06161, RELAWM01536, AWM; Geoffrey Serle, *John Monash: A Biography*, MUP in association with Monash University, Melbourne, 1982, p. 330.

6 Mrs R Hull (mother) to CEW Bean, 29 Mar. 1932,

AWM43, A401; CEW Bean, *The AIF in France 1917* (1933), Angus & Robertson, Sydney, 8th edn 1939, notes 112 and 46, pp. 770, 895; *Newcastle Morning Herald and Miners' Advocate*, 24 Sept. 1917; Desmond Mountjoy, Stid: An Australian Soldier Boy, in his *The Melody of God and Other Papers*, Constable & Company, London, 1923, p. 28.

7 AWM, REL01625; Ernest Henry Forty, personal dossier, NAA: B2455, Forty EH; Sir John Monash, *The Australian Victories in France in 1918*, Hutchinson & Co, London, 1920, p. 123.

8 CEW Bean, *The Anzac Book*, Cassell, London, 1916; KS Inglis, The Anzac Tradition, *Meanjin Quarterly*, no. 1, Mar. 1965; DA Kent, The Anzac Book and the Anzac Legend: CEW Bean as Editor and Image-maker, *Historical Studies*, vol. 21, no. 84, Apr. 1985; KS Inglis, *Sacred Places: War Memorials in the Australian Landscape*, MUP, Melbourne, 1998, pp. 75, 78–9; comment by Brigadier General Charles 'Digger' Brand, *The Daily Telegraph (DT)*, 4 May 1921.

9 *Education Gazette and Teachers Aid (EGTA)*, Feb., Mar. 1916, pp. 30, 57, Apr. 1917, p. 51.

10 *Education Gazette (EG)*, Nov. 1917, p. 256.

11 Serle, *John Monash*, pp. 299–300, 323.

12 Serle, *John Monash*, quoting Monash pp. 315, 359; CEW Bean, *The AIF in France: During the Allied Offensive*, Angus & Robertson, Sydney, 1942, pp. 876–7; Bill Gammage, *The Broken Years: Australian Soldiers in the Great War* (1974), Penguin, Melbourne, 1975, pp. 86, 208–209, 277.

13 CEW Bean, *In Your Hands, Australians* (1918), Cassell, London, 2nd edn 1919, p. 8; *All British Sentinel* (Adel.), 1 Jan. 1918, p. 17, renamed *The British Sentinel*, 2 Sept. 1918, p. 4, 1 May 1919, p. 8.

14 FB Smith, *The Conscription Plebiscites in Australia 1916–17* (1965), Victorian Historical Association, Melbourne, 2nd edn 1966; KS Inglis, Conscription in Peace and War, 1911–1945, in Roy Forward and Bob Reece (eds) *Conscription in Australia*, UQP, Brisbane, 1968, pp. 31, 33.

15 Inglis, quoting Hughes, Conscription in Peace and War, p. 38; John Robertson, *Anzac and Empire: The Tragedy & Glory of Gallipoli*, Hamlyn, Melbourne, 1990, pp. 265–7; Joan Beaumont, Australia's War, in Joan Beaumont (ed.), *Australia's War 1914–18*, Allen & Unwin, Sydney, 1995, pp. 48–9.

16 David J. Gordon, Britishers, Keep Your Flag Flying, *All British Sentinel*, 1 Dec. 1917, p. 26.

17 Slogan popularised and probably coined by Archbishop Mannix, Alan D Gilbert, Protestants, Catholics and Loyalty: An Aspect of the Conscription Controversies, 1916–17, *Politics*, May 1971, vol. VI, no. 1, p. 16; Jeff Kildea, *Tearing the Fabric: Sectarianism in Australia 1910 to 1925*, Citadel Books, Sydney, 2002, pp. 140–41, 35; Robson, *The First AIF*, pp. 173–74.

18 Kevin Livingston, Terence McGuire and the Manly Union 1914–24, *Australasian Catholic Record*, vol. XLVIII, no. 3, July 1971, p. 239.

19 Kildea, *Tearing the Fabric*, pp. 162, 170, 145–6, 165–6; Gilbert, Protestants, Catholics and Loyalty, p. 22; *DT*, 22 Nov. 1917; LL Robson, The Origin and Character of the First AIF, 1914–1918: Some Statistical Evidence, *Historical Studies*, vol. 15, no. 61, Oct. 1973, p. 741.

20 Judith Brett, *Australian Liberals and the Moral Middle Class: From Alfred Deakin to John Howard*, CUP, Cambridge, 2003, pp. 44–51.

21 Inglis, *Sacred Places*, p. 191; HO Arnold-Forster, *The Citizen Reader for the Use of Schools* (1886), adapted for Australian children (1906) by CR Long, Cassell, Melbourne, 1912, pp. 18–19, original emphasis; *EG*, Aug. 1911, p. 191, Oct. 1916, p. 224; Appendix 1.

22 Appendices 1 and 2.

23 SA *Education Act 1916*; *Victoria Parliamentary Debates*, 15 June 1915, p. 837; *NSW Parliamentary Debates*, 8 Aug. 1917, p. 460.

24 *SA Parliamentary Papers*, 1905, no. 44, p. 25.

25 SA *Education Act 1915*; *SA Parliamentary Debates*, 5 Oct. 1915, pp. 1138, 1140, 6 Oct. 1915, p. 1214, 26 Oct, 1915, p. 1540.

26 *EG*, Oct. 1916, p. 224; Appendix 1; *SAPD*, 1 Nov. 1916, pp. 1786–7, 7 Nov. 1916, p. 1886, 9 Nov. 1916, p. 1965; *The Register* (Adel.), 4 Sept. 1916; *SA Education Act 1916*.

27 *EG*, Dec. 1916, p. 377, Nov. 1917, p. 256; Circular, Minister of Education, Victoria to registered schools, 23 Aug. 1916, and responses, VPRS 10298, box 9, Public Record Office Victoria (PROV).

28 Teacher, Bower Public School (formerly Lutheran) near Eudunda, to Director, early August 1917, Maughan to teachers, 31 July 1917, GRG 18/2/1917/1955, State Records SA (SRSA); Director to inspectors, 28 Apr. 1917, and replies, GRG 18/2/1917/1569, SRSA.

29 Elizabeth Kwan, The Australian Flag: Ambiguous symbol of nationality in Melbourne and Sydney, 1920–21, *Australian Historical Studies*, vol. 26, no. 103, Oct. 1994.

30 *The Argus* (Melb.), 10 May 1920; *The Advocate* (Melb.), 25 Mar. 1920, p. 9.

31 *The Argus*, 21 Mar. 1921.

32 Eileen Whitelaw, Daisy Hill via Maryborough, to Premier, Victoria, 18 Apr. 1920, Secretary, Education Department to Premier, 21 May 1920, VPRS 1163, box 513, file 1675, VPRO.

33 RSL (NSW) Executive's view, *DT*, 5 May 1921; Senior Chaplain James Green to editor, *DT*, 9 May 1921.

34 Graham Freudenberg, *Cause for Power: The Official History of the New South Wales Branch of the Australian Labor Party*, Pluto Press in association with NSW ALP, Sydney, 1991, p. 136; Proceedings of the Municipal Council of Sydney, 16 Nov. 1920, Council of the City of Sydney Archives.

35 *DT*, 5 July 1921.

36 *The Geelong Advertiser*, 8 June 1921; shire and municipal councils, in particular from Taree, 1 June 1921, to Under-Secretary, Education Department, NSW, 17 May to 13 June 1921, Miscellaneous 20/12809 file 42098, Archives Office of NSW.

37 *DT*, 5 May, 25 Apr. 1921.

CHAPTER 4
THE RED AND THE BLUE

1 PJ Wallace, original emphasis, 8 June 1916, and response to Prime Minister's Department (DPM), 20 Apr. 1917, National Archives of Australia (NAA): A461, B336/1/1 part 2; Correspondence, Local Government Association and DPM and Department of the Navy (DN), 18 June to 22 July 1921, NAA: A461, D336/1/1 part 1.

2 Premier's Office, Tasmania to DPM, 19 Jan. 1915; Postmaster-General's Department to DPM, 5 July 1921, NAA: A461, D336/1/1 part 1.

3 *Education Gazette*, Oct 1921, p. 164, *The Shire and Municipal Record*, 26 Sept. 1921, p. 589, *The Sydney Morning Herald*, 13, 15 Oct. 1921.

4 DPM to DN, 26 Aug. 1921, correspondence, Town Clerk, Sydney, DPM and DN, 12 Oct.–14 Dec. 1921, NAA: A336/1/1 part 1.

5 Correspondence, Coleraine Fallen Soldiers' Memorial Fund Committee, Department of Defence (DD) and DPM, 7 May 1923 to 14 Apr. 1924, NAA: A461, B336/1/1 part 2.

6 DPM, 'Flags – Commonwealth and Others', 20 July 1923; Defence response, 17 Dec. 1923; circular, 31 Jan. 1924, NAA: A461, A336/1/1 part 1.

7 Returned Sailors and Soldiers Imperial League of Australia (NSW) to RSSILA, 22 Mar. 1924, RSL Papers, MS 6609/1/1697B, National Library of Australia; Llewellyn Atkinson for Bruce to state premiers, 3 May 1924, NAA: A461, A336/1/1 part 1.

8 Air Board Agenda no. 106 and attached correspondence, RAAF Historical Section, DD; Hughes, quoted by WJ Hudson and MP Sharp, *Australian Independence: Colony to Reluctant Kingdom*, MUP, Melbourne, 1988, p. 68.

9 Bruce, quoted by Hudson and Sharp, *Australian Independence*, pp. 75, 95, 99–100.

10 Parliament House – Position of Flags, NAA: A2514, P239; Royal Visit Cabinet Committee to Department of Home & Territories, 25 Mar., 1927, Flags to be Flown, NAA: A6976, 16.

11 Royal visit, opening of Parliament House ceremony, awaiting the arrival of the Royal Party, NAA: A3560, 7188; Introduction by Max Middleton in H Septimus Power, *The Art of H. Septimus Power*, Rigby, Adelaide, 1974, p. 9.

12 Official Secretary, Governor-General, to Secretary, DPM, 18 Dec. 1951, NAA: A2880, 6/14/10; Note, 'Governor-General's Proposed Flag', 21 Jan. 1931, NAA: A461, K336/1/1.

13 Governor-General's Flag and attachments, Private Secretary to the Queen to Official Secretary, Australian Governor-General, 8 Feb. 1996, Office of the Official Secretary to the Governor-General, file 2002/276, Government House.

14 RSSILA to Prime Minister, 8 Apr. 1931, NAA: A461, K336/1/1.

15 Hudson and Sharp, *Australian Independence*, pp. 125–9.

16 DD to DPM, 24 Mar. 1932, re *King's Regulations* and *Admiralty Instructions* of Aug. 1931, NAA: A461, Y336/1/1; Military and Official Secretary, Governor-General to Secretary, DPM, 3 Feb. 1936, NAA: A461, K336/1/1.

17 RSL (Vic.) to Director of Education, 21 Jan. 1929, VPRS 794, box 1127, 29/1882, Public Record Office Victoria (PROV); *Education Gazette & Teachers' Aid*, July 1932, p. 171, 26 Apr. 1933, p. 85; Appendix 2; News Cuttings Book 12, pp. 179–181, 198, RSL Papers, RSL (Vic.).

18 Board of Directors, ANA (Vic.) to Education Department, 2 Sept. 1930 and response, 5 Sept. 1930, VPRS 794, box 1145, 30/13624, PROV.

19 Minutes of meeting, 11 Aug. 1922, Metropolitan Committee, ANA (Vic.); see entries for the three men in *Australian Dictionary of Biography*, vols 8, 9, 12, pp. 377, 324, 581.

20 Henry Lawson, 'Freedom on the Wallaby', 1891, 'As Ireland Wore the Green', 1891; Katharine Massam, The Blue Army and the Cold War: Anti-Communist Devotion to the Blessed Virgin Mary in Australia, *Australian Historical Studies*, vol. 24, no. 97, Oct. 1991, pp. 422–423.

21 AA Dunstan, Premier, Vic. to JA Lyons, PM, 23 Feb. 1939, NAA: A461, A336/1/1 part 2.

22 *Young Witness*, 20 Apr. 1945, p.1; Note by TJC [Collins], 7 Mar. 1939, NAA: A461, A336/1/1 part 2.

23 Secretary, DPM to Secretary, DD, 5 June 1939, and response, 21 June 1939, NAA: A461, B336/1/1 parts 5, 3; Note (original emphasis) on revised paper, Flying of Flags, 9 Aug. 1940, NAA: A336/1/1 part 2; Konrad Kwiet, Inter-war German Community Life, in James Jupp (ed.), *The Australian People: An Encyclopedia of the Nation, Its People and Their Origins* (1988), Cambridge University Press, Cambridge, 2001, p. 375.

24 *Victoria Parliamentary Debates (VPD)*, 19 Nov. 1940, pp. 1605, 1600.

25 *VPD*, 29 Oct. 1940, p. 1317; 19 Nov. 1940, p. 1595.

26 *VPD*, 11 Nov., 1941, p. 1677; 27 Nov. 1941, p. 2096; 30 Oct. 1940, p. 1357; 23 Sept., 1941, p. 959; *The Teachers' Journal*, 20 Nov. 1940, p. 421; *VPD* 19 Nov. 1940, p. 1621.

27 Dunstan to Menzies, 16 Jan. 1941, NAA: A461, A336/1/1 part 2.

CHAPTER 5
CHOOSING BETWEEN ENSIGNS

1 Elizabeth Kwan, Blue Over the Red: Australia's Victorian Flag Legacy and Menzies' Decision, *Crux Australis*, vol. 13/4, no. 56, Feb. 2000.

2 General Secretary, UAP, to Menzies, 9 July 1940, Collins, draft reply for Secretary, Prime Minister's Department (DPM) to External Affairs Department, 18 Oct. 1940, WB, DPM to Collins, 23 Oct. 1940, National Archives of Australia (NAA): A461, D336/1/1 part 3.

3 'Commonwealth Flags', DPM, 21 Nov. 1940, NAA: A461, A336/1/1 part 2.

4 1, 11, 28 Nov. 1940, NAA: A461, A336/1/1 part 2.

5 General Secretary, UAP (NSW), 9 July 1940, Lucas to Menzies, 27 June 1941, NAA: A461, D336/1/1 part 3.

6 Circular, 29 Oct. 1941; DPM to Commonwealth Investigation Bureau, 25 Nov. 1941, NAA: A461, B336/1/1 Pt 3; *The Sydney Morning Herald*, 6 Nov. 1941.

7 16 Mar. 1939, NAA: A461, D336/1/1 part 3.

8 Hodgson, 18 Feb.1941; The Commonwealth Flag, 14 and 15 Mar. 1941; Collins to Howard Beale, Army Education (later MHR for Parramatta with an interest in the flag), 8 Apr. 1941, NAA: A461, A336/1/1 part 2.

9 ANA (NSW), 23 February 1943, NAA: A461, D336/1/1 part 4.

10 ANA (NSW) 1 June 1943; Defence Department to Department of Air, 11 Oct. 1943; Australian Military Forces, 31 Oct. 1947, NAA: A705, 85/1/158.

11 Beale to Chifley, 14 Feb. 1947, NAA: A461, A336/1/1 part 3.

12 Press statement; UPA, 3 Apr. 1947, NAA: A461, A336/1/1 part 3.

13 Chifley to John Dedman, Defence Minister, 5 Oct. 1949, Draft Report by Departmental Committee on Flags and their Usage in Australia, 24 Nov. 1949, NAA: A518, EC112/1 part 2.

14 Necessity of an Australian National Flag, n.d. but c. 1949, NAA: A462, 828/1/1 part 1.

15 Report of the Departmental Committee, Commonwealth of Australia Jubilee Celebrations, attachment to notice of meeting of Cabinet Sub-Committee on Jubilee Celebrations, 12 Oct. 1949, Calwell Papers, MS 4738/9/35/1949, National Library of Australia (NLA); DPM to NSW Premier's Department, 4 Nov. 1949, NAA: A461, O317/1/6.

16 A Calwell, review of Niall Brennan's *John Wren: Gamber – his life and times* (Hill of Content, Melbourne, 1971) in *The Herald* (Melb.), 4 Dec. 1971, in Folder Wren, John, Calwell Papers, MS 4738/21/Box 82.

17 Clive Parry, *Nationality and Citizenship Laws of the Commonwealth and of the Republic of Ireland*, Stevens & Son, London, 1957, pp. 550, 603; David Dutton, *One of Us? A Century of Australian Citizenship*, UNSW Press, Sydney, 2002, pp. 15–17; typescript, Calwell, Calwell Papers, MS 4738/23/Box 88.

18 Report of Representatives of Commonwealth and State Governments on Jubilee Celebrations, Canberra, 20 Mar. 1950, Menzies Papers, MS 4936/37/548/38, NLA; Agenda paper for first meeting of Education and Science Sub-committee, 19 June 1950, NAA: A9645, C3/2.

19 Report of Representatives, Menzies Papers.

20 Attachment, Mills to Secretary, DPM, 5 May 1950, NAA: A461, O317/1/6; Australian Flags, Submission no. 113, 26 May 1950, Director-General to Secretary, DPM, 27 Nov. 1950, NAA: A462, 828/1/1 part 1; Minutes of meeting of Cabinet, 4 Dec. 1950, Fourth Menzies Ministry – folder of minutes of Cabinet meetings, NAA: A4638, set 1.

21 Correspondence between Mills, Bean and Director-General Commonwealth Jubilee Celebrations, 13 Dec. 1950 to 14 Mar. 1951, NAA: A1361, 21/1/7 part 1.

22 Records relating to Commonwealth Jubilee, MS 1874, NLA; *Commonwealth Jubilee 1901–1951 Bicycle Relay*, GRG 18/2, 1951/311, State Records SA (SRSA).

23 As reported to the Secretary, DPM by Director-General of Jubilee Celebrations, 27 Nov. 1950, NAA: A462, 828/1/1 part 1; WC Taylor to Secretary, DPM, 27 Apr. 1951 and response, n.d., NAA: A461, O317/1/6.

24 Public Executive Officer to Assistant Secretary (Administration), DPM, 5 Jan. 1951, Secretary, DPM to PM, 30 Apr. 1951, NAA: A462, 828/1/1 part 1.

25 DPM to Office of Education, 22 Dec. 1952, NAA: A1361, 21/1/7 Pt 2; Evans to Secretary, Commonwealth Jubilee Celebrations Council, 6 June 1950, NAA: A9645, C3/2.

26 EJ Nuttall to PM, 27 Jan. 1953, WC Taylor, to Secretary, DPM, 28 Oct. 1952, NAA: A462, 828/1/7.

27 Correspondence and drafts, Education Office and DPM, 2, 17 Mar., 1953, NAA: A1361, 21/1/7 part 2.

28 26 Mar. 1953, GRG 18/2/1950/1706, SRSA; *Education Gazette*, Apr. 1953, p. 103; Appendix 1.

29 *Commonwealth Parliamentary Debates*, pp. 367–8, 816–17; Flags Bill, NAA: A462, 828/1/31.

30 *Recollections of a Bleeding Heart: A Portrait of Paul Keating*, Vintage, Sydney, 2002, p. 126.

31 See, for example, Janet Holmes à Court, Ausflag Director, *Constitutional Convention Hansard*, 10 Feb. 1998, p. 578; Carol A Foley, *The Australian Flag: Colonial Relic or Contemporary Icon?*, Federation Press, Sydney, 1996, p. 131. Foley, in suggesting that Lambert was 'the champion of the Australian Blue Ensign in the 1920s', cited my 1994 *Australian Historical Studies* article The Australian Flag: Ambiguous Symbol of Nationality in Melbourne and Sydney, 1920–21. But as far as my evidence showed (p. 300), Lambert used the red, not blue, ensign. Ralph Kelly, Ausflag Director, stated to author, 1 July 2005, that Ausflag took its cue from a general comment in Menzies' *Afternoon Light: Some memories of men and events*.

32 EJO, Attorney-General's Department, 22 Mar. 1954, NAA: A462, 828/1/31; *Flags Act 1953*, www.founding-docs.gov.au, 15 Jan. 2004.

CHAPTER 6
SEARCHING FOR AUSTRALIAN SYMBOLS

1 Attachment, Australian National Flag, Acting Secretary, Prime Minister's Department (DPM) to Commonwealth

Office of Education (COE), 3 July 1953, DPM to Director, COE, 25 June 1956, National Archives of Australia (NAA): A1361, 21/1/14 part 1; *The Australian National Flag*, DPM, Canberra, 1956 and editions of 1971, 1977, 1979, 1981, 1982, 1985, National Library of Australia (NLA).

2 *Education Gazette*, Feb. 1956, p. 79.

3 Official Secretary to the Governor-General to Secretary, DPM, 15 Dec. 1958, NAA: A2880, 6/14/10.

4 Correspondence between Joint House Department and DPM, Aug. 1954–Oct. 1971, NAA: A6728, 124 part 1.

5 Secretary, DPM to Director, COE, amended certificate attached, 21 May 1963, and response, 30 May 1963,

Newspaper (Canberra), 21 May 1981, in A91/33059 Pt 3, DD (sa).

19 Rick Grebert, *The Australian Army Slouch Hat and Rising Sun Badge*, NSW Military Historical Society, Mosman, 2002 , pp. 116–123; ER Garrett, The Badge with a History, *Australian Army Journal*, no. 185, Oct. 1964, pp.17–20, 22–23.

20 ER Garrett, Background, project 'Australian Army Insignia', Brief for MGO, 20 Oct. 1966; Military Board Minutes No. 241/1968, 19 July 1968, No. 75/1969, 14 Mar. 1969, A8455/2/10 Pt 1, DD (sa).

21 Australian Joint Service Symbol, Secretary, Chiefs of Staff Committee (COSC), to Principal Administrative Officers'

Committee (Personnel) (PAOC-P), 27 Oct. 1967, HQ 96/39814 Pt 1, DD (sa); PAOC-P Minute, Agendum No. 30/67, 26 Feb. 1968 and supplement No. 1, CSOC Minute, 19 June 1968, Minister's approval in Acting Secretary, Department of the Army to Secretaries, Departments of Navy, Air, 31 Dec. 1971, Australian War Memorial, 121 59/P/1.

22 Mark McKenna, *The Captive Republic: A History of Republicanism in Australia 1788–1996*, Cambridge University Press, Cambridge, 1996, p. 224.

23 Report by Ulrich Ellis on Design for Badge, Flag and Distinguishing Symbol for New England Movement, 16 June 1949, University of New England and Regional Archives, A547, 330–2 badges; RS Parker, New States for Australia, *Proceedings of the Australian Institute of Political Science*, Spring Forum, Armidale, 1–2 Oct. 1955, pp. 3–7.

24 Thomas v Brown and another, *Intellectual Property Reports*, vol. 37, 1997, pp. 212–19; *The Advertiser* (Adel.), 9 Apr. 1997.

25 Tent Embassy, Flag in David Horton (ed.), *The Encyclopaedia of Aboriginal Australia: Aboriginal and Torres Strait Islander History, Society and Culture*, Aboriginal Studies Press, Canberra, 1994; Tony Burton, Indigenality and Australian Vexillography, *Crux Australis*, vol. 10/4, no. 44, Oct./Dec. 1994, pp. 177–8, also Tjuringa Dreaming: Revolutionary Flags of the Australian Aboriginals 1971–1997 – Heralds of Change, draft paper, XXI International Congress of Vexillology, Buenos Aires, Argentina, 31 July to 5 Aug. 2005.

26 *The Sun-Herald* (Syd.), 27 June 1971, Anthem and Flag Quests, 9 Nov. 1971, Lavett to Editor, *The Australian*, 21 Sept. 1972, NAA: AA1975/370, 2, Publicity folder.

27 Roy Morgan to Lavett, 21 Sept. 1972, NAA: AA1975/370, 4, Ten Best Entries folder; Gallup Polls on the National Anthem, Parliamentary Library to Department of Administrative Services, 13 Oct. 1976, EB80/5765, Department of Prime Minister and Cabinet (DPMC) (sa).

28 ID Emerton, Assistant Secretary, DPMC, 29 Jan. 1974, NAA: A463, 1973/2555; *The Daily Telegraph* (Syd.), 20 Nov. 1972.

29 Draft, Australian National Anthem, Parliamentary Branch, Department of Special Minister of State (DSMOS) c. Feb. 1974, NAA: A463, 73/2555; *CPD*, 8 Apr. 1974, p. 1110.

30 *CPD*, House of Representatives, 12 Apr. 1973, pp. 1373–4; Press release, 8 Mar. 1974, EB80/5765; Lavett to members of the Australian National Anthem and Flag Quests Committee, 19 Apr. 1974, NAA: A750, 1972/54.

31 Issues involved in introducing an Australian national anthem, First Assistant Secretary, DSMOS, to Principal Private Secretary, Prime Minister, 6 Apr. 1974; press statement, 18 Apr. 1974; communications, Prime Minister's Office, DSMOS, DPMC and the Governor-General, 2–23 Apr. 1974, NAA: A463, 1973/2555.

32 Official Words for the National Tune 'Advance Australia Fair' or a National Song, Joint Submission by Ministers for Administrative Services, and Home Affairs and Environment, Dec. 1981, HON83/4979/01 DPMC (sa).

33 Harold Scruby, interview with author, 16 Sept. 2004, tapes in the author's possession; www.ausflag.com.au, 8 Sept. 2004; Ralph Kelly, Filibuster: The Century-Long Australian Flag Debate, *Crux Australis*, vol. 14/1, no. 57, Jan./Mar. 2000; on 21 Dec. 1992 the company became Ausflag Ltd, Australian Securities & Investments Commission, 21 July 2005.

34 Extract of minutes of meeting of ANFA steering committee, 21 Apr. 1983, from John Vaughan; *ANFA Newsletter*, Aug. 2003; National Secretary, RSL to Henry Farrell, later honorary secretary, ANFA (Victoria), 26 July 1983, RSL media release, Canberra, 4 Oct. 1983, *Newsletter*, ANFA (Queensland), May 1996, Papers of Henry Farrell, MS 9869/Box 1/folder 1, NLA; www.australianflag.org.au, 16 Sept. 2003.

35 John Vaughan, interview with author, 15 Sept. 2004, tapes in the Mitchell Library; *The Sydney Morning Herald (SMH)*, 6 Oct. 1983.

36 *History and Meaning*, brochure on the Australian flag, ANFA (Victoria) Melbourne, 1984, Papers of Henry Farrell, MS 9869/Box 2/folder 8, NLA.

37 *The Australian*, *SMH*, 6 Oct. 1983; John Edwards, The Boxing Kangaroo: Apotheosis of a Myth, *The Flag Bulletin*, no. 112, vol. xxiv, no. 4, July–August 1985, p. 133.

CHAPTER 7
BRITISH OR AUSTRALIAN?

1 In the first verse 'Australians all' replaced 'Australia's sons'; in the second, 'this Commonwealth of ours' replaced 'our youthful Commonwealth', and 'those who've come across the seas' replaced 'loyal sons beyond the seas', Sir Asher Joel KBE AO, former member of the National Australia Day Committee, to Assistant General Manager, Awards and National Symbols Branch (ANSB), Department of Administrative Services (DAS), 30 Jan. 1996, EB80/5765 DAS, special access (sa).

2 David Dutton, *One of Us? A Century of Australian Citizenship*, UNSW Press, Sydney, 2002, p. 17.

3 Brief for Prime Minister (PM), National Symbols …, 16 Nov. 1983, HON83/4979/02, Department of Special Minister of State (DSMS) (sa).

4 Governor-General to PM, 1 Dec. 1983, HON83/4979/01, DSMS (sa); Notes relating to copyright of *Waltzing Matilda*, HON83/4979/02.

5 PM to RSL, 17 Apr. 1984, HON83/4979/01; Minute Paper, Executive Council, 16 Apr. 1984, proclamation, 19 Apr. 1984, HON83/4979/02.

6 Scruby, interview with author, 16 Sept. 2004, tapes with author; Ralph Kelly, Filibuster: The Century-Long Australian Flag Debate, *Crux Australis (CA)*, vol. 14/1, no. 57, Jan.–Mar. 2000, pp. 31–2, 36–7.

7 June 1982, March 1992, Finding No. 3055, 17 Feb. 1998.

8 National President, RSL to Chief of the General Staff, 30 July 1990, A91/33059 part 2, Defence Department (DD) (sa).

9 Australian Army Badge and Army Emblem, Army Office to commands, 6 Sept. 1990, A91/33059 Pt 2, DD (sa).

10 Australian Army Badge and Army Emblem, Army Office to commands, 6 Sept. 1990, CGS to Minister, 18 Oct. 1990, p. 1 in A91/33059 Pt 2, p. 2 in A8455/2/10 Pt 1, DD (sa).

11 *The New Rising Sun Badge*, Directorate of Army Information, A91/33059 Pt 2; Army Office to commands, 3, 11 Feb. 1992, cleared news release, 18 Feb. 1993, A91/33059 Pt 3, DD (sa).

12 Chief of the Defence Force to Minister, 29 June 1999, HQ96/39814 Pt 1, DD (sa).

13 Don Watson, *Recollections of a Bleeding Heart: A Portrait of Paul Keating*, Random House, Sydney, 2003, pp. 111–14, 123; *The Weekend Australian (WA)*, 2–3 May 1992.

14 The Torres Strait Islander Flag, www.aiatsis.gov.au/lby/fct_shts/aus_flag.htm, 13 Jan. 2005.

15 Morgan Poll Finding for March 1992, No. 3055, 17 Feb. 1998; *WA*, 2–3 May 1992.

16 *WA*, 2–3 May 1993.

17 In June 1992, 32 per cent of Australians wanted to remove the Union Jack from the Australian flag, 39 per cent wanted to change the flag, Morgan Poll Finding No. 3055, 17 Feb. 1998.

18 *The Sydney Morning Herald (SMH)*, 3, 9 June 1994; *WA*, 4–5 June 1994.

19 Irving Saulwick and Associates poll of 28–29 June 1994 of 1000 votes on the question 'Should we keep the Australian flag as it is now, which included the British flag in its design or change it for some new design which would exclude the British flag?', EB80/5765, Department of Administrative Services (DAS) (sa).

20 Adrian McGregor, *Cathy Freeman: A Journey Just Begun*, Random House, Sydney, 1998, p. 165.

21 *SMH*, 26 Aug. 1994; *The Australian*, 15 Aug. 1994.

22 DAS to ATSIC, 17 Feb. 1994, Walker to Tickner, 12 July 1994, ATSIC to DAS, 15 Dec. 1994, Tickner to Walker, 13 Jan. 1995, 95/6315, Department of Immigration and Multicultural and Indigenous Affairs (DIMIA) (sa).

23 Paras 4.92–94, ATSIC, Canberra, 1995; *The Canberra Times (CT)*, 5 July 1995; 95/3882, DIMIA (sa).

24 *The Northern Territory News*, 3 July 1995; *The Australian*, 5 July 1995; Statement, PM, 4 July 1995, 95/3882.

25 *Commonwealth of Australia Gazette*, nos S 258 and S 259, 14 July 1995; DAS to ATSIC, 7 Feb. 1995, DAS to Attorney-General's Department, 15 Mar. 1995, 95/6315; Herald-McNair poll: 66 per cent of voters supported or strongly supported the Government's decision, *SMH*, 19 July 1995.

26 *The Mercury* (Hobart), 8 July 1995; ATSIC to DAS, 7 Apr. 1995, 95/6315; Thomas v Brown and Another, 37, *Intellectual Property Reports*, 1997; *SMH*, 27 Jan. 1997.

27 *Policies for a Coalition Government*, Liberal Party of Australia, Canberra, 1996; Judith Brett, The New Liberalism, in Robert Manne (ed.) *The Howard Years*, Black Inc. Agenda, Melbourne, 2004, p. 80.

28 Vaughan to Minister for Administrative Services (MAS), 16 April 1996, A463, 1996/4855, DAS (sa).

29 Gareth Hall reported view of Department of Prime Minister and Cabinet (DPMC) in file note, 6 May 1996, Hall's draft speech for MAS (for the Samuel Griffith Society Conference), 16 May 1996, 96/4759 DPMC (sa); Newspoll, Oct. 1994, *The Australian*, 20 June 1996.

30 Brief for MAS, 17 Apr. 1996, and response, HON96/0056 DAS (sa); Brief for PM, 24 Apr. and response, 25 Apr. 1996, 96/3294 DPMC (sa); PM to MAS, 30 May 1996, 96/4759; 21 and 28 June 1996.

31 John Edwards, Flags in the News, *CA*, vol. II, No. 4/10 Apr. 1986, p. 3.

32 Correspondence, ANFA (Vic.) and ADF, 1988–89, 3MD 88/6428, DD (sa).

33 CDF letter in Brief for CDF, National Flag Ceremony Incident, 8 Sept. 1992, DM 87–35058 part 1, DD (sa).

34 Secretary, ANFA (Queensland) to Major T Lyle, Gallipoli Barracks, Enoggera, 11 Aug. 1992, and Defence Centre Brisbane to Secretary, ANFA (Queensland), 26 Aug. 1992 in Brief for CDF, DM 87–35058 part 1. The ANFA president read the DC-B letter out to a gathering of 200 in King George Square, Brisbane, to cries of 'Shame, shame' and 'Blame Keating': Military boycotts flag-raising to duck controversy, *The Australian*, Flag-raising row flares: angry attack on premier and PM, *The Courier-Mail*, 4 Sept. 1992.

35 Vaughan to Project Officer, National Symbols, DAS, 28 Feb. 1995, HON94/00301/02, DAS (sa); Vaughan to MAS, 16 Apr. 1996, A463, 1996/4855, and to PM, 31 May 1996, 96/3294; PM to MAS, 22 Aug. 1996, A463, 1996/4855.

36 Scruby to PM, 28 Mar. 1996, HON97/0206, DPMC (sa).

37 52 per cent, as against 44 per cent, Feb. 1998, Finding No. 3055, 17 Feb. 1998.

38 Vaughan to PM, 12 Apr. 2000, 2001/2650, DPMC (sa).

39 Centenary of Federation Victoria to Prime Minister's Office (PMO), 8 Jan. 2001, Notes for file, National Symbols Officer (NSO), DPMC, 10 July 2001, 2001/2650.

40 File note, NSO, DPMC and NSO to PMO, 27 July 2001, ANSB, DPMC to Vaughan, 30 July 2001, NSO draft proposal, 2 Aug. 2001, NSO, DPMC to PMO, 7 Aug. 2001, 2001/2650.

41 Transcript, 3 Sept. 2001, 2001/2650; perhaps it reflected the brief on the flag for the PMO, prepared by Parliament's researchers familiar with author's work.

42 ANSB, DPMC to Vaughan, 30 July 2001, NSO, DPMC to PMO, c. late July 2001, 2001/2650; Henry Parkes, *The Federal Government of Australasia: Speeches Delivered on Various Occasions (November 1889–May 1890)*, Turner and Henderson, Sydney, 1890, p. 75; Vaughan to PMO, 29 Aug. 2001, A463, 2001/5357, DPMC (sa); Douglas Cole, 'The Crimson Thread of Kinship': Ethnic Ideas in Australia, 1870–1914, *Historical Studies*, vol. 14, 1971, p. 520.

43 www.flagaustnat.asn.au/importantfacts.php, 23 July 2005. The ANFA presented the site as 'a shortened version of a Project Sheet prepared by the Victorian Education Department for its Centenary of Federation "Federation 100 Projects"'. The association's first question and answer came from *National Flag Day – September 3*, a resource for Studies of Society and Environment by the Victorian Education Department; the second question and answer appears to be from the association.

44 Vaughan to NSO, DPMC, 8 Aug. 2001, NSO's notes of conversation with Vaughan, 28 Aug. 2001, 2001/2650; Vaughan, interview with author, 15 Sept. 2004; Vaughan to PMO, 29 Aug. 2001, Vaughan to Senator Bill Heffernan, Parliamentary Secretary to Cabinet, 23 Oct. 2001, NAA: A463, 2001/5357.

45 Vaughan to Nelson, 28 Nov. 2001, attachment to ANFA fax to Department of Education, Science and Training (DEST), 15 Mar. 2002, ES02/11141, DEST (sa); ABC TV *7.30 Report*, 3 Aug. 1992.

46 Notes of discussion, NSO and author, 4 and 5 Dec. 2001, in author's possession; Notes of meeting between Senator Heffernan and Nigel Morris, ANFA President (ACT), ANSB, DPMC, 12 Dec. 2001, Heffernan to Vaughan, 18 Dec. 2001, Morris to Heffernan's staff, 9 Dec 2001, NAA: A463, 2001/5357.

47 Assistant Secretary, Quality Schooling Branch (QSB) to Group Manager, Schools, DEST, 8 Apr. 2002; Ministerial Briefing, 21 Apr. 2002, ES02/11141.

48 Civics Education Group Chairman, Dr John Hirst, Reader in History, La Trobe University, to author, 5 June 2002; Hirst consulted author by telephone about 'Background notes' section only of Teachers' Notes, 18 June 2002 – author saw draft of the Teachers' Notes for the first time on 5 July, too late to comment before printing; DEST provided ANFA's Vaughan and Morris with a draft for comment on 17 June 2002; David Brown, Senior Project Manager, CC to author, 10 July

2002; Australian Flag – Teacher Notes, drafts 2 to 5, 3–24 June 2002, CC.

49 Teachers' comments on draft, c. 11 June 2002, annotations by Hirst and Brown on drafts, 7, 19 June 2002, Assistant Director, LCES, DEST, to Brown, 19 June 2002, CC; Morris to Assistant Director, LCES to Morris, 3 June 2002, ES02/11141; the National Archives of Australia website, which gives the history behind the *Flags Act 1953*, was also not included, see www.foundingdocs.gov.au, 15 Jan. 2004; Assistant Director, LCES to author, 19 June 2002: 'I am confident ANFA would have set us straight if we had included incorrect information in the first draft.'

50 *Our National Flag … since 1901 Teachers' Notes*, Curriculum Corporation, Commonwealth of Australia, Melbourne, 2002, p. 4.

51 Compare Evans' *The History of the Australian Flag* (1918), Melbourne, n.d., with his statement of 23 January 1959, History of the Australian Flag, Mitchell Library; Vaughan and Morris to Assistant Director, Languages and Civics Education Section (LCES), DEST, 18 June 2002, ES02/11141.

52 Group Manager, Schools to Assistant Secretary, QSB, DEST 26 Apr. 2002, correspondence between Vaughan, Morris and Assistant Director, LCES, 17 May to 2 July 2002, Nelson to School Principals, final draft, May 2002, ES02/11141; Assistant Director, LCES to Brown, 19 June 2002, CC; www.curriculum.edu.au/democ/newsletter, 7 Sept. 2004.

53 *The Australian*, 25 Oct. 2002; *WA*, 26–27 Oct. 2002; *CT*, 29 Oct. 2002; *The Age*, *SMH*, 26 Jan 1994.

54 Nelson, *North Shore Times*, 6 Nov. 2002, 7 July 2004; Ministerial Briefing, 30 Oct. 2002, ES03/10834, DEST (sa).

55 Nelson to Education Ministers, Government MPs, 4 Nov. 2002, ES03/10834.

56 Replies from Tasmania., NSW, Qld, NT, ACT, SA 6 Dec. 2002 to 28 Jan. 2003, ES03/08927, DEST (sa); Victorian Government Schools Reference Guide; response through members for Riverina and Indi to Nelson, 18 Nov., 12 Dec. 2002, ES03/08927.

57 The Australian Government's Agenda for Schools, 22 June 2004, www.dest.gov.au/ministers/nelson/jun_04/npm_220604, 23 June 2004 ; Ministerial Briefing, 30 Oct. 2002, ES03/10834; www.smh.com.au/yoursay/2004/06/23/index, 23 June 2004; *The Age*, *The Australian*, 23, 24 June 2004; *CT*, 26 June 2004.

58 *The Age*, *SMH*, 24 June 2004; Senate Employment, Workplace Relations and Education References Committee, *Commonwealth Funding for Schools, 2004*, p. 75; Marilyn Harrington, Schools Assistance (Learning Together – Achievement Through Choice and Opportunity) Bill 2004, Bills Digest no. 50, 29 Nov. 2004, p. 8.

59 Schools Funding, Briefing Book for the 41st Parliament, Parliamentary Library; James Jupp, *The English in Australia*, CUP, Cambridge, 2004, p. 191.

CONCLUSION

1 Morgan Poll Finding No. 3055, 17 Feb. 1998.

2 'The Young Queen', *The Review of Reviews for Australasia* (Melb.), Nov. 1900, p. 577.

3 *The Daily Telegraph* (Syd.), 25 Apr. 1921; *The Advocate* (Melb.), 25 Mar. 1920, p. 9; *The Bathurst Daily Argus*, 20 May 1905; *The British Sentinel* (Adel.), 2 Sept. 1918,

p. 4, 1 May 1919, p. 8; KS Inglis, The Term 'Australian', in James Jupp (ed.) *The Australian People: An Encyclopedia of the Nation, Its People and Their Origins* (1988), CUP, Cambridge, 2001, pp. 755–7.

4 James Jupp, *The English in Australia*, CUP, Cambridge, 2004, pp. 192, 198; David Dutton, *One of Us? A Century of Australian Citizenship,* UNSW Press, Sydney, 2002, p. 17.

5 RT Appleyard et al, Immigration since the Second World War, in Jupp (ed.), *The Australian People*, pp. 62–85; Jupp, *The English in Australia*, pp. 188–191, 201; Stuart Ward, *Australia and the British Embrace: The Demise of the Imperial Ideal*, MUP, Melbourne, 2001, p. 254.

6 David Goldsworthy, *Losing the Blanket: Australia and the End of Britain's Empire*, MUP, Melbourne, 2002, p. 1; Elizabeth Kwan, Journal, 17 Aug. 1997; *The Australian*, 22 July, 2 Aug. 2005; *The Weekend Australian*, 6–7 Aug., 3–4 Sept. 2005.

7 James Curran, *The Power of Speech: Australian Prime Ministers Defining the National Image*, MUP, Melbourne, 2004, pp. 242, 246.

8 Cynthia Banham and Amanda Morgan, Up Go Those Flag Sales as the Radio Boys Rally Round, *The Sydney Morning Herald*, 5 Apr. 2003.

9 George Megalogenis, *Faultlines: Race, Work and the Politics of Changing Australia*, Scribe Publications, Melbourne, 2003, pp. 54 (drawing on ABS census material), 55 (referring to James Forrest et al, Everywhere Different: A Geography of Racism in Australia, paper, Institute of Australian Geographers' Conference, Canberra, July 2002).

10 *The Sentimental Nation: The Making of the Australian Commonwealth*, OUP, Melbourne, 2000, dedication.

11 Mike Steketee, Turnbull Stars in Double-cross on Flag, *The Australian*, 20 Aug. 2004; Ausflag: The Flag Debate: The Turnbull Letters, www.ausflag.com.au/debate/turnbull.html, 16 July 2005.

APPENDIX 1

1 *Education Gazette,* Aug. 1911, p. 191; Oct. 1916, p. 224; May 1939, p. 144; 'Declaration of Loyalty', Apr. 1953, p. 103; 'Loyal Affirmation', Feb. 1956, p. 79.

APPENDIX 2

1 Elizabeth Kwan, Saluting the Flag: Patriotism in Australian Schools, *Crux Australis*, vol. 17/3, no. 71, Oct. 2004, especially pp. 141–3; Elizabeth Kwan, Which Flag? Which Country? An Australian Dilemma, 1901–1951, PhD thesis, Australian National University, 1995, pp. 321–8.

2 *Education Gazette and Teachers' Aid,* supplement, Oct. 1901.

3 *Education Gazette* (Adel.), Aug. 1911, p. 191.

4 *Education Gazette* (Syd.), Nov. 1917, p. 256, June 1922, p. 131.

5 *Education Office Gazette*, Dec. 1919, p. 452; *South Australia Parliamentary Debates*, 30 July 1924, p. 54.

6 Saluting the Flag, *The Argus*, 25 Mar. 1933.

7 Lines taken from Shakespeare's *Richard II*, *Education Circular*, May 1924, p. 209.

8 Director of Education, Tasmania, to Director of Education, SA, 31 May 1930, GRG 18/2/1930/1342, State Records of SA.

SOURCES AND
select bibliography

The chapter notes indicate the range and detail of sources used for this book. Those seeking more detail for the period 1901 to 1951 will find it in my PhD thesis Which Flag? Which Country? An Australian Dilemma, 1901–1951, Australian National University, 1995.

Commonwealth government records held in the National Archives of Australia and within departments (made available to me through the special access provisions of the *Archives Act 1983*) have been especially valuable. The main ones relating to flags and other national symbols are listed below. A select bibliography indicates the wider context.

SPECIAL ACCESS RECORDS

DEPARTMENT OF DEFENCE
88/04141/XXPYR, Australian White Ensign Adoption – Flying of by Ships & Establishments.
A91/33059 parts 1, 2, 3, The General Service Badge (Rising Sun Badge).
A8455/2/10 part 1, The General Service Badge New Pattern.
A4090, A8455/4/25, Insignia – the Australian Army (The General Service Badge) – Redevelopment.
DM 87–35058 parts 1 and 2, General Rules relating to the Australian National Flag and the Joint Services Flag.

HQ96/39814 part 1, Proclamation of the Joint Service Flag.
CN99/9158 part 1, Committees – Higher Defence Committees – Chiefs of Staff Committee (COSC) – Proclamation of a Joint Service Flag.
3MD 88/6428, Aid – Civil Community Aid to Australian National Flag Association Flag Raising Ceremony 3/9/89.
N91–1881 part 1, Naval Historical Series.

DEPARTMENT OF EDUCATION, SCIENCE AND TRAINING, INCLUDING THE CURRICULUM CORPORATION
ES02/11141 and ES04/01703, School Education – Programme Management 3050. Civics and Citizenship Education: 2001/2002 – Project Management for 'Our National Flag … since 1901'. Video Replication and Distribution to Schools.
ES03/08927, ES03/10834 and ES04/01706, School Education – Programme Management 3050 Civics and Citizenship Education: 2202/2204 Flagpole Provision to Schools – Coordination & Ministerials.
Teachers' Notes for the Australian National Flag Association video, 'Our National Flag … Since 1901': project specifications, drafts, comments, 21 May to 28 June 2002, Curriculum Corporation.

DEPARTMENT OF IMMIGRATION AND MULTICULTURAL AND INDIGENOUS AFFAIRS

95/3882, Proclamation of Aboriginal and Torres Strait Islander Flags under the *Flags Act 1953* OIA [Office of Indigenous Affairs].

95/6315, Proclamation of the Australian Aboriginal Flag – Key Documents Legal Section OIA.

96/1963, Purchase and Distribution of Aboriginal and Torres Strait Islander Flags. Council for Aboriginal Reconciliation CAR ARB [Aboriginal Reconciliation Branch] OIA.

DEPARTMENT OF THE PRIME MINISTER AND CABINET

A463, 1996/4855, Proclamation of 3 September as Australian National Flag Day.

A463, 2000/0995, Australian Defence Force Ensign Proclamation ANS.

A463, 2001/5357, Flag Ceremonies in Schools Oath of Allegiance ANS.

2001/2650, Re-enactment of First Flying of Australian National Flag Melbourne, 3 September 2001 ANSB [Awards and National Symbols Branch].

AUSTRALIAN FLAGS BOOKLET

HON92/00081, HON92/00081/02, Australian National Flag History 1992.

HON92/00210, Australian National Flag booklet – 1993 [1995] edition.

HON94/00301, HON94/00301/02, HON94/00301/03, HON94/00301/04, Australian National Flag Book Consultancy Proposal.

98/1630, Australian Flags Booklet – second edition, ANS.

CORRESPONDENCE SUPPORTING AND OPPOSING CHANGE TO THE FLAG

92/2975, Proposed New Australian Flag General Representations.

96/1735, Representations on a New Australian Flag Government Division.

HON96/0074, Australian National Flag Ministerial Replies 1996.

HON97/0206, HON97/0206/02, HON97/0206/03, Australian National Flag Ministerial Replies.

97/3576, Australian National Flag Representations 1997 ANS.

98/1083; 98/1328–1331; 98/2893; 98/3963, Australian National Flag Representations, ANS.

FLAG LEGISLATION

HON88.11, Flags Amendment Bills.

HON96/0056, *Flags Act 1953* Plebiscite.

96/4759 and 96/4760, *Flags Act 1953* Plebiscite ANS.

HON96/00078, HON96/00078/02 and HON96/00078/03, Protection for Australian National Flag.

96/2093; 96/3294, Australian Flag Legal and Administrative Review Branch.

NATIONAL ANTHEM

EB80/5765, History of the National Anthem and National Tune.

HON83/4979/01and HON83/4979/02, National Anthem National Tune 1983 Policy.

NATIONAL ARCHIVES OF AUSTRALIA RECORDS

CABINET SECRETARIAT

A5839, 603 Cabinet Minute – New Ensign for the Royal Australian Navy – without memorandum.

COMMONWEALTH ARCHIVES OFFICE

A750, 1972/54, Australian National Anthem & Flag Quests Committee – Survey of Records.

AA1975/370, 1 – AA1975/870, 8, National Combined Anthem and Flag Quest Committee records.

COMMONWEALTH OFFICE OF EDUCATION

A1361, 21/1/7 parts 1, 2, Miscellaneous – Commonwealth Jubilee – Flags for Schools.

A1361, 21/1/14 part 1, Miscellaneous – Rules for Flying Australian National Flag.

DEPARTMENT OF AIR

A705, 85/1/158, RAAF – AMP [Air Member for Personnel] – Australian Flag – Flying of at Funerals.

DEPARTMENT OF DEFENCE

A4090, 218/1/13 part 1 [Proposed] One Flag policy for Australia ... DGSPP aspect.

A5954, 1185/4, CID Secret Document: 1 Co-operation between the Naval Forces of the United Kingdom and Dominions; 2 The Status of Dominion Fleets and the Flag to be Flown.

MP84/1, 1874/1/28, Saluting Flag.

MP178/2, 2115/1/57, Memorandum of Conference between the British Admiralty & Representatives of the Dominions of Canada & Australia.

MP472/1, 1/13/4322, Query by ANA Western Australia Branch re: non-flying of Australian flag at inspection of 'Melbourne'. Navy Office.

DEPARTMENT OF EXTERNAL AFFAIRS

A1, 1905/4192, Practice in regard to flying of both state & Commonwealth flags on Public Buildings.

A1, 1908/433, Flags on Commonwealth Buildings.

A6, 1901/133, Despatch & Correspondence re Seal and Flag.

A6, 1901/134, Federal Flag.

A8, 1901/208/8, Design of Federal Flag by AW Thompson.

A8, 1902/135/13, Correspondence 1902: Dissatisfaction in NSW ANA with design of Australian flag and seal.

A518, EC112/1 part 2, Flying of Flags – Territories – General.

DEPARTMENT OF THE PRIME MINISTER AND CABINET

A461, A336/1/1 parts 1–3, Commonwealth Flags – Uses of.

A461, B336/1/1 parts 1, 2, Commonwealth Flag.

A461, B336/1/1 parts 3, 5, The Commonwealth Flag – Requests for Information.

A461, BG317/1/6, Commonwealth Jubilee Celebrations. Education & Science Sub-Committee Jubilee Meetings.

A461, D336/1/1 parts 1–4, Commonwealth Flags – Display on Public Buildings.

A461, H317/1/6, Commonwealth Jubilee Celebrations – Suggestions and Offers of Co-operation.

A461 K336/1/1, Flags for Governor-General.

A461, M317/1/6, Commonwealth Jubilee Celebrations. Issue of Jubilee Medal.

A461, O317/1/6, Commonwealth Jubilee Celebrations 1951. Presentation of Flags to Schools.

A461, Y336/1/1, Flags to be Flown by Naval Vessels in Foreign Ports.

A462, 828/1/1 part 1, Australian Flag – Correct Use – Policy.

A462, 828/1/7, Origin of the Australian Flag.

A462, 828/1/31, National Emblems – Flags – Legislation to Declare an Australian National Flag.

A462, 828/3/8 part 1, Requests for Commonwealth Coat of Arms.

A463, 1963/1990, Australian Flag Certificate for Schools and Organisations.

A463, 1973/2555, National Anthem Quest – Administrative Procedures.

A9645, C3/2, Meetings of Education and Science Sub-Committee (Commonwealth).

GOVERNOR-GENERAL

A2880, 6/14/10, Ceremonial, Policy and Procedural –
Flying of Flags – Blue Ensign – Australian National Flag,
Legislation, Rules etc.

A11085, B7/5, Governor of New South Wales – July 1913 –
Ceremonial Parade – State Governors making arrangements direct with local Military Authorities [. . .] .

JOINT HOUSE DEPARTMENT

A6727, 37, Flags [and flagpoles].

A6728, 124 parts 1 and 2, Flags and Flagpoles.

PARLIAMENT HOUSE CONSTRUCTION AUTHORITY

A8107, Documents relating to the Parliament House Design
Competition prepared for entrants and general publications, all records in series.

SELECT BIBLIOGRAPHY

Alomes, Stephen, *A Nation at Last? The Changing Character
of Australian Nationalism 1880–1988*, Angus &
Robertson, Sydney, 1988.

Australian Flags (1995), Ausinfo, Canberra, 1998.

Birrell, Robert, *A Nation of Our Own: Citizenship and Nation-
building in Federation Australia*, Longman Australia,
Melbourne, 1995.

Brett, Judith, *Australian Liberals and the Moral Middle Class:
From Alfred Deakin to John Howard*, Cambridge
University Press, Cambridge, 2003.

Cashman, Richard, *Sport in the National Imagination:
Australian Sport in the Federation Decades*, Walla Walla
Press in conjunction with The Centre for Olympic
Studies, UNSW, Sydney, 2002.

Colley, Linda, *Britons: Forging the Nation, 1707–1837*, New
Haven, Yale University Press, 1992.

Cunneen, Christopher, *King's Men: Australia's Governors-
General from Hopetoun to Isaacs*, George Allen & Unwin,
Sydney, 1983.

Curran, James, *The Power of Speech: Australian Prime
Ministers Defining the National Image*, Melbourne
University Press, Melbourne, 2004.

Davidson, Alistair, *From Subject to Citizen: Australian
Citizenship in the Twentieth Century*, Cambridge
University Press, Cambridge, 1997.

Davison, Graeme, *The Use and Abuse of Australian History*,
Allen & Unwin, Sydney, 2000.

Dermody, Kathleen, *A Nation at Last: The Story of Federation*,
Australian Government Publishing Service, Canberra, 1997.

Dutton, David, *One of Us? A Century of Australian
Citizenship*, UNSW Press, Sydney, 2002.

Foley, Carol, *The Australian Flag: Colonial Relic or
Contemporary Icon?* The Federation Press, Sydney, 1996.

Gammage, Bill, *The Broken Years: Australian Soldiers in the
Great War* (1974), Penguin Books Australia, Melbourne,
1975.

Goldsworthy, David, *Losing the Blanket: Australia and the End
of Britain's Empire*, Melbourne University Press,
Melbourne, 2002.

Hirst, John, *The Sentimental Nation: The Making of the
Australian Commonwealth*, Oxford University Press,
Melbourne, 2000.

Hudson, WJ and Sharp, MP, *Australian Independence: Colony
to Reluctant Kingdom*, Melbourne University Press,
Melbourne, 1988.

Inglis, KS, *Sacred Places: War Memorials in the Australian
Landscape*, The Miegunyah Press, Melbourne, 1998.

Jupp, James (ed.) *The Australian People: An Encyclopedia of
the Nation, Its People and Their Origins* (1988),
Cambridge University Press, Cambridge, 2001.

Jupp, James, *The English in Australia*, Cambridge University
Press, Cambridge, 2004.

McKenna, Mark, *The Captive Republic: A History of
Republicanism in Australia 1788–1996*, Cambridge
University Press, Cambridge, 1996.

Manne, Robert (ed.) *The Howard Years*, Black Inc Agenda,
Melbourne, 2004.

Smith, Anthony D, *The Ethnic Origins of Nations*, Blackwell,
Oxford, 1986.

Souter, Gavin, *Lion and Kangaroo: The Initiation of Australia*
(1976), The Text Publishing Company, Melbourne,
2000.

Ward, Stuart, *Australia and the British Embrace: The Demise
of the Imperial Ideal*, Melbourne University Press,
Melbourne, 2001.

White, Richard, *Inventing Australia: Images and Identity
1688–1980*, George Allen & Unwin, Sydney, 1981.

Znamierowski, Alfred, *Flags Through the Ages: A Guide to the
World of Flags, Banners, Standards and Ensigns*,
Southwater, London, 1999.

Znamierowski, Alfred, *Flags of the World: An Illustrated Guide
to Contemporary Flags*, Southwater, London, 2000.

ILLUSTRATION CREDITS

1.14 National Library of Australia nla.pic-an13117280–16.
1.15 John Lumley; National Archives of Australia: A1721, 43; A1721, 44 and A8,1901/208/22.
1.16 Ralph Kelly, Flag Society of Australia.
1.17 National Library of Australia, nla.pic-an23504847.
1.18 State Library of Victoria; from *Education Gazette and Teachers' Aid*, Nov. 1900, *The School Paper*, Class IV, Dec. 1900.
1.19 Newspaper collection, Mitchell Library, State Library of New South Wales; from *The School Paper*, Class III, July 1901.
1.20 Newspaper collection, Mitchell Library, State Library of New South Wales; from *Town and Country Journal*, 25 May 1901.
1.21 State Library of Victoria; from *Education Gazette and Teachers' Aid*, Oct. 1901 supplement.
1.22 National Library of Australia, nla.pic-an23398139.
1.23 State Library of Victoria.
2.1 Newspaper collection, Mitchell Library, State Library of New South Wales.
2.2 Battye Library, 4323B/20 (62, 042P).
2.3 National Archives of Australia: A1861, 721.
2.4 Melbourne Cricket Club Museum reg. no. M7083.
2.5 National Library of Australia, PIC/Album 340/43.
2.6 State Library of Victoria.
2.7 National Library of Australia, nla.pic-an8334416.
2.8 National Archives of Australia: A6661, 40; permission to reproduce the Commonwealth Coat of Arms granted by the Department of the Prime Minister and Cabinet.
2.9 Permission to reproduce the Commonwealth Coat of Arms granted by the Department of the Prime Minister and Cabinet.
2.10 Mitchell Library, State Library of New South Wales.
2.11 CT Stannage (*The People of Perth: A Social History of Western Australia's Capital City*); National Library of Australia.
2.12 News Ltd.; National Library of Australia.
2.13 National Archives of Australia: A1861, 2201.
3.1 James Northfield Heritage Art Trust © and National Library of Australia, nla.pic-an7721244.
3.2 State Records of South Australia, GRG 32/16/33.
3.3 National Library of Australia, nla.pic-an14107674.
3.4 National Library of Australia, nla.pic-an23708998.
3.5 Australian War Memorial Negative Number REL/15959.
3.6 Australian War Memorial Negative Number P01095.001.
3.7 State Library of South Australia, SLSA: PRG 29/40/6/1.
3.8 Australian War Memorial Negative Number H00563.
3.9 National Library of Australia.
3.10 State Library of South Australia, SLSA: PRG 903.
3.11 State Library of South Australia.
3.12 National Film and Sound Archive, a division of the Australian Film Commisssion; still from the film *Ireland Will Be Free*.
3.13 National Film and Sound Archive, a division of the Australian Film Commisssion; still from the film *Ireland Will Be Free*.
3.14 Max Leason; newspaper collection, State Library of New South Wales.
3.15 News Ltd; National Library of Australia.
4.1 National Archives of Australia: A1861, 4470.
4.2 National Archives of Australia: A3560, 4859.
4.3 Australian Picture Library.
4.4 Ralph Kelly, Flag Society of Australia; approved by the RAAF Brand Manager.
4.5 Mitchell Library, State Library of New South Wales.

4.6 Historic Memorials Collection, Canberra; courtesy of the Parliament House Art Collection, Department of Parliamentary Services, Canberra, ACT.
4.7 Ralph Kelly, Flag Society of Australia.
4.8 National Library of Australia.
4.9 National Library of Australia, from *The Age*, 16 February 1938.
4.10 National Library of Australia; from *Victoria Government Gazette*, 9 July 1951.
4.11 National Library of Australia, nla.pic-an24460199.
5.1 Film World and Cinesound Movietone Productions, from the collection of the National Film and Sound Archive, a division of the Australian Film Commission.
5.2 National Archives of Australia: A1361, 21/1/7 part 2.
5.3 Film World and Cinesound Movietone Productions, from the collection of the National Film and Sound Archive, a division of the Australian Film Commission.
5.4 Film World and Cinesound Movietone Productions, from the collection of the National Film and Sound Archive, a division of the Australian Film Commission.
6.1 Ralph Kelly, Flag Society of Australia.
6.2 Ralph Kelly, Flag Society of Australia; approved by the RAAF Brand Manager.
6.3 Ralph Kelly, Flag Society of Australia.
6.4 ALP National Secretariat, Liberal Party of Australia, and National Library of Australia, Australian Federal Elections Campaign Ephemera, 1970 part 2, 1977 part 3.
6.5 National Archives of Australia: A6135, K25/5/93/141; A1500, K24654.
6.6 Ralph Kelly, Flag Society of Australia; approved by the RAAF Brand Manager.
6.7 The Office of the Chief of Army (1991) and the author (all).
6.8 Ralph Kelly, Flag Society of Australia.
6.9 Carol Molnar; and Jonathan King, *The Other Side of the Coin: A Cartoon History of Australia*; National Library of Australia.
6.10 National Library of Australia, Australian Federal Elections Campaign Ephemera, 1961 part 2.
6.11 Max Ellis, a trustee of the New England New State Movement and the University of New England and Regional Archives, A1800, 1.
6.12 University of New England and Regional Archives, A547, and News Ltd.
6.13 Ralph Kelly, Flag Society of Australia, by permission of the author Harold Thomas 1971©.
6.14 History Trust of South Australia and Elizabeth Kwan, *Living in South Australia: A Social History*, vol. 2, National Library of Australia.
6.15 Ralph Kelly, Flag Society of Australia; Australian Olympic Committee.
7.1 Ralph Kelly, Flag Society of Australia, and Ausflag.
7.2 Geoff Pryor, *The Canberra Times* and National Library of Australia, nla.pic-an23407558.
7.3 Ralph Kelly, Flag Society of Australia.
7.4 Ralph Kelly, Flag Society of Australia.
7.5 Australians for Constitutional Monarchy.
7.6 Sturt Krysgman; National Library of Australia.
7.7 Geoff Pryor, *The Canberra Times* and National Library of Australia, nla.pic-vn3259231.
7.8 Cathy Wilcox.
7.9 National Australia Day Council; from *Annual Report*, National Australia Day Council, 1988, 1993,

National Library of Australia.

7.10   Australian Labor Party National Secretariat.
7.11   Ansett Australia; from *Ansett Frequent Flyer News*, Nov.
        1994–Jan. 1995; Boeing 767 model, Ken & Janet
        Bond's collection.
7.12   Sport. The Library.
7.13   Ausflag.
7.14   Bill Leak; National Library of Australia.

7.15   Ralph Kelly, Flag Society of Australia, and Ausflag.
7.16   George Sponiar, Australian National Flag Association.
7.17   George Sponiar, Australian National Flag Association.
7.18   Peter Nicholson, www.nicholsoncartoons.com.au
7.19   *Border Mail*, Albury.
7.20   Geoff Pryor and *The Canberra Times*.
7.21   Bill Leak.
8.1   Supplied by the author.

ACKNOWLEDGMENTS

Many people and organisations assisted me in my search to explain Australians' changing relationship to their national flags since 1901. That quest began with my master's thesis, Making 'Good Australians': The Work of Three South Australian Educators, at the University of Adelaide, then developed as a doctorate, Which Flag? Which Country? An Australian Dilemma, 1901–1951, under the expert guidance of professors Ken Inglis and Barry Smith at the Australian National University. A study grant from the University of South Australia assisted my archival work in Canada. The report of one of my examiners, Dr Bill Gammage, was especially useful in initiating this book.

Critical in bringing my study up to date was the willingness of four government departments – Defence; Education, Science and Training (including the Curriculum Corporation); Immigration and Multicultural and Indigenous Affairs; and Prime Minister and Cabinet – to make their recent records available to me under the special access provisions of the *Archives Act 1983*. The richness of those resources was invaluable, and underlined the importance of public servants keeping such records. At the same time, I acknowledge that the views, interpretations and conclusions based on department records are my own and do not necessarily reflect those of the relevant department.

The illustration credits and notes indicate the many individuals and organisations that readily assisted me with images. In this regard I would especially like to acknowledge the National Archives of Australia (which provided its images and a range of other assistance); National Library of Australia; Australian War Memorial; Defence Department; Old Parliament House; National Film and Sound Archive; National Capital Authority; Government House, Canberra; Joint House Department, Parliament House, Canberra; and state libraries in New South Wales, Victoria, South Australia and Western Australia. In preparing those illustrations I relied on the skills of Rob Armstrong, graphic designer.

Those with a particular interest and expertise in flags were also helpful, especially the Flag Society of Australia's Ralph Kelly – who provided the drawings of the many flags in the book – Tony Burton, John Vaughan, Ralph Bartlett and George Poulos, the last of whom introduced me to the society. I appreciate the willingness of Harold Scruby, executive officer of Ausflag, and John Vaughan, national spokesman for the Australian National Flag Association, to be interviewed about the role of their organisations.

I am indebted to the Department of the Senate's grant of leave without pay for the time needed to research and write this book, and to the encouragement of Cleaver Elliott, Ann Millar and Wayne Hooper.

Three colleagues read my manuscript: Ken Inglis, a constant source of encouragement and wisdom; John Hirst, who sees issues so clearly; and Ralph Kelly, who has the keen eye of a vexillologist. Ian Hancock also read parts of the text. Their thoughtful and incisive comments were invaluable in my revision of the text. Any remaining shortcomings of the book are my own.

I thank Angela McAdam and Alex Bellis of the National Archives of Australia, who helped establish the project; and the staff of UNSW Press, especially Dr Robin Derricourt, Mary Halbmeyer, Dr Heather Cam and Di Quick (designer), and also Neil Thomson (editor) and Catherine Page (proofreader and indexer) for producing this book with enthusiasm and skill.

Last but by no means least, I am most grateful for the patience and support of friends and family, especially Ping and Anna, who have lived with this book for some years.

INDEX

Page numbers in bold indicate an
illustration or caption

Aboriginal and Torres Strait Islander
    Commission (ATSIC) 128, 133–34
Aboriginal flag 118–19, **118**, **132**,
    133–34
Admiralty (British) 14, 18, 22, 23, 49,
    54, 79, 86, 150
Advance Australia Fair 29, 111,
    119–21, 123, 124
All British League 64, 68
allies' days 95
America *see* United States
American flag **42**, 95, **137**
American Legion 121
American patriotic salute 30
Anglo-Australians 25, 32, 37, 122, 148
Anglo-Irish war **70**, 72, 75
Anglo-Japanese alliance 43
Ansett 131, **131**
Anzac Book, The (Bean, ed.) **62**, 62
Anzac Day 63, **63**, 72, 73, **87**, 120,
    124, 127, 135, 143
Ausflag 7, 10–11, 121–22, 125, **125**,
    128, 133, **137**, 138–39, 142, 143,
    153, 156, 158
Australasian Federation League of NSW
    19, **21**
Australasian League flag 14, **15**
Australasian Olympic Team 46, **48**
Australia Day 48, 50–53, 119, **131**
'Australia first' 38, 65, 66, 76
Australian Anti-War League 34
Australian Army 115, **116**, 126, **126**,
    136
Australian Capital Territory flag 118
Australian Comforts Fund 57, 60
Australian Commonwealth Ensign 6,
    23 *see also* blue ensign (Australian)
Australian Commonwealth Merchant
    Flag 6, **23** *see also* red ensign
    (Australian)
Australian Commonwealth Military
    Forces 115, **116**
Australian Communist Party 75, 95,
    103
Australian Defence Force **116**, 126,
    136
Australian Defence Force Ensign **116**,
    126
Australian Flag Society of 2003 11
Australian Flags (1995) 10, 134, 136
Australian Heritage Society 121
Australian Imperial Force (AIF) 55, 60,
    63, 64, 126
Australian Labor Party (ALP) 40, 65,
    111, **111**, 120, 121, 130, **131**, 158
Australian National Anthem and Flag
    Quests Committee 119, 153

Australian National Flag 100, 106 *see
    also* blue ensign (Australian)
Australian National Flag, The (1956–)
    7–8, 9–10, 108–9, 111–13
Australian National Flag Association
    (ANFA) 7, 10, 11, 121–22, 128,
    134, 136–44, **144**, 155–56, 158
Australian National Flag Day *see*
    National Flag Day
Australian Natives Association (ANA)
    18, 32, 34, 37, 43, 44, **45**, 48, 49,
    55, 88, 89, 96, 151
Australian Republican Movement 128
Australian Republican Party **116**, 117,
    139
Australian Workers' Union 75
'Australians' 38, 47, 64, 68, 72, 77,
    102, 148, 154
Australians for Constitutional
    Monarchy 128, **129**

'baggy green' **44**
Balfour Report 83, 86
Barton, Sir Edmund 16, 18–22, 31,
    33, 35, 40, 139, 151
Bathurst, NSW 37, 39, 53
Beale, Howard 97, 106
Bean, Charles 62, 64, 101–2
Beazley, Kim 124
Beckett, William 91
Bellear, Sol 133
bicentenary (1988) 121, 124, 125,
    127, 158
Birdwood, General Sir William 60, 61
blue ensign (Australian) 23, **84**;
    burnt 148; given to schools
    99–102, **101**, 152; myths 104, 141;
    origins 5, 6; precedence 78–79,
    106, **107**, 108; proclaimed as
    national flag 98, 100, 107; restric-
    tions lifted 94, 95–96; use in war
    57–60, 61, **61**, 63, 92–96, 130;
    Victorian support for 88–92; vs red
    ensign 81–82, 84–85, 97
blue ensign (British) **14**
blue ensign (NSW) 15, **15**
blue ensign (Victorian) 15, **15**
Boer War 25, 30, 35, 51, 152
Bolshevism 74–76, **75**
bonfires 37, 39
boxing kangaroo flag 122, **122**
Britain (United Kingdom of Great
    Britain and Northern Ireland) 5, 6,
    13, 14, 54, 78, 83, 96, 154
British arms **19**, **44**
British Army 63–64
British Empire/Commonwealth of
    Nations 25, 28, 35 68, 78, 91, 109,
    113, 150, 154 *see also* imperial
    sentiment

British Empire League (BEL) 34–35,
    36, 37, 39, 41, 152
British Empire Union 64, 76
British nationality 35, 38, 47, 102
Bruce, Stanley Melbourne 83
Bull, John 52
Burton, Tony 10

cadets, school 24, 28, **31**
Cain, John 89
Calwell, Arthur 9, 99, 105–6, 107
Canada 16, 30, 79, 83, 86, 90, 110,
    114, **137**, 158
canton 14
Capital Hill, Canberra 110, **112**, 112
Carruthers, Joseph 35–36, 38, 39
Catholic church 50–53, 65, 106
Catholic Federation 65–66
Catholic–Labor link 36, 66, 75
Catholic schools 27, 39, 50–51, 53,
    69
Catholics 36, 37, 53, 65, 66, 70–71,
    72, 89–90, 128, 154, 158
Cayley, Frank 9
Centenary Flag 140, **141**, 155
centenary of federation 12, 133,
    139–41, 158
ceremony (flag-raising in schools) 8,
    30–31, **31**, 63, 69, 76–77, 88, **89**,
    144–48, **145** *see also* salutes
Chifley, Ben 97, 98–99, 152
China 25, 103
citizen's crown 44
citizenship 67, 69, 123, 154, 155
citizenship ceremonies 8, 99, 105, 157
Civics Education Group 142–43
class, social *see* middle class; working
    class
coats of arms 43–45, **44–47**, 82, **82**,
    84, 110, 115
Cold War 103
Collins, Tom 90, 92, 94, 96
colonial badges 14–15, **15**
colonial ensigns 15, **15**, 98, **137**
Commonwealth Coat of Arms 43,
    45–46, **46**, **47**, 110, 115, 156
Commonwealth/state control of schools
    99–103, 104–5, 145–48, 152, 156
Commonwealth Games 120, 133
Commonwealth of Australia **18–22**,
    44–45
Commonwealth of Nations *see* British
    Empire
Commonwealth Office of Education
    100, 101, 110
Commonwealth Parliament 24, 27, 29,
    32, 82, 84–85, 112
Commonwealth Star 18, 19, **23**, 43,
    46, **46–47**, **85**, 86, 115–16, 126,
    131, **139**, 156–57, 158

communism 73, 75, 76, 77, 89, 95, 100, 103, 106
competitions: Ausflag (1985–86; 1993) 125, **125**, 133; Ausflag (1997–2000) 138–39, **139**, 156; Commonwealth government (1901) 5, 16–19, **21**, 104; Commonwealth government (1973) 120; *Herald Standard* (1900) 16, **16**, 24, 26; Lavett's (1971) 119, 120; *Review of Reviews for Australasia* (1900) 16
conscription (WWI) 64–66, 86, 89
conservative resurgence 126, 135–48
Constitution 92, 107, 128, 135
'Cooees' 57
Cook, Sir Joseph 40, 77
Council for Aboriginal Reconciliation 133–34
'country' 30, 67
Country Party 89, 90, 92
Cronulla Beach, NSW 148
Crouch, Richard Armstrong **31**, 31–32, 34, 41, 86, 150
Crown 86, 115, 116, **116**, **126**
Crux Australis 11
Curriculum Corporation 143
Curtin, John 95, 96, 98, 158

Dante's four virtues 143
Deakin, Alfred 41, 43–45
defence 35, 40, 43, 49, 83, 154
Delegate, NSW 57, **58–59**
Depression, the 88, 89
Discovering Democracy Programme 142–44
dominion flags 78, 79, **137**
Dorrington, Annie 17, **21**
Downer, Alexander 130, **130**
Duke and Duchess of Cornwall and York **20–21**, **22**, 27, 45, 139
Duke and Duchess of York 84
Dunstan, Albert **88**, 89–94, 105, 106, 145, 152

Eager, Clifden 91
Easter Uprising (Ireland, 1916) 66, 71
Education Act 1941 92
Education (Patriotic Ceremonies) Act 1940 92
Edward VII (King) 22–23, **22**, 30, **33**
Elizabeth II (Queen) 105, 106, **107**
Ellis, Ulrich **117**
Empire (British) 25, 28, 78 *see also* imperial sentiment
Empire Day 34–41, 47–48, **49**, 50–53, 68, 152
English flag 14
ensigns 4–6, 14 *see also* blue ensign; red ensign; white ensign
ethnicity 37, 65, 66, 67–69, 72, 77, 148, 149, 151, 157
Eureka flag 14, **15**, 89, 105, 106, 157, **157**
Evans, Ivor 17, **21**, 104, 143

federation **17–21**, 24, 32, 35, 156 *see also* centenary of federation; jubilee of

federation
federation flag **5**, **15**, **18**–19, 21–22, **21**, **22**
fireworks 37, 39
Fisher, Andrew 46, 151
Fitchett, Dr William 16, 26, 31
flag days 6, 79, 95 *see also* National Flag Day
'flag-flapping' 7, 27
flagpoles 145–47, **146**
flag-raising ceremony *see* ceremony (flag-raising in schools)
Flag Society of Australia 10, 11
flags (origin) 14
Flags Act 1953 6, 7, 8, 105–6, 109, 123, 124, 133, 135, 149, 152–53
fly 14, 78
Flying of Flags (paper) 90
Foley, Carol 11–12
Fort-street Public School **29**, 39
forts 32, 41
Fraser, Malcolm 120–21, 123
Free Trade Party 36, 37, 40
Freeman, Cathy **132**, 133, 134
fundraising badges (WWI) 57, **63**

Gair Manufacturing Company 94
Gallipoli 55, 59, 62–64, 68, 126, 143
Geelong, Vic. 25, 37, 76
Geneva Convention on the High Seas (1958) 113
Gentil, Frank 139, **139**
George, Lloyd 64
George V (King) 49, 86
German-Australians 67–68, 69, **91**, 91
God Bless Our Lovely Morning-land 51, 52
God Save the King 29, 39
God Save the Queen 105, 111, 117, 119–21, 124
Government House 86, 109
governors-general 49, 54, **54**, **85**, 86, 109, 120, 124
Grand Army of the Republic (US) 30
Guy Fawkes 37, 66

Hanson, Pauline 138, **138**
Harbonnières (France) 61
Harris, Sir John 89
Hawke, Bob 121, 123, 124, 125, 158
Hawkins, Leslie 17, **21**
Higgins, HB 25
Hines, Sir Colin 121
Hirst, John 157
Hodgson, William, 95–96
Hogan, Ned 89
hoist 14
Howard, John 6–7, 134, 135, 136, 138, 139–40, 144, **146**, 149, 155, 156, 158
Hughes, WM (Billy) 59, 60, 64, 65, 81, 83
Hull, Lt Arthur 60, 61, **61**

identity, national *see* national identity
immigrants 30, 40, 103, 147, 154,

155, 156, 157
imperial conferences 49, 81, 83
imperial sentiment 24, 25, 38, 56, 64, 96
independence 35, 36, 38, 78, 83, 85, 86, 96, 110, 154
indigenous rights 30, **118**, 119, 128, 133, 155, 157
Iraq war 148, 156
Ireland Will Be Free 72–73
Irish-Australians 36, 37, 39, 50–51, 65, 72
Irish flags 52, 70, 71
Irish Free State 83
Irish Home Rule movement 50, 52, 66, 71
Irish republicanism 74, 77 *see also* Sinn Fein
Isaacs, Sir Isaac 86

jack 14
Jacka, Albert 8, 86
jackstaff 13, 14, 54
Japan **42**, 96, 111, 154
Jehovah's Witnesses 92
joint service flag 115–16, **116**, 126
jubilee of federation 93, 98–103

kangaroo **46–47**, **114**, 114–15, **116**, 122, **122**, 126
Keating, Paul 6, 7, 127–30, **130**, 134, 149, 153, 158
Keep the Union Jack A-flyin' 76
Kelly, Ralph 10, 11
King *see* Edward VII (King); George V (King)
King and Empire Alliance 73, 74, 76
King's Regulations 32, 86
kinship, crimson thread of 32, 140, **141**, 153, 155
Kipling, Rudyard **20**, 26–27, 33, 154
Kokoda 127
Korean war 100, 152, 156

Labor Party 66, 67–68, 89, 106, 127, 135, 151 *see also* Australian Labor Party; NSW Labor Party
Lambert, Bill 75, 76, 81
Lavett, John 119, 120, 122, 153
League of Empire 36, 41, 152
Leagues of Loyalty 66, 70
Lebanese-Australians 148
Leeper, Dr Alexander 69, 70, 72
Liberal–Country Party coalition 99, 100, 127, 135, 136, 138, 145, 148
Liberal Party 35–36, 65, 69, 106, 111, **111**, 135, 142, 157–58
logos 111, **111**, 131, **131**
Long, Michael 155
Loyal Orange Institution 51
loyalty 28, 35, 38, 43, 55, 64, 65, 69, 86, 103, 157 *see also* Leagues of Loyalty
Loyalty Despatch Bicycle Relay 102
Lumley, William 19, **23**
Lutheran schools 68, 69

Lyons, Joseph 86, 90

Mabo decision 128
Mafeking siege 25, 51
Making Our Flag (ANFA, 1992) 142
Mannix, Archbishop Daniel 65–66, 70–71, 72, 99
Margaritis, George **139**
Maughan, Milton 68
May Day 73, 76
Meath, Lord 35
Men from Snowy River, The 57, **58–59**
Menzies, Robert 8, 90, 94–96, 98–99, 101–2, 103, 105–10, **107**, 152, 156, 158
Merchant Shipping Act 1894 113
middle class 27, 36, 65
Mills, Prof RC 100, 102
Mitchell Giurgola and Thorp Architects 112
monarchists 128
Monash, Lt Gen. Sir John 8, 60, 61, 63–64, 86
Moran, Cardinal Patrick 36, 50–53, **52**
Morris, Nigel 11
Murdoch, Keith 64
Murray River flag **15**

Namok, Bernard **128**
national anthem 68, 69, 105, 111, 119–21, 123, 124
National Australia Day Committee/Council 123, **131**
National Capital Development Commission 110
national colonial flag 15
National Council for the Centenary of Federation 12
National Flag Day 122, 136, 139, 141, **144**, 155
national identity 32, 40, 63, 77, 131, 137, 138, 149
national sentiment 22, 32, 36, 38
nationalism 64, 116, 126, **147**, 148
Nationalists 65, 66, 69, 74, 76, 77, 78, 81, 151, 158
nationality 34, 35, 38, 53, 55, 79, 90, 96, 102, 103, 113, 123, 148, 154, 158
Nationality and Citizenship Act 1948 99
nationhood 8, 32, **33**, 55, 102, 127, 153
Navigation Act 1920 33
Nelligan, Phillip 29, 39, 53
Nelson, Dr Brendan 142–46, **144**, **146**, 155, 156
'New Australians' 99, 100, 154
New England New State Movement **117**, 118
New Zealand 22, 46, 65, 79, 90, 158
Northern Territory flag 118
NSW ensigns 15, **15**
NSW Labor Council 73
NSW Labor Party 35–36, 38, 40, 51, 74–77
NSW schools 29, 38, **42**, 47, **52**, 53, 63, 69, **144**, **146**

Nuttall, Egbert J 17, **21**, 104

Old Guard 76
O'Reilly, Maurice 50–53
Olympics: London (1908) 46; Stockholm (1912) **48**; Antwerp (1920) 46; Paris (1924) 82, **82**; Melbourne (1956) 117; Munich (1972) 119; Montreal (1976) 120; Sydney (2000) 125, 158; Athens (2004) **122**
One Nation Party 138
Opening of Federal Parliament at Canberra, 9 May 1927 (Power) **85**
opinion polls *see* polls
Our National Flag...Since 1901 (ANFA, 2000) 142

Page, Sir/Dr Earle 82, 90
palls 8, 86, 96, 98
Parkes, Henry **21**, 32, 34, 140, **141**
Parliament House 8–9, **82**, 84–85, **84**, **85**, 98, **103**, **107**, 110; new **112**, 112
patriotism 24, 27, 38, 41, 43, 47, 51, 53, 64, 69, 79, 90, 92, 99, 144, 147
Pearce, George 49, 54
pledges *see* salutes
polls 12, 117, 120, 121, 125, 128, 130, 131, 134, 135, 138, 140, 153
Polygon Wood, Battle of 60, **61**
post offices 32, 79, 95
postcards (WWI) 60, **60**, **61**
Power, Septimus 84–85, **85**
precedence of flags 78–82
private schools 26–27, 39, 69, 92, 100, 147, 148
Prohibition of Discrimination Act 1966 119
Protestant associations 35, 39, 66, 70, 71, 72, 73, 74, 95, 97
Protestant schools 27, 69, 147
Protestants 36, 37, 39, 50, 51, 53, 65, 66, 71, 72, 95, 151, 154, 157, 158
public schools 8, 26–29, 63, **89**, 100, 159

Queen *see* Victoria (Queen); Elizabeth II (Queen)
Queen's flag for Australia **108**, 109

RAAF ensign **83**, 83, 110, **111**, 114, **114**, 150
racism 148, 155
reconciliation 133–34
recruitment posters (WWI) **56–57**
red ensign (Australian) 6, **23**, 33, **57**, 79, **85**, 85, **87**, 106, 113; use in war 9–10, **58–59**, 60, **63**, 93, 130
red ensign (British) **14**, 15, 22
red ensign (Victorian) 15, **15**, **17**
red flag (of socialist movement) 23, 73, **74**, 76
referendums 65–66, **117**, 118, 119, 135
Reid, George 35, 36, 40
republicanism 76, 127–30

Returned Sailors' and Soldiers' Imperial League of Australia 73 *see also* RSL
Returned Sailors' and Soldiers' Political League (RSSPL) 73, 76
rising sun 43, 44, **44–45**, 115, **116**, 126
Royal Air Force ensign **83**, 110, 150
Royal Australian Air Force ensign *see* RAAF ensign
Royal Australian Navy 54, 110, **111**
Royal Commonwealth Society 121
Royal Crest **85**, 86, **126**
Royal Exhibition Building, Melbourne 18, **19**, 24, 27, 136, 141
Royal Navy 43, 55, 83, 86, 110
Royal Society of St George 37, 68
royal standard 86, **108**, 109
RSL 11, 73, 74, 76, 82, 88, 121, 124, 126, 136, 142, 151, 155
RSSPL 73, 76
Rule Britannia 56, 76

salutes: ANFA flag promise 142; governor-general **49**, 54, **54**; gun 39; military 49; naval 54, 150; in public schools 30, **31**, 92, 159; South Australian 8, 67–69, 105, 109, 159; *see also* ceremony (flag-raising in schools)
Sargood, Sir Frederick **24**, 24–29, 33, 102, 139, 152, 155
Schools Assistance Act 2004 147
Scottish societies 37, 44–45
Scruby, Harold 7, 11, 121, 125, 142, 158
Scullin, James 86
sectarianism 36, 37, 51–53, 65, 66, 151
self-reliance 36, 38
Shipping Registration Act 1981 113
Sinn Fein 66, 70, 71
Skippy badge 115, **116**
Smith, Bruce 37, 40, 41
Smout, Arthur 9
socialism 23, 36, 37, 73
soldier–settlers 81, 88, 95
Sons of Australia 76
South Africa 25, 35, 79, 83, 86, 114, **137**
South Australian schools 8, 36, 38, 47, 63, **67**, 67–68, 104–5, 109
Southern Cross 13, **15**, 16, 18, 114, 125, 131, 143, 156
Southern Cross flag *see* Eureka flag
St Andrew cross 13
St George cross 13, 14, 16, 18–19, **27**, 43, 44, 85, 110
St Patrick cross 13
St Patrick's Day 51, 70–72, 73, 99
St Stanislaus' College 29, 50, 52
state badges 15, **18**, **19**, 45, **45**, 46, **47**
state flags **15**, 82, 94
State School Flag Committee 26
Statute of Westminster 1931 86, 91, 96
Stephen, Sir Ninian 124
Stevens, William 17, **21**
Stokes, Wayne **125**, 125

Tasmanian government 79
Tate, Frank 41
telegraph signal 26, 27, 141
temperance movement 35
Tent Embassy 119
Thomas, Harold 118–19, 134
Thompson, Frederick **16**
Tickner, Robert 133
Torres Strait Islander flag 128, **128**, 133–34
trade unions 36, 65
Trinity Grammar School 69
Tucker, Mark **125**, 125
Turnbull, Malcolm 128, 158

Union Jack **13**, 22, **27**; burnt 73, 76; given precedence 78–85, **80**, **82**, **84–85**, 92, 93, 102, **103**, 104, 152; given to schools 24–29; national flag 6, 25, 95, 102; origin 13; 'right...to fly' 90, 105–6; symbolism 25–26, 28–29, 96, 138, 155–56; use in Britain 22–23; use in schools 67, **67**, 68, 69, **89**, 91; use in war 56, **56**, 59, 62, **62**, 63, **63**
Union of Soviet Socialist Republics 95

United Australia Party (UAP) 86, 90, 91, 92, 95, 158
United Kingdom *see* Britain
United Nations 100, 126
United States 30, **42**, 43, 95, 96, 99, 103, 110, 111, 117, 136, **137**, 146, 154
upper hoist 14

Vaughan, Crawford 68
Vaughan, John 7, 9, 11, 121–22, 136, 139, 140, 142, **144**, 156, 158
Verran, John 68
vexilloid 14
vexillology 14
vice-regal representatives 49, 54, 120, 124 *see also* governors-general
Victoria (Queen) 34
Victoria Cross winners 70–71, 72
Victorian ensigns 15, **15**
Victorian schools **28**, **31**, 36, 38, 63, 69, 73, 88–92, **89**, **145**
Vietnam War 110–11, 115
Viner, Ian 134
voting rights 30, 35, 157

Walker, Frank 10, 133

war memorials 62, 67
Watson, Chris 32, 36, 151
wattle 38, **47**
Wesley College 27, 69
Western Australian public schools 48, **49**
White Army 88
white ensign (Australian) **23**, 43, 49, 110, **111**, 150
white ensign (British) 13, **14**, 54, 86, 110, 150
Whitlam, Gough 120, 124, 158
Wilton, Gen. Sir John 115–16
Women's Liberal League 35, 37
women's voting rights 30, 35
working class 29, 36, 65, 76
World War I 55–69, 79, **80**, 151
World War II 93–96, 114
Wren, John 71, 72, 89, 91, 99

Xavier College 27, 39

yardarm **82**, 82
'Young Queen, The' (Kipling) **20**, 33